Talking to Strangers

IMPROVING AMERICAN DIPLOMACY

AT HOME AND ABROAD

Monteagle Stearns

A Twentieth Century Fund Book

PRINCETON UNIVERSITY PRESS

PRINCETON, NEW JERSEY

The Twentieth Century Fund sponsors and supervises timely analyses of economic policy, foreign affairs, and domestic political issues. Not-for-profit and nonpartisan, the Fund was founded in 1919 and endowed by Edward A. Filene.

Copyright © 1996 by The Twentieth Century Fund, Inc.

Published by Princeton University Press, 41 William Street, Princeton, New Jersey 08540

In the United Kingdom: Princeton University Press, Chichester, West Sussex

All Rights Reserved

Fourth printing, and first paperback printing, 1999

Paperback ISBN 0-691-00745-4

The Library of Congress has cataloged the cloth edition of this book as follows

Stearns, Monteagle, 1924—

Talking to strangers : improving American diplomacy

at home and abroad / Monteagle Stearns

p.   cm.

"A Twentieth Century Fund book."

Includes bibliographical references and index.

ISBN 0-691-01130-3

1. United States—Foreign relations—1989– 2. United States—Relations—Foreign Countries. 3. United States—Foreign relations administration. 1. Title.

E840.S715 1995

327.73—dc20   95–24342

This book has been composed in Times Roman

The paper used in this publication meets the minimum requirements of ANSI/NISO Z39.48–1992 (R 1997) (*Permanence of Paper*)

http://pup.princeton.edu

Printed in the United States of America

4 5 6 7 8 9 10

Chapter 1 contains material originally published in a different form in the July 1989 issue of *World Monitor* magazine under the title "Managing the 90s."

Talking to Strangers

Contents

Foreword   ix

Preface   xiii

Acknowledgments   xxi

Abbreviations   xxv

CHAPTER ONE
The New Frontiers of American Diplomacy   3

CHAPTER TWO
The Diplomacy of Reason   20

CHAPTER THREE
The Diplomacy of Doctrine   38

CHAPTER FOUR
The Diplomacy of Process   55

CHAPTER FIVE
Diplomacy as Representation   72

CHAPTER SIX
Diplomacy as Management   92

CHAPTER SEVEN
Diplomacy as Communication   112

CHAPTER EIGHT
Diplomacy as Negotiation   132

CHAPTER NINE
Improving the Reach of American Foreign Policy   148

CHAPTER TEN
Improving the Grasp of American Diplomacy   164

Notes   179

Index   193

Foreword

AFTER five decades, the United States has realized the central goals of its foreign policy: the defeat of Soviet communism and the triumph of democratic capitalism. For the first time in its history America stands as the predominant and unchallenged power on the planet. The costs of the cold war were immense—indeed, the current national convulsions about the federal debt are, in a sense, a past-due bill for the trillions spent on the cold war military establishment. But the triumph of American ideas and power has not been an occasion for dancing in the streets. Instead, the nation seems uncertain of whether it is on course at all, questioning the value of "mixed capitalism" as an economic system and even the legitimacy of the republican form of government.

In this context, perhaps it is not surprising that those who did the patient, hard work of advancing the American cause in international affairs have not been the subject of parades and awards. Instead, the foreign policy establishment sometimes seems more like a tempting target of political opportunity than an exemplar of public service. Part of the problem is that the end of the struggle with the Soviet Union has muddied the crystal clarity of America's mission around the globe. Today, our interests, though far-flung, are more connected to domestic affairs; they are more narrowly security oriented and more explicitly economic than at any time since before World War II.

Despite our enjoyment of relative prosperity, public discourse is filled with disquiet about the state of the nation. Participation in community affairs is down, and trust in leaders of any kind is perhaps at an all-time low. Government officials especially are seen by many as a major obstacle to full realization of the American Dream.

When this view of the nation is combined with our unique and persistent notion that in the public sector professionalism is of limited use, or even likely to have pernicious effects, the education and training of our representatives for service abroad is bound to suffer.

The long-term implications of this eccentricity are too important to be brushed aside. If America is to maintain its effectiveness in international affairs, we need an effective cadre of Foreign Service officers.

With that necessity in mind, the Fund turned to Monteagle Stearns, former United States ambassador to Greece and to the Republic of the Ivory Coast. His distinguished career in the Foreign Service provides a foundation of experience that informs the thoughtful discussion in this work of the place of diplomacy and the diplomatic corps in promoting the interests of the United States.

Stearns traces the development of American diplomacy from the early days of the Republic, a tradition that glows with names like Ben Franklin, Thomas Jefferson, and Charles Francis Adams. Indeed, part of Stearns's story is how seldom such eminence is recognized in the generations that follow. Still, the foundations of a "distinctively American" approach to diplomacy emerge with vivid clarity. These insights sharpen Stearns's observations concerning the development and implementation of more recent foreign policy. And they ensure that his prescriptions for diplomacy in the post–cold war era are firmly grounded in the realities of the American experience.

Of course, steady, patient diplomacy has never been likely to be confused with either political heroism or media celebrity. Stearns has much to say about what the reality of our media-driven democracy means for the lives and careers of those who actually serve in the Foreign Service. The way we choose, train, promote, reward, and punish our foreign policy professionals has, like the policies they advance, a special American flavor. Indeed, any program for upgrading the diplomatic corps or enhancing its influence makes sense only if it fits the particular, rough-edged version of democratic capitalism of the United States.

Ensuring that this nation has the talent and expertise it needs to secure our future is a subject that should be of great concern to all Americans. The Fund has explored the problem of recruiting and retaining high-quality government managers in *The Government's Managers*, a report on the senior executive service, and is currently looking at the presidential appointment process.

The force of Monteagle Stearns's arguments, as well as the quality of his past contributions, requires the attention of those who care about American effectiveness in international matters. On behalf of the Trustees of the Twentieth Century Fund, I thank him for his efforts.

Richard C. Leone, President
The Twentieth Century Fund
May 1995

Preface

DIPLOMACY is both servant to and master of foreign policy: servant because the diplomat's role is to carry out the instructions of political policymakers, master because what the diplomat cannot accomplish, policymakers will usually have to do without. The ambivalence inherent in this relationship explains why diplomats and policymakers are such uneasy partners in the enterprise of foreign affairs. It also explains why a book about the practice of diplomacy must also to some extent be a book about the making of foreign policy. How well diplomats and policymakers work together, and how justly each appreciates the contribution of the other to the policy-making process, will in the end determine the effectiveness of an administration's foreign policy.

Serving as United States minister to China in the 1920s, John Van A. MacMurray explained how he saw his role in a letter to Under Secretary of State Joseph C. Grew:

> I conceive my functions to be those of the shipmaster and local pilot whose business it is to do the actual navigation under general order from you who are the shipowners . . . that in a certain reach there is not enough water to float the ship and that nobody except the pilot is in a position to prescribe a speed or a course to be followed with reference to water level, currents, winds, or other local conditions.[1]

This is still the way most professional diplomats see their role and the contribution they are in a position to make to their nation's foreign policy. The ultimate destination of the ship, its cargo, its tonnage, and its means of defending itself are principally the responsibility of the shipowners. Getting the ship to its destination safely is, or should be, the primary responsibility of the diplomatic pilot.

This is rarely the case in practice; in American foreign affairs since World War II, almost never. Even in the 1920s, in carrying out the unadventurous policies of the Coolidge administration at a time when the strategic displacement of the United States was much less than it is today and the dangers of ignoring local conditions were much more apparent, diplomatic pilots found their advice frequently unheeded by policymakers at home. MacMurray's letter to Grew was actually occasioned by MacMurray's frustration over instructions from the State Department that reflected little or no comprehension of local conditions in China; instructions that, in his words, often "made me stop my engines and lose steerage when fighting a heavy current."

In admonishing the State Department to pay closer attention to Chinese realities, MacMurray had one advantage denied to modern envoys. He was conducting diplomacy before the communications revolution had created the illusion of the "global village." For the nonspecialist, China was still a remote region with an inscrutable culture, a country to be interpreted by experts and photographed by the *National Geographic*. Today, the ability of satellite television to disseminate the image of distant events almost as they occur misleads us into believing that we know the rest of the world better than we do. Images conveyed in real time are not necessarily reality, or at least not necessarily intelligible reality. It was Scottish filmmaker John Grierson who criticized the educational value of filmed newsreels by saying "they mistake the phenomenon for the thing in itself."

The same criticism applies with even greater force to telecasts of world events. Television coverage of the occupation of Tiananmen Square by Chinese students in the winter of 1989, for example, provided a compelling glimpse of one dramatic moment in the history of modern China but not an understanding of the process that led up to it or an accurate forecast of the events that followed it. The same can be said of television coverage of the Gulf War. In both cases, the "phenomenon" assumed greater importance than the process that produced it. Impact news reporting of this kind affects policymakers just as it affects the public, but it is an unstable foundation for policy. Effective foreign policy needs to look behind the appearance of events. It needs to address the process of change rather than the phenomena that change periodically throws to the surface of world affairs.

To argue, as this book does, that professional diplomacy is essential to the formulation of effective foreign policy is not to say that the views of diplomats should (or could) be determining in so complex a decision-making process. It is not to argue that foreign policy should (or could) be immune from political pressures and debate, or that it is too complicated to be entrusted to any but a foreign policy elite. Enlarging the role of the professional diplomat in policy-making would be no more elitist than enlarging the role of the professional journalist in the makeup of American newspapers. Diplomats are the journalists of foreign policy. The notion that foreign policy can be made coherent without them is as unrealistic as it would be to have a newspaper office staffed only by columnists and editorial writers.

In fact, for the past fifty years the evolution of foreign policy–making in the United States has been away from reliance on the skills of professional diplomacy, which include specialized knowledge of the history, language, and culture of foreign societies, and toward reliance on technical and managerial skills and on the more theoretical prescriptions of political science. The communications revolution, with its foreshortened historical perspective, its preference for phenomena over processes, and its habit of generalizing from specific events, has accelerated the trend. As a result, information (which, we are told, travels on a superhighway) easily overtakes knowledge (which generally travels on a winding footpath). By most reckonings, the American public, with more information available to it than ever before, is less knowledgeable about foreign affairs than it was fifty years ago.

Does this matter? The argument advanced in succeeding chapters is that it does. The cold war had the effect of bisecting the globe into Communist and non-Communist sectors, or trisecting it, if one takes literally the concept of a "Third World." Whether the globe was divided into two or into three parts, however, the geography of the cold war oversimplified the map of the world and accustomed us to thinking about it in highly generalized and schematic terms. In places like the former Yugoslav and Soviet republics we are becoming acutely aware of some of the trouble spots omitted from cold war maps, just as we are beginning to see that in such areas policymakers are often no more knowledgeable than the general public. There will be no lack of problems in the future that send us scurrying to our atlases to locate a new Chechnya or Nagorno-Karabakh.

Even the particular problems of familiar regions were deprived of their individuality during the cold war, as though we were looking at them through the wrong end of the telescope. Their significance was assessed primarily in terms of their potential to destabilize the superpower equilibrium. The differences of two NATO allies, Greece and Turkey, in the Aegean and over the Mediterranean island republic of Cyprus, for example, were taken seriously in Washington only when they seemed to be pushing the two countries to the brink of war. Under the zero-sum conditions of cold war diplomacy, the United States repeatedly intervened to defuse crises but tended to deprecate the importance of the grievances underlying them. Greek-Turkish differences have still to be resolved, and the two countries' ability to reach solutions unaided has been further weakened by violence in the Balkans that is itself aggravated by years of cold war neglect.

In today's international environment, whether a threat to American interests arises from differences between NATO allies or from despots assembling nuclear weapons in the wilderness, a new rationale for U.S. foreign policy is clearly needed. Or perhaps rather than a new rationale, a new way of looking at foreign policy, seeing it not as a way of countering a monolithic threat from outside the United States but as a way of coping with the problems of daily life *inside* the world community. Rather than a new, all-purpose doctrine, closer and more perceptive observation of our surroundings may be called for.

This is as true of economic as of political or military issues. To compete successfully in the world market, American manufacturers and the American government need to know more about the world. Foreign competition is too strong to enable us to continue selling left-hand-drive vehicles to right-hand-drive countries. We are also learning that trade agreements do not automatically become effective when they are signed. Enforcing them demands as much diplomacy as does negotiating them, and frequently more familiarity with local conditions. A recent press report on the problems involved in persuading the Chinese to take effective action to protect copyrights and patents shows how complex trade diplomacy has become: "Bringing about change no longer means policing what nations do at their borders . . . but rather meddling deeply in the inner workings of another country's economy, its power structure and its laws."[2] Viewed from this perspective, foreign policy (and diplomacy) take on a different coloration. If containment and military deterrence were the twin objectives of cold war strategy, their opposite faces—diplomatic interaction and suasion—are likely to figure more prominently in the strategy that succeeds it. This emerges not only from the changed appearance of the strategic landscape but from changed American expectations of foreign policy. Having prevailed in the cold war, Americans rarely advocate that the United States retreat into isolationism or abdicate its role of world leadership, but fewer still are willing to see U.S. forces take the lead in peacekeeping operations or to continue paying in other ways the full price of world leadership. The ability to win partners and organize coalitions has become essential in confronting military threats; in confronting nonmilitary threats like the spread of communicable diseases or environmental pollution, it has always been essential.

The character of U.S. world leadership, together with the resources and skills needed to sustain it, was bound to change as the world changed. As the cold war was winding down, one American commentator wrote of the United States: "Few nations in history have combined such raw military and economic muscle with so parochial a view of the rest of the globe as does modern America."[3] One may quarrel with the phrase "few nations in history." The island empires of Great Britain and Japan were more parochial in outlook than the United States, mainly because their populations were more homogeneous and less tolerant of diversity. Nevertheless, it is hard to dispute that American world leadership has been characterized more by military and economic power than by diplomatic finesse or political perceptiveness. Until the Nixon administration took into its own hands the day-to-day management of relations with the Soviet Union, this was the area where professional diplomats were most influential in shaping cold war policy. The price of miscalculation was too high to dispense altogether with experts who had firsthand knowledge and experience. This was so even when their advice was not followed. George F. Kennan has often complained that policymakers misconstrued his containment strategy to mean almost exclusively military containment; as a result, they consistently underestimated the importance of nonmilitary factors in Soviet affairs and were afflicted by tunnel vision when they looked at the rest of the world. Certainly, the predominant characteristic of American foreign policy during the cold war was single-mindedness; the litmus test for any policy initiative was how it would affect the balance of military power with the Soviet Union.[4]

A different, more versatile approach to foreign policy is indicated today. Decentralization, flexibility, and wide peripheral vision are more valuable attributes than the capacity for massive retaliation in a world that looks increasingly like the bustling, crawling, creeping Pennsylvania farm that Kennan described in his memoirs: "The farm includes 35 acres and a number of buildings. On every one of those acres, I have discovered, things are constantly happening. Weeds are growing, gullies are forming, fences are falling down, paint is fading, wood is rotting, insects are burrowing. Nothing seems to be standing still."[5]

A world where nothing is standing still, where everything needs attention but in different degrees at different times, is not a world whose problems can be clearly discerned from the summit, or that lends itself to single-issue diplomacy. Keeping up with the process of change, identifying incipient problems, and making an accurate initial appraisal of their likely effect on U.S. interests are best accomplished close up and from more than one vantage point. A well-equipped diplomatic service, intelligently led, sensibly managed, and logically deployed, can do this better than anyone else.

The central question addressed by this book is how well equipped, led, managed, and deployed American diplomacy is today. As a former career diplomat I have a healthy respect for the United States Foreign Service, a small corps of professionals numbering only a few thousand officers, many serving in dangerous and insalubrious posts that bear no resemblance to the diplomatic salons of popular imagination. Their services are usually unappreciated by policymakers and unknown to the general public until an American diplomat has the misfortune to be taken hostage or killed in the line of duty. The book's purpose, however, is not to celebrate unsung heroes. Changes are needed in the ways in which foreign policy is made, but also in the ways it is carried out. Traveling in relatively unknown seas, where navigation by cold war charts is no longer practical and new charts have yet to be drawn, neither the shipowner nor the pilot has reason for complacency. Nor do we, the passengers. In the pages that follow, I attempt to show how the craft can be made more seaworthy.

This is a book intended for the general reader concerned about foreign affairs as well as for specialists in the field. If changes in the structure, management, and priorities of American diplomacy are to occur, the power to effect them will come from outside the Foreign Service and probably from outside the State Department. I have as a result tried to avoid the language of diplomatic manuals and to present American diplomacy to the reader both in its historic context and from the standpoint of how it is practiced.

The book is divided into four main parts. The first chapter is introductory, discussing how traditional European diplomacy evolved, describing certain special features of the American approach to diplomacy, and analyzing changes in the international environment that affect fundamentally the diplomatic methods of all states. The next three chapters deal with historical phases of American diplomacy that embody distinguishing characteristics, grouped under the headings "the diplomacy of reason," "the diplomacy of doctrine," and "the diplomacy of process." Under the latter heading, the performance of the U.S. Foreign Service is compared with that of leading European powers. Then four chapters take up each of the core skills of diplomacy— representation, management, communication, and negotiation—and examine how well American diplomats have mastered them, how productively they use them, and how these skills fit into the policy-making process. The final two chapters provide conclusions and recommendations. The first of these chapters recommends ways to improve the use of diplomacy by policymakers, with particular reference to long-range policy planning, focusing policies on both global and regional problems, and introducing more continuity into the implementation of policies. The final chapter sets forth a series of recommendations designed to make American diplomacy a more effective instrument of foreign policy, starting with reforms in the State Department and concluding with reforms in the Foreign Service.

Acknowledgments

MY FIRST CONTACT with the Twentieth Century Fund was in 1950 when I was serving in my first Foreign Service post in Ankara, Turkey, and was presented with a copy of Thornburg, Spry, and Soule's *Turkey: An Economic Appraisal*, published the year before under the auspices of the Fund. It was an excellent study and I still consult it. My hope is that the authors' association with the Fund was as satisfactory as mine has been.

This book has been in preparation for three years, and over that time I have had many reasons to appreciate the support of the Twentieth Century Fund and its president, Richard C. Leone. Among his associates, past or present, I owe special thanks to my editor, Carol Kahn Strauss, who was as skillful in spotting logical lapses as grammatical ones. Thanks also go to David Aaron, Beverly Goldberg, and Michelle Miller for their assistance at various stages of the research and writing. As the book was nearing completion I benefited in the fall of 1994 from a seminar on portions of the manuscript, organized at the Council on Foreign Relations by the council's former director of studies, Nicholas X. Rizopoulos. In the final stage of preparing the manuscript for publication the oversight of Walter Lippincott at Princeton University Press and the editing of Anita M. O'Brien were especially valuable.

Among a distinguished group of foreign diplomats with whom I exchanged ideas while the book was in preparation, I would like to thank in particular André Ross, whom I first met in 1969 in Laos, where he was serving as French ambassador. He went on to represent France in Zaire, India, and Japan, retiring as secretary general of the Quai d'Orsay. It was Ambassador Ross who commissioned the report on the French Foreign Service prepared in 1987 under the chairmanship of Jacques Viot, at that time the French ambassador in London. The Viot report, which Ambassador Ross kindly made available to me, together with a number of comments of his own on contemporary

French diplomacy, proved of inestimable value. Other old friends, Wiegand Pabsch, the German ambassador to Argentina, and Alfred Cahen, the Belgian ambassador to France, have also been wonderful sources of intellectual stimulation and reflection on problems that all diplomatic services have in common. Needless to say, they bear no responsibility for my own comments and conclusions.

Numerous friends and associates from the United States Foreign Service have also read one or more chapters of the book in draft and have provided me with valuable comments. Among them are my erstwhile colleagues Morton I. Abramowitz, Robert M. Beaudry, Milton Kovner, Bruce Laingen, Stephen Low, Robert H. Miller, and Lannon Walker. In updating statistical data on the Foreign Service, another colleague, C. Edward Dillery, was extremely helpful. Among active Foreign Service officers, Robert T. Grey of the U.S. Delegation to the United Nations assisted me greatly in arranging appointments in New York, and Richard L. Jackson and Mark C. Lissfelt made valuable contributions to my thinking on various aspects of a Foreign Service career. I am especially indebted to Woodward Clark Price for the trouble he took to read the entire manuscript and to give me the benefit of observations made from the vantage point of an officer whose career is still largely before him. Discussion of policy planning in the book was greatly sharpened by the critical comments of Robert R. Bowie, a former director of the State Department's policy planning staff and professor emeritus of international relations at Harvard. Once again, if the reader finds errors of fact or judgment in the book, the responsibility is mine, not theirs.

Among several academic friends and associates with whom I discussed the book, Stanley Hoffmann of Harvard, Alan Henrikson of Tufts, and Robert L. Paarlberg of Wellesley made especially helpful comments. I am also grateful to Bruce Yenawine, director of the Connecticut River Museum and an admiring student of Benjamin Franklin, as I became, for steering me in the right direction to learn more about the accomplishments of the first and finest of U.S. diplomats.

During most of the period of research and writing, I have been fortunate to be either an associate or an affiliate of the Center for

International Affairs at Harvard. Whether in having access to the incomparable Harvard libraries, attending seminars, or participating in corridor discussions, my association with CFIA has greatly enriched the content of this book.

Once more I owe special thanks to my wife, Toni, who took time away from her own writing to give me the benefit of her fine editorial eye and perceptive comments.

Abbreviations

AFGE	American Federation of Government Employees
AFSA	American Foreign Service Association
AID	Agency for International Development
BENELUX	Belgium, the Netherlands, and Luxembourg
CCPS	Comprehensive Country Programming System
DCM	Deputy Chief of Mission
DGP	Director General, Foreign Service
EU	European Union
FAS	Foreign Agricultural Service
FCS	Foreign Commercial Service
FSI	Foreign Service Institute
FSO	Foreign Service Officer
HUMINT	Human Intelligence
INN	International Negotiation Network
IO	Bureau of International Organization Affairs, U.S. State Department
LCE	Limited Career Extension
NAFTA	North American Free Trade Agreement
NATO	North Atlantic Treaty Organization
NFATC	National Foreign Affairs Training Center
NGO	Nongovernmental Organization
NSC	National Security Council
SALT II	Strategic Arms Limitation Treaty
SES	Senior Executive Service
SFS	Senior Foreign Service
SIGINT	Signals Intelligence
S&T	Science and Technology
UNEP	United Nations Environmental Programme
UNHCR	United Nations High Commissioner for Refugees
USIA	United States Information Agency
USUN	United States United Nations Mission (New York)

Talking to Strangers

The New Frontiers of American Diplomacy

> Foreign policy can raise or lower the cost of your
> home mortgage, can give you a job, and can take it
> away. Foreign policy can affect the air you breathe.
> Foreign policy can determine the future of American
> security and the fate of American values.
> *(Winston Lord, National Press Club, July 22, 1992)*

THE LOSS of an enemy can be as disorienting as the loss of a friend. The collapse of communism has revealed a world that existed virtually unseen while the attention of Americans was riveted on the superpower confrontation. It is a world as unfamiliar to generations schooled in the cold war as the universe revealed by Copernicus was to generations schooled to believe that the Earth stood motionless at the center of the universe while other bodies in the Solar System revolved around it. And just as the heliocentric universe of Copernicus transformed the science of astronomy, so the post–cold war world requires a new approach to international relations and to diplomacy.

Nations are not constellations and diplomacy is not a science. The best we can hope to develop is an international system centered on the proposition that on a shrinking globe the common problems of nation-states deserve as much attention as do their individual problems. The frontiers of American diplomacy will have to undergo significant expansion, even as the core skills of the diplomatic profession—representation, management, communication, and negotiation—are significantly improved.

American diplomacy struggled to meet the needs of the old world. It will require drastic reform to meet those of the new. The United States may be the only remaining military superpower, but in its approach to diplomacy it too often looks like the only remaining banana republic. There is a great deal that is wrong with the way we formulate, implement, and manage U.S. foreign policy. Ingenuous zeal replaces knowledge of the history and dynamics of other cultures;

enthusiasm and frenetic activity replace patience and intelligent skepticism; and the illusion that foreign affairs is a series of excellent adventures replaces the reality that it is a turbulent but flowing process of change and synthesis. In the American vernacular, "diplomatic" usually means insincere and evasive, "undiplomatic" honest and straightforward.

Professionalism is prized in the United States in virtually all professions except diplomacy. So are the rewards of merit. The reason that neither is thought essential to the conduct of U.S. foreign policy lies in our history, our national temperament, and our form of government. It also lies in misconceptions we have about what diplomacy is intended to achieve, how it is most effectively employed to protect our national interests abroad, and what the proper relationship should be between professional diplomats and political policymakers.

Our closest allies take diplomacy more seriously than we do. So do our adversaries. In its day, even the Soviet Union, not a state that relied on diplomacy if intimidation was an option, managed its foreign service less cavalierly than do most American administrations. In the training they gave their young diplomats, especially language training, the Soviets were light years ahead of us. Typically, promising candidates for the Soviet Foreign Service were identified in secondary school and, after passing their entry examinations, spent five and a half years in a diplomatic prep school (the Moscow State Institute for International Relations). The orientation training of U.S. Foreign Service officers, including language training, is less than a year. Officers are lucky to get more than a year or two of additional training in their entire careers.

Much will have to be changed in our diplomacy to meet the needs of a rapidly changing world, starting with our mistaken assumption that, under the skin, all peoples are just like us and are prevented from agreeing with us, when they do not, only by their misguided leaders. This appealing but simplistic view of human nature helped put us up the Mekong without a paddle in Indochina and later into the Somali desert to feed starving children, some of whom ended up shooting at us or being shot. It complicates our efforts to place American relations with Russia on a new, more constructive basis because it fails to take sufficiently into account a fundamental truth expressed by

Aleksandr Solzhenitsyn when he returned to Russia in 1994 after twenty years of exile. National renewal, he said, would not result from simply grafting onto Russia the experience of the West because "Our life, spiritual and otherwise, must be formed from our own tradition, our understanding, our atmosphere."[1]

Indeed, American tradition, understanding, and atmosphere are not universally applicable. Consider how the national ethos is embodied in the American western film genre, a native art form that carries within it, as one critic has observed, "habits of perception that shape our sense of the world."[2] *The Man Who Shot Liberty Valance*, for example, a 1962 John Ford film that often turns up on late-night television, perfectly reflects what might be termed the iconographic American view of conflict, conflict resolution, and diplomacy. It is also unique among westerns in that the protagonist actually *becomes* a diplomat. James Stewart returns in retirement to the town of Shinbone, where years before he first hung out his shingle as a lawyer. A lawless cowtown when he first arrived, Shinbone has grown and been civilized in the years since Stewart was beaten up and humiliated by a gang of ruffians, led by Lee Marvin, whom the young lawyer tried ineffectually to bring to justice. Stewart had finally redeemed his honor when he shot it out with Marvin and was credited by the townspeople with killing him. The renown Stewart achieved as the man popularly supposed to have "shot Liberty Valance" is sufficient, we are led to believe, to launch him on a brilliant career of public service that includes terms as governor and United States senator and is crowned by his appointment as ambassador to the Court of St. James. Only at the end of the film, in a flashback, do we learn that law and order was brought to Shinbone not by Stewart but by John Wayne, the film's true hero, who had arranged for a sidekick to shoot the villainous Marvin from a concealed vantage point and for Stewart to get the credit.

The film is an expression of the abiding American distrust of those whose professional goal is compromise—usually lawyers or diplomats (or, in the case of the Stewart character, both). By temperament and tradition, we are less likely to regard diplomacy as the achievement of national objectives by means short of the use of force than as compromising objectives that the use of force would more reliably achieve. In the circumstances, it is not surprising that presidents and secretaries of state so often resort to images of the western frontier when they discuss American foreign policy. Dean Rusk said of the Cuban missile crisis, "we were eyeball to eyeball and the other guy blinked"; in an interview with an Italian journalist Henry Kissinger compared himself to the "lone cowboy"; spokesmen for the Nixon administration described its withdrawal strategy from Vietnam as "backing out of the barroom shooting." The language in each case is intended to suggest uncompromising diplomacy and the ability to go it alone.

During the period of the cold war, American foreign policy focused on the containment of the Soviet Union and its satellites. As long as the United States was able to maintain the level of preparedness that defense and intelligence analysts said was necessary for military parity with the Soviet Union, the objectives to be achieved by diplomacy, except in the field of arms control, were distinctly secondary. In a pinch, as Kissinger once said, we could "overwhelm problems with our resources."

In a different world, whose ground rules have yet to be defined, our ability to achieve national objectives by means short of force—by means that do not require disproportionate expenditure of our resources—will be of prime importance. The military success of the United States in the Gulf War does not invalidate this estimate. In the first place, the financial cost of the war was defrayed by substantial contributions extracted from our allies by a diplomatic effort as intensive as the military campaign it supported. In the second place, President Bush's claim that military action against Iraq was necessary to create "a new world order" looks decidedly premature and has not, in any event, been followed by action on an equivalent scale in other trouble spots.

DIPLOMACY OF THE GULF WAR

We do not know whether the Gulf War will prove to be the first police action of the new world order or, as now seems more likely, the last of the old. Whichever it is, the Bush administration showed that it was far more comfortable waging the war than defining its precise objectives and the outcome that would fully justify it. Having wooed the Iraqi dictator with agricultural export credits and conciliatory words up until the eve of his invasion of Kuwait, the administration never quite recovered its balance. The impression was unavoidable that in withdrawing the hand of friendship it had extended to Saddam Hussein and turning it into a clenched fist, the administration had failed to take into consideration all of the consequences of military intervention and all of the alternatives to it.

The Gulf War, in fact, illustrates the tendency of American foreign policy to define military actions not in the Clauswitzian sense of a "continuation of policy by other means" but as the final phase of policy beyond which there is only victory or defeat. Our diplomacy was most effective when it was working to create and sustain a consensus supporting military action. When it came to the diplomatic and political ends to be served by the Gulf War, the attention of senior administration officials seemed to wander and their voices to become more discordant. Diplomatic planning to anticipate the likely effect of the war (on the Iraqi Kurds and Shiite Moslems, or on Saddam Hussein himself) appeared to be almost nonexistent. The problems created for Turkey, first by the massive influx of Iraqi Kurds, then by stirring up the grievances of Turkish Kurds, seem to have taken the administration by surprise. One need not conclude from this that the administration's failure lay in its refusal to march into Baghdad and overthrow Saddam Hussein. On the contrary, it can be argued that such an outcome would have saddled the United States and its allies with responsibilities for the occupation and governance of Iraq that they were incapable of discharging. What can be said is that having prudently chosen more limited objectives, the administration should have shunned the language and tactics of total warfare and better weighed the political consequences of the policy it adopted.

While a fresh approach to the Arab-Israeli problem emerged from the dust of battle, it seemed to come almost as an afterthought and to capitalize too slowly on the altered balance of power in the region. There were signs that the State Department's Middle Eastern specialists, several of whom had received more public censure than their political superiors for carrying out the administration's policy of improving relations with Saddam Hussein before the Gulf War, were not consulted by the administration's leadership or informed of its intentions.

Foreign policy cannot work in this fashion. The absence of trust and the increasingly cluttered and obstructed lines of communication between top administration officials and their career staffs at home and abroad contribute greatly to the lack of foresight and follow-through that characterizes many of our recent foreign policy initiatives. They account as well for the often spasmodic and superficial quality of American diplomacy after the triumphs of the Marshall Plan and the Truman Doctrine.

THE VIENNA CONVENTION AND AMERICAN MORALITY

The traditional purpose of diplomacy is succinctly expressed in the preamble to the 1961 Vienna Convention on Diplomatic Relations in which the signatories, including the United States, after affirming their respect for the principles of the United Nations Charter "concerning the sovereign equality of States, the maintenance of international peace and security, and the promotion of friendly relations among nations," go on to express their belief "that an international convention on diplomatic intercourse, privileges and immunities [will] contribute to the development of friendly relations among nations, *irrespective of their differing constitutional and social systems.*"[3] The scope of diplomatic action is carefully circumscribed by Article 41:

> Without prejudice to their privileges and immunities, it is the duty of all persons enjoying such privileges and immunities to respect the laws and regulations of the receiving State. They also have a duty not to interfere in the internal affairs of that State. All official business with the receiving State entrusted to the [diplomatic] mission by the sending State shall be conducted with or through the Ministry for Foreign Affairs of the receiving State or such other ministry as may be agreed.[4]

No attempt is made to distinguish moral shades of sovereignty—whether power was acquired democratically or by inheritance or by coup d'etat—nor between just and unjust laws. The assumption behind the Vienna Convention is that diplomacy is the method by which sovereign states, equal under international law, conduct business with each other. This same assumption underlies all diplomatic conferences since the Treaty of Westphalia in 1648 that have sought to codify the rules of international conduct. Westphalia created a "states system," which, it was thought, would improve the prospects for peace in Europe by acknowledging the sovereign powers of rulers within their own borders and restraining them from interfering in the internal affairs of other states. It was hoped that this would prevent a recurrence of the religious wars that had convulsed Europe for more than a century. If confessional issues were treated as domestic affairs they could be removed from the diplomatic agenda and there would be one less *casus belli* to trouble the peace of Europe.

The American diplomatic method, which will be examined in detail in subsequent chapters, has never fully embraced so limited a view of the scope of foreign affairs. From the time Woodrow Wilson justified American entry into the First World War on the grounds that it would make the world "safe for democracy," to Ronald Reagan's denunciation of the Soviet "evil empire," American presidents have insisted, and the American public has expected, that foreign policy serve some purpose larger than regulating the nation's external affairs. The United States has been, in other words, resolutely pre-Westphalian in declaring the aims of its foreign policy even as it has accepted the restraints on diplomatic practice embodied in the Vienna Convention and its predecessors.

The tension this produces in the relations of American policymakers and American diplomats has been evident in every administration since Wilson's and has appeared to grow rather than abate. While congressional attitudes on individual foreign policy issues vary, the weight of congressional opinion has also tended to be pre-Westphalian in the sense that moral judgments on the conduct, whether internal or external, of foreign states come easily to members of Congress and carry few political liabilities at home. When Con-

9

gress in 1976 charged the State Department with the responsibility for preparing annual public reports evaluating the human rights record of each country receiving U.S. military or economic assistance, the Carter administration welcomed the move as consistent with its own desire to make respect for human rights in other countries a prime objective of U.S. foreign policy. It was American diplomats who were unenthusiastic about what they called "human rights report cards" and who predicted (correctly) that the administration would have trouble coming up with an accurate yardstick and applying it with consistent objectivity.

In carrying out U.S. foreign policy, American diplomats need to square the restraints of the Vienna Convention with the expectations of the political leadership and the public. The fit is never comfortable. It contributes to the ambivalence with which the profession of diplomacy is viewed in the United States and to the amount of fiddling with the machinery of foreign affairs that goes on in the name of making American diplomacy "responsive" or bringing it "up-to-date." Viewed from the standpoint of the Vienna Convention, American diplomats have generally been more up-to-date than foreign policy commentators and opinion leaders who seemed to be advocating a return to the religious warfare that Europe had abandoned in the seventeenth century as too Manichaean and too costly.

Limitations of Traditional Diplomacy

The thesis of this book is not by any means, however, that the world would be a safer place and its affairs more easily regulated if only states uniformly observed strict adherence to the rules of the Vienna Convention. Traditional diplomacy, well intentioned though it is, civilized as it tries to be, is simply not equipped to address the kinds of international problems that are emerging or, more accurately, are becoming visible after the cold war. The Vienna Convention, with its convenient distinction between internal and external affairs, leaves too many problems uncovered, including perhaps the most important one taught to us by World War II, that the punishment foreign tyrants mete out to their own people eventually will be extended to the rest of us if they are given the chance.

On a more practical and immediate plane, the way states deal with each other and the problems they need to solve have probably changed more in the last forty years than in the previous four hundred, since the time, that is, when the rudiments of modern diplomacy first began to take shape in Renaissance Italy. Diplomatic forms have changed too, of course, but surprisingly little, in either the last forty years or the last four hundred. Diplomacy now as then is basically the conduct of a dialogue between states through their authorized representatives. The principal difference is not in the central objective of diplomacy—which remains the enhancement of national security—or in the conception that diplomats have of their functions—which are still governed by centuries-old conventions that survive because they are reciprocal and have been found to be practical—but in the new ways in which national security is being defined and the new lines of communication available to the leaders of modern states when they practice diplomacy.

Modern Diplomacy and the Nation-State

The diplomatic dialogue today takes place through resident embassies and consulates, at international conferences, through hundreds of international organizations that have proliferated since World War II to address specialized problems or areas, and increasingly in direct talks between the leaders of states themselves.

One might assume that the ability of leaders to communicate face-to-face or by telephone would simplify the task of reaching agreement. The practice has certainly become widespread. Its popularity during the Bush administration can be inferred from the fact that, by an informed estimate, the presidents of the United States and Turkey alone exchanged no less than forty telephone calls between the opening of the Gulf crisis in August 1990 and the end of that year.[5] Such exchanges, however, do not invariably speed the wheels of diplomacy. The result may even be to slow them down. Taken in conjunction with the tendency of states to identify threats to their national interest in much wider, and often more arcane, spheres of activity, including actions by other states whose effect in earlier periods of international life would have been regarded as purely internal, personal diplomacy can lead to delay and misunderstanding. Few leaders have the time to master a detailed brief or to probe for hidden reservations or nuances in the position of a foreign counterpart. Since the substantive talks of leaders are limited by competing demands and time-consuming ceremonies, understanding in depth is rare and the outcome can be colored by personal chemistry or by factors irrelevant to the problem under discussion. A former Canadian ambassador to the United States has described how the mutual dislike of President Reagan and Prime Minister Trudeau complicated his efforts to achieve agreement on the acid rain problem—a good example of the kind of contemporary international dispute that goes far beyond the diplomatic guidelines of Westphalia and Vienna. Resolution of the acid rain controversy required, among other things, changes in U.S. domestic legislation, something only the American Congress could effectuate, and to move the dispute toward agreement the Canadian ambassador had to revise drastically his own somewhat traditionalist view of what constituted interference in the internal affairs of another state.[6]

However the dialogue between sovereign states is conducted, whether by leaders directly or through embassies and other intermediaries, there is a common assumption that the nucleus of international affairs is the sovereign nation-state, which enters into the dialogue and accepts its conventions and restraints voluntarily, fulfills negotiated obligations scrupulously, and does not resort to war except in self-defense. These may be said to be the rules of the diplomatic game, defining what amounts to the playing field for states wishing to participate in it. Rules similar to those observed today were first codified in 1815 at the Congress of Vienna, although many of them, like the reciprocal privileges and immunities customarily bestowed by states on foreign envoys to facilitate communications with their governments, can be traced back to the Greek city-states. The rules of this game, like those of any other, may be broken by individual states, but the assumption further holds that states that break them flagrantly and frequently will be expelled from the field, forceably if necessary.

The practitioners of modern diplomacy until the end of the First World War tended, in the words of British diplomat and author Harold Nicolson, to be men who "possessed similar standards of education, similar experience and a similar aim"—men who "desired the same sort of world."[7] It is remarkable how serviceable the system remained even when the players became more diverse and made a point of rhetorically rejecting the rules of the game. The leaders of the Soviet Union after the Bolshevik revolution were extravagant in their denunciations of traditional diplomacy as a bourgeois device intended to perpetuate the global privileges and inequities of capitalism. They abolished all traditional diplomatic titles in 1918 and decreed that chiefs of Soviet diplomatic missions abroad should be known as "plenipotentiary representatives," not ambassadors or ministers. Nevertheless, in practice the Soviet Union eventually came to accept the utility of diplomatic discourse and to observe its conventions,[8] as have any number of Third World states that also considered diplomacy reactionary in purpose and decadent in style. The United States itself held this view in the early years of American independence, as will be seen in the next chapter.

It was not that revolutionary and Third World leaders "desired the same sort of world" as their counterparts in the industrialized states. It was simply that they recognized that traditional diplomacy afforded the most reliable lines of communication between states even when it failed to produce agreement. Since revolutionary and newly independent states were, if anything, more sensitive to the prerogatives of sovereignty and quicker to discern external threats to it than were older, more complacent states, they could also see more advantages than not in participating in the established states system. They tried to make the older states abide by the rules they had themselves created, especially by discouraging the interference of one state in the internal affairs of another. All the states in the system, in other words, whatever their economic development and political philosophy, prized their own sovereignty enough to acknowledge that of others—to acknowledge that all were independent states functioning in an interdependent system. Because the nation-state remained the nucleus of international affairs, traditional diplomacy remained the preferred method of conducting international business. Paradoxically, it was the cold war, during which relations and negotiations between the superpowers dominated the global scene, that camouflaged—while aggravating—the changes in the structure of international affairs that we can now see are deeply threatening to the ability of traditional diplomacy to address its most important challenges.

NATIONALISM AFTER THE COLD WAR

The world emerging from the cold war is characterized by ethnic and cultural nationalism, as well as by economic and social transnationalism. Both characteristics are in some degree incompatible with the authority and competence of the contemporary nation-state and, accordingly, with familiar diplomatic practices and priorities. The splintering of states like the Soviet Union and Yugoslavia requires new rules of the game if stability and peace are to be restored to the peoples these lapsed sovereignties once comprehended, and to the geographical space they still occupy. How does the restructuring of these formerly independent political units affect the traditional reluctance of states to intervene openly in the internal affairs of other states? If external borders have previously been treated as legally sacrosanct, what should the attitude of the international community be toward internal borders? What exactly are the rights of minorities under international law, and who is to judge when self-determination is justified in becoming secession?

There are no easy answers to these questions. At the time the United States recognized Slovenia and Croatia in 1992, Yugoslavia had existed as a nation-state almost as long as the United States had at the time of the American Civil War, when the critically important objective of Union diplomacy was to prevent international recognition of the Confederacy. How, in consequence, should diplomats square their responsibilities in the domain of state-to-state relations with their responsibilities in the field of human rights? For policymakers struggling to define national interests in their wider context, such dilemmas are no less painful. How high a price can the United States afford to pay in its trade relations with undemocratic states, for example, in the hope of achieving progress in the entirely unrelated fields of constitutional or social reform? It was an issue that dogged American relations with the Soviet Union in the past and seriously complicates relations with China today.

While the collapse of Yugoslavia and the Soviet Union have been termed "implosions" because most of the violence is directed inward, that does not mean other states are not also profoundly affected. The flow of refugees out of combat zones in eastern Europe and many other parts of the world shows that the internal problems of states can easily spill over on their neighbors. Yet contiguous states, acting alone or bilaterally, cannot hope to control the accelerated flight of refugees that ethnic nationalism has generated. Indeed, the problem is overwhelming the resources both of neighboring states and of the United Nations High Commissioner for Refugees (UNHCR). Global homelessness challenges the competence and compassion of the international community as much as the homeless of our cities challenge national and municipal authorities. New mechanisms, authorities, and programs are badly needed in both areas.

ECONOMIC TRANSNATIONALISM

Economic transnationalism makes different but equally strong demands on the authority of the contemporary nation-state. Former Secretary of State George Shultz used to illustrate the increasingly multinational character of American manufacturing by quoting from a shipping label on a crate of integrated circuits produced by a company in the United States: "This product contains components made in one or more of the following countries: Korea, Hong Kong, Malaysia, Singapore, Taiwan, Mauritius, Thailand, Indonesia, Mexico, the Philippines. The exact country of origin is unknown." Unknown also is the exact effect of this trend on American national interests. If the integrated circuits made by the American firm contain components manufactured in Malaysia and Mauritius, for example, the firm—and by extension the American government and the American economy—has a tangible stake in the economic stability of Malaysia and Mauritius. And wherever the integrated circuits are to be sold, the United States has both a need for assured access to the market and a stake in its vitality. Some models of American automobiles contain so many foreign-made components that Congress is considering the feasibility of requiring manufacturers to list them to enable purchasers to know when they are really "buying American."

The difficulty in gauging who wins and who loses—whether jobs or profits—as manufacturing becomes more multinational accounts for much of the bitterness with which the North American Free-Trade Agreement (NAFTA) was debated in 1993. This transformation of production is matched by a transformation of the world capital market, where, by one estimate, a trillion dollars is electronically transferred through the system every day. Both in its innovations in manufacturing and in capital transfer the new system provides great flexibility and responsiveness, but whether the system represents for the states participating in it mutual reinforcement or mutual vulnerability will depend on the skill with which it is operated by governments, multinational corporations, banks, and international agencies, none of which has much past experience in managing an international system in which the nucleus of power is not preemptively that of the nation-state.

SOCIAL TRANSNATIONALISM

One could add many other examples of problems that do not need passports to cross international frontiers: environmental pollution, including acid rain and depletion of the ozone layer, nuclear and conventional arms proliferation, the transmission of the AIDS virus, international terrorism, and the drug trade are a few that come readily to mind. The questions raised for diplomats by these transnational problems relate, on the one hand, to the kinds of expertise they need to keep up with them and, on the other, to the ways available to them, if they are accredited to a foreign government rather than an international organization, to reconcile their bilateral with their multilateral responsibilities. Serving in a state whose government one suspects of being lax in combating the activities of terrorist groups, how far is the diplomat justified in going to do the anti-terrorist job that the host government—or, in the terminology of the Vienna Convention, the "receiving" government—is failing to do? When the diplomat tries to judge the adequacy of a foreign government's efforts to control the spread of the AIDS virus or drug trafficking or atmospheric pollution, how much inside information is needed, and how far can he or she afford to go in acquiring it? Collecting information in some of these areas will be new and legitimate targets for intelligence agencies, but the diplomat will still have difficult decisions to make for which there are no clear precedents or guidelines—certainly none provided by the Vienna Convention.

Many of these problems will require states to work together in new ways, investing a larger fraction of their sovereignty in existing or still-to-be-created international authorities that possess the skills, continuity, and scope to address problems unknown to traditional diplomacy or unrecognized by it. The enlarged possibilities for effective international cooperation that have opened up with the end of the cold war will be wasted if states are unable to protect their vital common interests as effectively as they do their vital competing interests.

Clearly, if the world of the cold war was Shinbone, the world that has succeeded it is not. The quest for security and justice no longer leads to a showdown between two armed antagonists in a dusty street. The problems we face have few up-or-down solutions. This is a teeming, divided world with a population crowded into a space too small for it, rapidly consuming its own substance, and afflicted by problems it barely understands. It is a world where compromise is not contemptible but a condition for survival.

WHY AMERICAN DIPLOMACY MATTERS

None of the changes occurring in the structure of international affairs implies, however, that the nation-state is defunct or that its powers of action and decision will be delegated to international bureaucracies.

Multinational agencies are only as strong as their members permit them to be, and their capacity for independent action is almost nil. The United Nations has only the capability its members provide to enforce the resolutions passed by them. Nation-states are still the principal actors and the only enforcers. Indeed, what we are seeing is not the demise of nation-states but their proliferation. There will be more bilateral diplomacy, not less. To cite only one example, the United States has replaced a single embassy in Moscow with fifteen in the capitals of all the former soviet socialist republics.

But the successor states to the Soviet Union, to Yugoslavia, and to who knows how many other uneasy unions of distrustful tribes will be weaker and less effectual than the polities they replace. They will need more assistance to become contributing members of the world community. Greater diplomatic effort will be required of the older and larger states if effective coordination in addressing common problems is to be achieved, even supposing that agreement can be reached on what they are and what causes them. Nor can we assume that the ethnic homogeneity of the new states will assure their tranquility and simplify their problems of national security. It was Lord Acton in the nineteenth century who advanced the view that wherever geographical boundaries coincided with ethnic ones, chauvinism, xenophobia, and racism were potential threats to liberty. Looking at the wars of nationalities in ex-Yugoslavia and the Caucasus (or, for that matter, in the ethnic neighborhoods of American cities), who would be likely to argue with him?

This, of course, will place greater responsibilities on the more secure and powerful states than they have had to shoulder in the past. It will in particular challenge the United States, still the richest and most powerful actor in the states system, to make good its claims to be seeking a more just as well as a more peaceful world. The universality with which Americans like to cloak their country's foreign policy, misplaced as it has sometimes been, can be an advantage to policymakers in creating new structures of international cooperation and to diplomats in making them work.

The quality of American diplomacy will matter more than ever—to ourselves and to others. That is why it deserves a close look at this time to determine what its distinctive traits are, how it evolved into its present form, and whether that form is adequate to the challenges ahead. Where the American diplomatic method is inadequate, how can it be strengthened? And, where adequate, how can it be better used as an instrument of American foreign policy?

The Diplomacy of Reason

> The most complete victory is to cause the enemy
> to relinquish his purpose without suffering loss to
> yourself.
> *(Belisarius)*

BEFORE CONSIDERING whether the contemporary world requires a
new diplomacy, and specifically a new American diplomacy, to cope
with problems that differ in kind as well as degree from those confronted by earlier states systems, the origins of American diplomatic
practice must be examined to determine if there is a distinctively
American diplomatic method.

THE AMERICAN TRADITION

We should begin by recognizing that Americans, from the earliest
days of independence, have consciously sought to avoid European
diplomatic models. We have seen ourselves, rightly or wrongly, as
practitioners of a new diplomacy, born of the Enlightenment, in
which the power of reason would replace military power and distinctions between personal and state morality would be narrowed if not
entirely eliminated. The founders of the republic sought alternatives
to the use of military force to achieve national objectives. The
Louisiana Purchase established a precedent for the later Gadsden and
Alaska purchases. The founders disliked the concept of a balance of
power, in large part because they recognized that European wars, including those fought on the American continent, were waged to preserve or restore it.

The American desire to conduct foreign affairs in a different way
extended to diplomatic forms. Scorning the elaborate uniforms worn
by European diplomats, the first American representatives abroad

made an impression by their simplicity of attire. After independence, presumably as a reassurance to European monarchies, the United States adopted diplomatic and consular uniforms (the senior American envoy's tricornered hat to be decorated with a white ostrich feather, "not standing erect, but sewed around the brim"[1]), but it abandoned them after the Civil War. Associating the title of ambassador with the rule of kings and the etiquette of courts, the United States did not accord the rank to its senior diplomats until 1893, appointing instead ministers plenipotentiary. The first diplomatic history of the United States, published in 1826, notes that "the pre-eminence of ambassadors manifests itself chiefly in the particular ceremonial of their reception in the country where they are appointed to reside. They are entitled to speak at the audiences they obtain, with heads covered—to keep a canopy or throne in their dwellings, etc."[2] More significantly, the author goes on to say that the faculty of representing his sovereign "an American minister cannot well possess, for he represents nothing but the nation."

This sense of conducting ourselves differently from Europeans, of being more high-minded than they, more democratic and more scrupulous in our observance of international law, continued to permeate American diplomacy even after it became apparent that the United States was as capable of acting out of self-interest as any other state, and as likely to disregard international law when it did not suit the national purpose. The moral pretensions of American diplomacy are nevertheless as essential to its character as the pragmatism with which most American governments have conducted it. The dichotomy developed early.

BEN FRANKLIN, DIPLOMAT

The first American diplomat is generally considered to have been Benjamin Franklin. After serving eight and a half years in France, initially as an American commissioner, then as American minister, he was succeeded in 1785 by Thomas Jefferson, who represented the United States in Paris for almost five years. No other explanation may

21

be necessary for the trust we have placed ever since in the virtues of amateurism in the practice of diplomacy.

In reality, Franklin and Jefferson, quite aside from their remarkable qualities of intellect and character, were no amateurs. By the time he arrived in France in 1776, Franklin had already served twice in quasi-diplomatic capacities in England. His two London missions, totaling a period of more than fifteen years, were from 1757 to 1762 to negotiate on behalf of the Pennsylvania Assembly differences with the proprietary Penn family, and from 1764 to 1775 to act as agent, first for Pennsylvania, ultimately for Georgia, New Jersey, and Massachusetts as well, in their increasingly difficult relations with the British government. All of these missions were in varying degrees unsuccessful, but they made of Franklin a knowledgeable, tough-minded and infinitely patient diplomat of whom John Adams would later write: "Who, in the name of astonishment, in all America, at that time had a knowledge of courts? Franklin alone had resided in England as a despised and scorned agent at the Court of St. James's. His manners, address, learning, knowledge, and good sense were acknowledged by all who conversed with him."[3]

Despite Franklin's experience and superb diplomatic skills, his mission to France from 1776 to 1785 can be said to have established a precedent for everything that has gone wrong ever since in the management of American foreign policy.[4] He was consistently frustrated by slow, divided, or nonexistent decision making at home; his credibility was undermined by the appointment of incompetent and badly informed supernumeraries whose responsibilities duplicated (when they did not triplicate or quadruplicate) his own; his authority on issues central to his mission was threatened by the despatch of special envoys who knew little about France but were said to be closer to the thinking of the American government than Franklin; he was inundated by administrative and consular minutiae; and after he had successfully completed his assignment he was unjustly attacked for giving away too much to the French.

Franklin began his French mission as one of three commissioners, as American independence was still unrecognized by France at the end of 1776 when he arrived there. His two colleagues were the free-wheeling Silas Deane of Connecticut, who had already made one trip to France the year before to obtain supplies for the Continental Army, and the self-important and vindictive Arthur Lee of Virginia. Franklin was already a well-known figure of the Enlightenment in France and was quickly able to establish relations of confidence with the French foreign minister, the Count de Vergennes. However, he never managed to resolve the problem of redundant lines of communication, which were further complicated at home by the existence of two committees of the Continental Congress responsible for foreign affairs, the Committee of Secret Correspondence and the Secret Committee. On a personal level, Franklin's relations with Deane remained fairly harmonious, despite Deane's political intriguing and financial speculation, but Franklin earned the implacable enmity of Lee, who professed to believe him corrupt and whom Franklin, in turn, according to one student of his French mission, considered a "lunatic."[5]

Deane's replacement in 1778 by John Adams did not improve the situation, since Adams, though more intelligent than Deane and less conniving than Lee, disapproved of Franklin's disorderly work habits and considered him dissipated in his social life. Adams and Franklin, however, agreed on one thing, the folly of hydra-headed diplomacy, "whose hazard," said Franklin, "is in proportion to the number."[6] Little did he know how fortunate he was in comparison to some of his successors. At one time after World War II, the United States maintained five senior officials in Paris with the rank of ambassador.

FRANKLIN'S STYLE

Problems arising from the dissimilar temperaments and conflicting egos of the commissioners were compounded for Franklin by the impossibility of obtaining timely and accurate information on the progress of the war and, when news finally arrived, strong differences of opinion among the commissioners about the best way to present it to the French. Deane, Lee, and Adams were all activists whose inclination was to multiply the number of American démarches and alarm the French with the specter of a negotiated peace with Britain on terms short of independence if France did not openly commit itself to the American cause. Franklin, whose disposition was to avoid wrangling with his fellow commissioners or with the French if possible, went along with this approach at first but quickly decided that it was counterproductive. Similarly, when news of the surrender of Fort Ticonderoga to the British was published in the London papers in August 1777, Franklin resisted Deane's recommendation that the French be presented with an ultimatum—either France side openly with the United States or the Americans would sue for peace. It was well that he did. By early December the news of Bourgoyne's surrender at Saratoga had reached France and the military picture had changed entirely. Franklin and Vergennes signed treaties of commerce and alliance within two months.

Franklin's approach to the French (which his colleagues, especially Adams, regarded as indolent) was in fact a reflection of his growing conviction that the French would make an open commitment when they were ready to go to war with Britain and not before. He saw no danger that France would side with its ancient enemy against the Americans or do anything deliberately to strengthen British prospects for victory. Accordingly, in his eyes, it was prejudicial to American interests to try to provoke an Anglo-French war before the French were ready to fight. At best such a tactic would damage the confidence of the French in American good faith; at worst it would precipitate a French defeat.

Years later, in 1784, Silas Deane described Franklin's attitude: "It is proper to observe that Doctor Franklin was from the first averse to warm and urgent solicitations with the Court of France. His age and experience, as well as his philosophical temper, led him to prefer a patient perseverance, and to await events, and to have the Court of France to act from motives of interest only."[7] Deane might have mentioned another virtue of Franklin's diplomatic style, his imperviousness to flattery. While serving as a colonial agent in England in 1767, Franklin had written skeptically to his son, William, of ingratiating remarks made to him by the French minister. In this he was more like Jefferson, who scorned flattery, than like his fellow envoy John Jay. After Jay negotiated an inconclusive and unpopular treaty with the British in 1794, a British minister observed, "Mr. Jay's weak side is Mr. Jay."

Dr. Franklin's strong side was unquestionably Dr. Franklin, and he displayed the qualities most prized (and most rare) in a diplomat today. He accurately and dispassionately appraised the French view of their own interests in the Revolutionary War; he refused to be stampeded into precipitate actions; he eschewed diplomatic activity for its own sake; and he presented the American case (as Jefferson would do later) less by lecturing the French than in pragmatic terms, to encourage them, in Deane's words, "to act from motives of interest only."

Franklin's diplomacy was effective in another way of which Jefferson's would be reminiscent. He took pains to learn how the French system operated, including the intricacies of the French budget process, knowledge of which enabled him to discourage American loan requests that were badly timed or unclearly and unpersuasively presented. Most importantly, perhaps, he mastered the French style of doing things. His proficiency in the language was apparently serviceable and amusing rather than fluent, but he was superbly equipped to meet the French on their own ground socially.

As a colonial agent in England, Franklin conducted diplomacy largely through journalism and the written word, but in France he adapted himself to the French preference for social discourse and conversation. Adams's sour comment that Franklin's round of dinners was a "scene of continual discipation"[sic][8] probably reveals more about his own social discomfort in France than about Franklin's excesses. Franklin enjoyed the French and they enjoyed him. The success of his mission was facilitated by his salon diplomacy, just as the tart-tongued, disapproving, and hyperactive Adams quickly depleted his influence and wore out his welcome in Paris in jarring diplomatic and social confrontations.

FRANKLIN'S "LOCALITIS"

The price Franklin paid for his success was a charge of Francophilia and lack of zeal in protecting American interests. He was attacked not only by Arthur Lee but by another bustling, freelance American diplomat in Europe, Ralph Izard of South Carolina, who later declared that "the political salvation of America depends upon the recalling of Dr. Franklin."[9] Izard had been appointed commissioner to Tuscany in 1777 without any consideration of whether he would be received there by the Tuscan court. When he was not, he turned up in Paris vainly hoping to introduce himself into Franklin's negotiations with Vergennes. Rebuffed by both Franklin and the French, he became, upon his return to the United States, one of Franklin's bitterest critics in the Continental Congress. The criticism and second-guessing took their toll. When a special envoy was sent to Paris to seek a new French loan in 1781, Franklin correctly concluded that he was being by-passed and offered his resignation. Fortunately, it was not accepted.

The suspicion that Franklin was overly partial to the French was unfair to him but comprehensible in the circumstances of revolutionary diplomacy. The United States was fighting for survival and needed French help but was reluctant to accept a relationship of dependency on a monarchy that did not share the ideals expressed in the Declaration of Independence. As a small, embattled, and internally divided confederation whose power did not compare to that of the major European states, the United States had reason to fear the consequences of overcommitting itself to France. The attitude is far less justified today when the charge of "parochialism" or "localitis" is still leveled at American diplomats who are deemed more familiar than they should be with a particular foreign culture.[10] In the constant shuffling of officers from one assignment to another in the modern Foreign Service, however, few stay long enough to risk contagion. As a result, few become real experts. Franklin's more than eight years in France and Jefferson's five contrast with the average tenure of three years to which contemporary American ambassadors are limited. The loss to American foreign policy in depth of knowledge and continuity is incalculable.

The best defense of Franklin from the charges of Izard, Lee, and others was made by Jefferson in a letter dated December 4, 1818:

> The fact that his temper was so amiable and conciliatory, his conduct so rational, never urging impossibilities, or even things unreasonably inconvenient to them [the French], in short, so moderate and attentive to their

difficulties, as well as our own, that what his enemies called subserviency, I saw was only that reasonable disposition, which, sensible that advantages are not all to be on one side, yielding what is just and liberal, is the more certain of obtaining liberality and justice.[11]

THOMAS JEFFERSON, DIPLOMAT

Jefferson when he arrived in Paris was younger (by thirty-seven years) than Franklin and much less experienced in the ways of foreign courts, but he had gained considerable experience in statecraft as a member for seven years of the Virginia House of Burgesses, a delegate to the Continental Congress, and governor of wartime Virginia from 1779 to 1781. Furthermore, Jefferson, like Franklin, had thought deeply about the relationship of the colonies to the mother country and to Europe. In 1774, at the age of thirty-one, he had written *A Summary View of the Rights of British America*, an essay based on his proposed instructions for the Virginia delegates to the Continental Congress. It was an angry but carefully reasoned indictment of British colonial policy, including the taxes and duties levied by the Crown on exports and imports that interfered with the colonies' freedom of commerce—a prerogative of statehood that became the foundation of Jefferson's philosophy of foreign affairs and which he worked tirelessly to promote during his service in France and later as secretary of state and president. Addressed as a warning and appeal to King George III, Jefferson's essay also expressed a view on the style appropriate to American diplomatic communication that later American diplomats, less gifted in composition than he, have often used less skillfully: "Let those flatter, who fear: it is not an American art."[12]

Jefferson's service in France was troubled by fewer problems in Franco-American relations than Franklin had faced, but there were internal French problems of which he was well aware. Jefferson was a careful and sympathetic observer of events leading up to the French Revolution, having early in his residency decided that the French court was out of touch with reality. As he wrote to Madison from Fontainebleau: "The king comes here in the fall always, to hunt. His court attend him, as do also the foreign diplomatic corps. But as this is not indispensably required and my finances do not permit the expence of a continued residence here, I propose to come occasionally to attend the king's levees, returning again to Paris, distant forty miles."[13]

The American government, preoccupied with domestic problems, was not greatly interested in internal French affairs that did not directly impinge on American interests, especially commercial. This changed when relations with revolutionary France worsened dramatically in the first term of Washington's presidency, by which time Jefferson was no longer in Paris. Instead, he was coping with them as secretary of state.

The high priority assigned by the Continental Congress to American commercial interests very much accorded with Jefferson's own and resulted in a masterpiece of economic analysis and reporting that should be required reading today for every young Foreign Service officer. Jefferson's *Observations on the Whale-Fishery*, conveyed to the French Foreign Ministry in 1788, brilliantly demonstrates his ability to master a complex subject (with which, as a Virginian, he must have been relatively unfamiliar) and to marshal exhaustively the most cogent and elegantly written arguments to support his thesis that exclusion of American whale oil from the French market worked against French interests. Throughout his démarche, Jefferson deftly develops a strategic rationale to bolster his economic arguments: "France had effectually aided in detaching the U.S. from the *force* of Great Britain. But as yet they seemed to have indulged only a silent wish to detach them from her *commerce*." He concludes:

> Whether then we consider the Arrêt of September 28 [closing the French market to American whale oil] in a political or a commercial light, it would seem that the U.S. should be excepted from its operation. Still more so when they invoke against it the amity subsisting between the two nations, the desire binding them together by every possible interest and connection, the several acts of favour of this exception, the dignity of legislation which admits not of changes backwards and forwards, the interests of commerce which require steady regulations, the assurances of

the friendly motives which have led the king to pass these acts, and the hope that no cause will arise to change either his motives or his measures towards us.[14]

Jefferson's efforts to reverse French exclusionary policies were largely successful, although he apparently had to contend not only with the French government, but with a clan of Nantucket whalers who had a privileged marketing arrangement in Dunkirk and may have colluded with French officials to keep other American whale oil off the French market.[15] The influence of special-interest lobbies on American foreign policy is obviously not a recent phenomenon.

Jefferson's démarche on the whale-oil issue was what we would today call "voluntary," although it clearly advanced an American interest that Jefferson knew to be important. The research and drafting were Jefferson's responsibility. His approach to the French did not have to be cleared with agencies and officials at home who might have worried about the vegetable-oil lobby, the dangers of overcommitting America to the French cause, or even the reaction of the rival Nantucket whalers. Action was taken by the man closest to the problem in the way he considered most likely to persuade the French government that its interests would be served by changing French policy, not, as is the case with too many contemporary démarches, in the way most likely to satisfy competing domestic bureaucracies that their individual interests are being protected.

Jefferson's *Observations* were comprehensive in their mobilization of the best arguments his versatile intellect could identify in every field relevant to the subject. In the more compartmentalized Foreign Service of the present, where an embassy is composed of specialists in several distinct but related areas—known collectively as the "country team"—the drafting of an aide-memoire of this kind would in all likelihood be delegated to the embassy's economic section, cleared, perhaps with minor additions or subtractions, by the political section, edited by the deputy chief of mission, and approved (if deemed worthy of his attention) by the chief of mission. Such a process does little for the style and persuasiveness of most official communications. The misconception that diplomacy is, or should be, the application of primarily technical skills to essentially technical problems reduces much contemporary diplomatic correspondence to the lifeless prose of a computer manual. It is rare for arguments to be presented vivaciously or within a context defined by more than one dimension of the national interest. Messages today move with the speed of light, but too often cast little.

Jefferson's diplomatic service in France is notable for more than his eloquence. He explored France indefatigably, from the bookstalls on the Seine to the French countryside, paying special attention to the condition of French agriculture. From his letters it is clear that he used the French language not only with officials but with villagers whom he encountered on his long walks. These conversations were a valuable opportunity to gain insights into the life of the peasantry in the ancien régime and, by extension, into the health of the expiring regime itself. In a letter to Lafayette he writes:

> From the first olive fields of Pierrelate to the orangeries of Hières, has been continued rapture to me. I have often wished for you [to accompany me]. . . . This is perhaps the only moment of your life in which you can acquire that knolege [*sic*]. And to do it most effectually you must be absolutely incognito, you must ferret the people out of their hovels as I have done, look into their kettles, eat their bread, loll on their beds under pretence of resting yourself, but in fact to find if they are soft.[16]

FRANKLIN AND JEFFERSON: DIPLOMATS OF THEIR TIMES

The exceptional qualities that characterize the diplomacy of Franklin and Jefferson suggest that great diplomats, like great soldiers, are a product of their times. The most productive periods in American diplomacy have been those when the American people faced, or thought they faced, the threat of national extinction. The diplomacy of the American Revolution was essentially a diplomacy of survival. Once it was recognized that the United States could not survive without foreign help—and Franklin was one of the first to see this—the only important questions left to decide were where and how to obtain it.

The issues confronting U.S. foreign policy were similarly clarified in later periods of national crisis, and American diplomats usually emerged who were equal to them. During the Civil War, Charles Francis Adams represented the United States with distinction in the critically important London embassy, and after World War II career diplomats like George Kennan and Charles Bohlen played vital policy-making roles and became national figures. Conflicts like the First World War, Korea, and Vietnam, on the other hand, which were not wars of national survival, although they were proclaimed so at the time, turned out to be as bad for diplomatic as for military reputations.

The Civil War Diplomacy of Charles Francis Adams

The Civil War, no less than the Revolutionary War, was a life-or-death struggle for the United States. The survival of the Union depended on the ability of the North not only to prevail on the battlefield but also to prevail diplomatically. It was essential to forestall recognition of the Confederacy by the Europeans. London was the key diplomatic salient, for if England recognized the South the continent would surely follow the English lead. The performance of Adams as United States minister at the Court of St. James shares many of the characteristics displayed by Franklin and Jefferson. Functioning in a much more hostile environment than they had encountered in France, his accomplishment in preventing English recognition of the Confederacy was no less significant than theirs in preserving the Union.

Charles Francis Adams was the grandson of John Adams, Franklin's cocommissioner in Paris, who later became the second president of the United States. Charles Francis Adams had spent much of his boyhood in Europe. His father, John Quincy Adams, served at various times as minister to the Netherlands, Prussia, Russia, and Great Britain. As secretary of state, he was the author of the Monroe Doctrine in 1824. Charles Francis Adams had therefore received a thorough grounding in diplomatic practice by the time he was appointed to London in 1861. It was apparent that he would need it from the moment he stepped off the ship at Liverpool to be informed that Britain had recognized the belligerency of the Confederacy. Adams's son Henry, accompanying his father to London as private secretary, described how his father reacted to the news: "The instructions [from Washington] . . . were clear and unmistakable and would have justified him and something more in at once refusing to hold any communications with the government here. . . . But he decided otherwise and determined not to do anything violent."[17]

Adams, in the tradition of his family, was strongly antislavery, although before the outbreak of war he had advocated a policy of moderation toward the South. He had expected that antislavery sentiment in Britain would work to the advantage of the Union and was disillusioned to find that British economic interest in trade with the Confederacy carried greater weight. Nevertheless, he set about cultivating friends where he could find them, reminding the British government ceaselessly of its obligations under international law, and discouraging actions in London or Washington that would rupture diplomatic relations. Confident that he knew his friends and adversaries, never reluctant to take the initiative, but invariably patient in his dealings with the British government, Adams remained alert but imperturbable through almost seven difficult years in London: "He showed no trace of excitement. His manner was the same as ever; his mind and temper were as perfectly balanced; not a nerve twitched."[18]

THE SPOILS SYSTEM

The challenge of great events can of course summon up greatness in individuals only if the quality is there to be summoned. Many of the other American envoys in European capitals during the Civil War were undistinguished political hacks, and Adams's staff in London, with the exception of his son, was little better. Henry Adams reports that "As Secretary of Legation the Executive appointed the editor of a Chicago newspaper who had applied for the Chicago Post-Office."[19]

To judge from the account of Charles Francis Adams, President Lincoln himself had given Adams's appointment to London little serious attention. When Adams, accompanied by Secretary of State Seward, was received by the president and expressed his gratitude for the appointment, Lincoln said he should direct his thanks to Seward. Then, instead of the discussion of Anglo-American relations Adams had been hoping for, the president, "stretching out his legs before him . . . with an air of great relief as he swung his long arms to his head[, said]:—'Well, governor [Seward] I've this morning decided that Chicago post-office appointment.'"[20]

Lincoln's attitude reflected the degree to which federal appointments by the time of the Civil War had become political plums. The emergence of rival political parties in the United States before the end of the eighteenth century had led to the practice of making federal appointments on the basis of party loyalty rather than merit. The practice became known as the "spoils system" and was publicly endorsed by President Andrew Jackson. The inefficiency and corruption that accompanied the system produced a widespread call for civil service reform after the excesses of the Grant administration and led in 1871 to the creation of the Civil Service Commission. Diplomatic appointments, however, continued to be made primarily on the basis of political patronage until the passage of the Rogers Act in 1924.

COMMERCE AND NEUTRALITY

In the long, unheroic intervals between times of crisis, routine diplomatic activity may not produce great diplomats but does define a state's underlying priorities in foreign policy and the structure of its diplomacy. So it was with the United States through most of the nineteenth century and the first decade of the twentieth. American leaders were preoccupied with the need to consolidate the position of the United States in the Western Hemisphere and to avoid becoming involved in European disputes. By the 1820s the promotion of American trade and the countering of threats to it had become, as Jefferson had foreseen, the most important responsibilities of American missions abroad. This, and the lack of interest on the part of the American government in pursuing political or military objectives beyond the hemisphere, had a tangible effect on the disposition of embassies and consulates abroad.

Historically, embassies have mainly been concerned with government-to-government relations and conditions in the host country that can have an impact on American interests. Embassy officials spend most of their time in direct dealings with their foreign counterparts and in analyzing and reporting on significant developments. Consulates, on the other hand, have historically been concerned with the protection and welfare of Americans abroad.[21] Consular officers have traditionally spent their time on passport and citizenship services and assistance to American businesses. In the contemporary Foreign Service lines between embassy and consular work are less clearly drawn, although much of the traditional pattern remains.

The emphasis on trade in the eighteenth century, and the increasing demands levied on consuls by the American seamen who steered cargoes to their destination, is shown by the multiplication of American consulates. In 1800 there were already 52; by 1860 there were 279; and by 1920 the number had risen to 368—268 more than existed sixty years later in 1980. By contrast, the corresponding figures for American diplomatic posts abroad were only 6 in 1800, 33 in 1860, and 45 in 1920.[22]

Reform of the Consular Service

It is therefore logical that the first attempts to insulate American missions abroad from the stultifying effects of the spoils system benefited consular, not diplomatic, appointments. Until 1856 consular officers were unsalaried but authorized to pocket their consular fees— the charges levied by consulates for the services they provided to Americans abroad. These could be substantial (Nathaniel Hawthorne averaged $15,000 a year during the four years he was American consul in Liverpool). This system, or rather lack of system, was easily abused because consular fees were not regulated by law. Complaints began to reach Congress that some consuls charged more than others for the same services. Sea captains and other Americans who relied on their services found many consular officials unqualified and undisciplined in the performance of their duties. In the Fillmore administration, Secretary of State William Marcy put the consular service on a salaried basis to reduce the temptation to overcharge for consular fees. However, as author of the phrase "to the victors belong the spoils," Marcy did little to improve the standards of recruitment for consular officers. It was in 1895 that the Cleveland administration finally introduced a system of competitive examinations to enable consular appointments to be made on the basis of merit. A few years later the McKinley administration adulterated the examinations as a way of reintroducing political patronage into the system. It was not until 1906, through the intervention of Secretary of State Elihu Root, that competitive examinations were made a permanent requirement for appointment to the consular service.

REFORM OF THE DIPLOMATIC SERVICE

Competitive examinations for entry into the American diplomatic service—as distinct from the consular corps—were not introduced until 1924 when the Rogers Act set up a professional Foreign Service by placing the consular and diplomatic functions under a single personnel system and establishing uniform regulations governing appointment, promotion, and retirement for officers of both services. It was an indication that the grim ordeal of World War I, and the repudiation of Wilsonian idealism after it, had convinced the country's political leadership that the United States needed earlier warning and a better grasp of world events that could affect American interests.

Testifying in support of the Rogers Act, Secretary of State Robert Lansing stated the case for a professional Foreign Service: "The European war came upon the United States in 1914 as a surprise chiefly because its Department of State through inadequate equipment had been unable to gather information and interpret it in a manner which would reveal the hidden purposes of the governments by which hostilities were precipitated."[23] Lansing could have documented his thesis with examples had he chosen to do so. The American chargé d'affaires in Austria-Hungary had reported the assassination of the Archduke Franz Ferdinand in Sarajevo in June 1914 without comment. As late as the last week of July 1914 the American ambassador to Germany was expressing the view that there would be no general European war. Nevertheless, Washington's "surprise" was due more to its own inattentiveness than to deficiencies in diplomatic reporting. Lansing was correct in saying that the State Department and the Foreign Service were ill-equipped in 1914 to discern the "hidden purposes" of the European powers, but it was the better-equipped Europeans who had blundered into the conflict. The British foreign secretary, Sir Edward Grey, was probably more accurate than Lansing when he told the American ambassador in London that the continent seemed to be "in the clutch of blind forces."

If the government to which a diplomat reports is not paying attention or finds the views of its emissaries too unwelcome, the most meticulously prepared messages will go unread and the most prescient warnings unheeded. Who in the Continental Congress had given Jefferson's political and economic reports on prerevolutionary France the attention they deserved? Who in Washington in 1978 was willing to prepare for the collapse of the shah's regime in Iran or even, ten years later, that of the Soviet Union?

The Real Case for Diplomacy

The reason to have a well-equipped State Department and Foreign Service in Lansing's day, as in our own, was not so much to ferret out secrets as to conduct a permanent conversation with other governments about conflicting and common interests. Avoiding unpleasant surprises is always an important purpose of diplomacy, but it is usually accomplished through close and careful observation of foreign conditions and the steady give-and-take of diplomatic exchanges. These, occurring over time, are more likely to provide governments with a cumulative sense of each other's intentions and capabilities than the search for concealed plans and conspiracies.

Lansing's advocacy of the Rogers Act was designed to appeal to congressional Europhobia, American disillusionment with the war, and the common belief that the United States had been drawn into it by the schemes of European governments. But he failed to cite the most important function of diplomacy, which is to provide reliable communications between states and regulate their problems in an atmosphere as free as possible of chauvinism, rancor, and morbid suspicion.

In 1925, after the Rogers Act was safely passed, it was left to Lansing's successor, Secretary of State Charles Evans Hughes, to make the real case for diplomacy (or rather, as he called it, the "new diplomacy"):

> In view of the multiplication of international questions and of the interrelation of political and economic problems, it should be apparent that the national interest demands thoroughly trained Foreign Service officers. . . . The new diplomacy requires not the divining of the intent of monarchs, the mere discovery and thwarting of intrigues, but the understanding of peoples. There must be intimate acquaintance with their interests, their problems, the conflicts of parties, the course of opinion. There must be ability to sift; to seize upon what is significant in the mass of news, of rumors, of assertion, of debate; to know the character and particular aims of men who control the actions of governments. For this, alertness and general adaptability will not suffice. One must have the equipment of the student of history and politics, and the democratic sympathies and cultural training which enable him to enter into the thoughts of peoples.[24]

Today we might want to supplement the inventory of skills desirable in a diplomat—more knowledge, for example, of global as distinct from national and international problems—but Hughes's is a description of diplomacy that is valid today and that Franklin, Jefferson, and Adams would have understood and approved.

The Diplomacy of Doctrine

> It was all very careless and confused. They were careless people, Tom and Daisy—they smashed up things and creatures and then retreated into their money or their vast carelessness, or whatever it was that kept them together, and let other people clean up the mess they had made.
>
> (*F. Scott Fitzgerald,* The Great Gatsby)

AMERICANS resist indoctrination but cherish doctrines. One result of this craving for general rules is that the inquiring, low-keyed approach to diplomacy advocated by Charles Evans Hughes seldom suits the style of American foreign policy. A doctrine is essentially a publicly announced rationale for policy. Doctrines are usually proclaimed to create a moral and legal foundation for decisions that have been reached on essentially pragmatic grounds. The tension between these two inclinations crackles through much of our diplomatic history.

If the strength of American diplomacy from its earliest days has been to look nonideologically at external reality and to assess it both pragmatically in terms of American interests and morally in terms of American values, its weakness becomes apparent whenever American leaders fail to get this balance right. Either they try to force external reality into an American context where our interests come to be determined disproportionately by our values (which may or may not be reliable guides in a foreign culture) or, conversely, they lose sight of the American context and allow our values to be determined disproportionately by our interests (which amounts to the kind of value-free diplomacy rejected by the founding fathers as incompatible with the republic's sense of moral purpose). Both approaches lead to foreign policy failures, the first because it produces policies incomprehensible abroad, the second because it produces policies indefensible at home.

The proper balance between pragmatism and moral certitude in American foreign policy is not easily arrived at because it changes according to the time, the problem, and the administration. It must also be defined *politically*, which means the balancing point will be calculated differently by different interest groups. Inevitably there is a cyclical effect. The perceived cynicism of the Nixon/Kissinger approach to foreign policy was succeeded by the perceived moralism of the Carter years. Beneath both, however, lies the fundamental American view of external relations, explicitly voiced by Jefferson, that foreign alliances are more likely to entangle than to strengthen us.

The Packaging of Foreign Policy

The conflict among foreign policy fears, expectations, and needs must be resolved by each presidential administration in its own way. Increasingly this has been done by giving foreign policy the status of a precept. The practice began in the nineteenth century with the Monroe Doctrine opposing the extension of European influence in the Western Hemisphere. It continued with the Ostend Manifesto on Cuba and the Open Door policy on free trade. The twentieth century opened with the Roosevelt Corollary to the Monroe Doctrine justifying U.S. intervention in the internal affairs of Latin American states to counteract "chronic wrongdoing." Woodrow Wilson's Fourteen Points were couched as precepts. Since World War II it has sometimes seemed that no administration could be credited with a foreign policy unless it was first credited with a doctrine. The Truman Doctrine on aid to Greece and Turkey was followed by the Eisenhower Doctrine on aid to the Middle East and the Nixon Doctrine on aid to regional hegemons. We have even begun to apply the label of doctrine to the foreign policies of others. The Brezhnev "doctrine," for example, was said to justify Soviet military intervention in the internal affairs of its socialist allies. More recently we have seen the Milosevic "doctrine" of ethnic cleansing in Serbian-populated lands of the former state of Yugoslavia.

In fact, most other states, and virtually all democratic states, avoid doctrines like the plague, believing that if a doctrine means what it says, the government is committing itself in advance to actions it may not wish to take when the time comes. If the doctrine does not mean what it says, other states will discover the truth soon enough, and the credibility of both the doctrine and the state that has proclaimed it will be needlessly damaged. It may be precisely because foreign policy doctrines appear to limit alternative courses of action by making the chosen policy look inevitable that American governments find them so attractive and Europeans do not. For Europeans, the more foreign policy options they can preserve, the better; for Americans, the more options, the more debate and the less likelihood of effective action.

To be sure, American governments, no less than European, want to preserve their freedom of action. But because Congress is more likely to challenge government policy than is possible in a parliamentary system, U.S. political leaders prefer to limit choices. So do their diplomatic subordinates. The so-called options papers prepared for American policymakers by lower-ranking officials in the State Department were once described by Henry Kissinger as "present policy bracketed by unthinkable alternatives."

A doctrine is customarily cast in generalized terms, leaving room to interpret it selectively, and is invested with strong moral content, which makes it harder to argue with than a policy presented in straightforward terms of self-interest. The Truman Doctrine providing military and economic aid to Greece and Turkey in 1947 might, for example, have been presented to Congress and the American public by the administration simply as a program of assistance to two states threatened by the Soviet Union that were considered important to the security of Western Europe and therefore to the security of the United States. Instead, as one of the doctrine's authors has written, when the question of public presentation was discussed, "The most striking thing about the ensuing discussion was the unanimous view that the new policy of the United States [to aid Greece and Turkey] should be presented to the public in terms of assistance to free governments everywhere that needed our aid to strengthen and defend themselves against Communist aggression or subversion."[1] Furthermore, casting a policy in apocalyptic terms offers the administration the advantage of inhibiting debate both after and *before* it is announced.

The same account of the genesis of the Truman Doctrine describes George Kennan's fruitless objections to the unlimited nature of the commitment apparently being undertaken:

> He objected strongly both to the tone of the message and the specific action proposed. He was in favor of economic aid to Greece, but he had hoped that military aid to Greece would be kept small, and he was opposed to aid of any kind to Turkey. It was nevertheless to the tone and ideological content of the message, the portraying of two opposing ways of life, and the open-end commitment to aid free peoples that he objected most. . . . It was too late. The decisions had already been taken and widely approved.[2]

Kennan was right in trying to calibrate the Truman Doctrine more accurately in terms of how the administration was actually prepared to apply it in other parts of the world (in China, for example, which fell to communism two years later without the administration's attempting to invoke the Truman Doctrine). Those who differed with him were right, however, in thinking that congressional and public support for the program would probably not be forthcoming if it was presented less grandiloquently. The packaging of foreign policy is almost as important as its content in a country like the United States, whose relative self-sufficiency makes going it alone look more feasible than it usually is and encourages administrations to announce their foreign policy decisions as though they were papal encyclicals. European diplomacy seems in contrast cynical and self-serving.

FACTORS SHAPING AMERICAN DIPLOMACY

Whatever importance the first American diplomats attached to symbolic distinctions, such as their reluctance to adopt European-style uniforms and the title of ambassador, American diplomacy was bound to differ significantly from the European model. It was shaped by an entirely different political system and geographical situation. European monarchies chose (and were usually able) to deal with each other secretly and were accountable mainly to themselves. Diplomacy was designed to preserve the security of states of comparable size and wealth, which existed in close proximity to each other, and whose best hope of survival was to stay accurately informed of each other's intentions and capabilities. Since no single state in the European system (except Switzerland) could effectively isolate itself from the others, and none (unaided) could long dominate the others, their collective security depended on their ability to correct imbalances of power before these became threatening to their individual security. It was a system that required the participants to recognize and accept that their safety lay not in isolation but in engagement. The divining of foreign intentions, the assessment of foreign capabilities, and the conclusion of foreign alliances, all within a closed system of confidential communications and secret negotiations, with no accountability before the fact and little after, were the essence of European diplomacy until the end of the First World War.

The European system was conspicuously ill suited to the policy-making processes of the American republic, as well as to its foreign policy objectives. Although the Continental Congress created its Committee of Secret Correspondence and its Secret Committee, the American government was from the beginning bad at keeping secrets (and has steadily gotten worse). Benjamin Franklin in Paris was so oblivious to the requirements of security that one commentator said his legation "was virtually an employment bureau for the British secret service."[3] The openness of the American system, and the checks and balances built into it by the founding fathers, were consistent with their concept of republican government, but not with old-school diplomacy. Even today, British and French diplomats are relatively well insulated from partisan political pressures and only assume full political accountability if they rise from the ranks to become foreign ministers.

For Europeans, the process of diplomacy is distinct from the formulation of policy. Officials are accountable for the policies they make and implement but not, except in rare cases, for the deliberations that lead up to them. It is a matter of wonder to Europeans that American diplomats can be summoned from their posts abroad to testify before a congressional committee on problems still under discussion with the government to which they are accredited. Equally con-founding to Europeans is the fact that American career officials are sometimes held more accountable by the legislature (and the courts) for failed policies or policies of dubious legality than are the political officials who authored them. This is because a European government will fall with the failure of a major policy initiative, as the Eden gov-ernment in Britain fell after Suez in 1956, and career officials are unlikely to become scapegoats for them. In the American system, however, where the government can survive its foreign policy fail-ures, there is a greater temptation to shift the blame for bad policy decisions to career officials, as the Bush administration tried to do when its courtship of Saddam Hussein exploded in the Gulf war. The American system calls for greater accountability at lower levels—which is appropriate in a democratic government—but it diminishes (inappropriately) the accountability of the president and his immedi-ate advisers. In the European system, greater accountability for elected officials comes at the expense of political continuity; in the American system, greater accountability for career officials comes at the expense of diplomatic continuity.

Nonentangling Alliances

Just as the American diplomatic process differs from the European, so do its objectives and assumptions. When George Washington in his farewell address stated that America's "detached and distant situation invites us to pursue a different course" from the Europeans, and when Thomas Jefferson in his first inaugural address called for "peace, commerce, and honest friendship with all nations, entangling alli-ances with none," they charted the course of American foreign policy for the next 150 years. Until the end of the Second World War the almost unchallenged assumption was that the security of the United States was best preserved by isolation from, not engagement in, the European system of alliances and its balance-of-power diplomacy. Even a progressive internationalist like Woodrow Wilson would not agree to a military alliance with Great Britain and France when the

United States entered the First World War in 1917. The United States became an associate of the Entente powers, not their military ally. Thus was the theoretical possibility of independent action preserved by the American government even as it committed its full military strength to the allied cause.[4] Traditional American diplomacy, reflecting this fundamental reluctance to be tied down, has been and, to a greater extent than is commonly supposed, still is a diplomacy of separation designed more to limit margins of cooperation with other states than to enlarge them.

The reader may here object that since World War II the United States has fully participated in the European alliance system, in fact has been to a great extent its architect. This is true, but with an important qualification. The most significant American commitment to European security is embodied in the North Atlantic Treaty. Yet Article 5, its key provision, which starts by asserting boldly that "The Parties agree that an armed attack against one of them in Europe or North America shall be considered an attack against them all," continues in a more equivocal vein to commit each signatory to assist other members only "by such action as it deems necessary." In contrast, the earlier Brussels Treaty Organization, negotiated in 1948 by Britain, France, and the BENELUX states—converted into the Western European Union (WEU) in 1954 to include the Federal Republic of Germany and Italy—is categorical in the commitment its signatories make to "afford the Party so attacked all the military and other aid and resistance in their power."[5]

The language of the NATO treaty is careful to preserve separateness by leaving a loophole in the commitment members make to assist each other; the WEU calls, at least rhetorically, for full engagement.[6] The test of an alliance is in its application, and NATO has been a far more influential instrument of diplomatic and security policy than the WEU. Nevertheless, the careful hedging of Article 5 of the NATO treaty reflects the American preoccupation with separateness as clearly as Article 5 of the WEU treaty reflects the European habituation to engagement.

The inclination toward separateness in the implementation of American foreign policy and the inclination toward doctrine in its formulation are constant elements that link the earliest phases in the development of the American diplomatic method with the latest. What has changed is the world role of the United States, and with it the bureaucratic apparatus by which American foreign policy is managed. Later chapters will deal with the growth of the bureaucracy, but both factors have strengthened our predilection for doctrinal foreign policy and affected the priorities we set for American diplomacy.

SELF-IMAGE AND SELF-INTEREST

The professionalism that was introduced into the practice of American diplomacy by the Rogers Act of 1924 was supposed to strengthen the pragmatic side of American foreign policy and reduce the danger of empty moralizing. The actual results have been more ambivalent. What George Kennan called the "moralistic-legalistic" aspect of American foreign policy is still highly visible, but so is a heightened sense of national self-interest. The ambivalence is essential to the way we see others and ourselves and has been present throughout our diplomatic history.

The Swiss or Scandinavian diplomatic model may have been what the founders had in mind for the United States after independence, but in practice American foreign policy rapidly became more assertive and muscular than reticent and aloof. A preference for neutrality in European conflicts and keeping our distance from the European balance of power has never meant that the United States was unmindful of its own power position in this hemisphere. In the nineteenth century the vital interests of the United States beyond its recognized borders lay not to the east, in Europe, but to the west and south where American foreign policy was anything but neutral and detached. The counterpoint to neutrality abroad was manifest destiny at home.[7] It is not by chance that the primary focus of American doctrines in the nineteenth century was Latin America and the Caribbean. By the twentieth century the territorial ambitions of the United States had largely been realized. Having in the process become a major power, the United States possessed national interests that were far too com-

45

plex and diversified to permit U.S. foreign policy the luxury of pursuing a completely different course from the Europeans.

Assertive diplomacy seems to fit the national character. So does the disposition to project a big image in the world. From its origins the United States has possessed a proselytizing impulse that was consistent with the founders' conviction that the United States would set democratic standards for the rest of the world. Though at variance with the prudence and pragmatism they advocated in foreign policy, the crusading spirit that so often animates American foreign policy doctrines grows out of that philosophical tradition.

In the words of the British politician and classicist Enoch Powell, "the life of nations no less than that of men is lived largely in the imagination." How a nation imagines itself will explain the sources of its external conduct as accurately as any accounting of its objective strengths and weaknesses. Most foreign policy triumphs and virtually all disasters are produced when nations try to give substance to their dreams. Large and small nations are subject to the same risks.

Russia's triumph, for example, lay in convincing itself, and for varying periods many others, that, in the guise of the Soviet Union, it represented a new, more just world order; its collapse came about because it brutalized the character of its regime and exhausted its resources trying to impose its vision on others. The British disaster at Suez was the result of pursuing an imperial dream even as the empire itself was being dismantled. The triumph of modern Greeks was winning their independence from the Ottoman Empire in 1828. A century later Greece sought to realize its "Great Idea"—the dream of resurrecting the Greek empire as it existed before the Ottoman conquest. The result was the Asia Minor disaster of 1922, unleashing social, economic, and political forces that buffet Greece to this day.

The list of states whose most significant foreign policy successes and failures were determined by the way they imagined themselves, and were imagined by others, could be extended indefinitely. It would of course prominently include the United States, which has so often explained its foreign policy initiatives as attempts to extend the "American dream" to less fortunate parts of the world.

It is in fact the imagined component of American foreign policy that explains the popular appeal of diplomacy by doctrine. If the utility of doctrines to presidential administrations lies in their ability to limit debate about foreign policy, their attraction to the public is that they seem to embody cherished American ideals. This aspect of doctrinal diplomacy can also be appealing to diplomats, who are not indifferent to the advantages of having a popularly acclaimed rationale for foreign policy, much of which is otherwise conducted in conditions of obscurity and popular misconception.

Even Henry Kissinger, the superrealist, when seeking confirmation as secretary of state before the Senate Foreign Relations Committee in 1973, interpreted American foreign policy in terms worthy of the great moralist, William Jennings Bryan,[8] who was one of his predecessors:

> These [foreign policy] challenges, though they appear as practical issues, cannot be solved in technical terms; they closely reflect our view of ourselves. They require a sense of identity and purpose as much as a sense of policy. Throughout our history we have thought of what we did as growing out of deeper moral values. America was not true to itself unless it had a meaning beyond itself. In this spiritual sense, America was never isolationist.[9]

Whether or not this represented Kissinger's own philosophy of foreign affairs (and in important respects it did not) is less interesting than the fact that he felt obliged to pay lip service to it in his testimony. To his credit, the diplomatic history of the United States reveals no Kissinger Doctrine, even though he must share responsibility for conceiving the misguided Nixon Doctrine of building up regional superpowers—a doctrine that today lies entombed with the shah of Iran. There is a difference between a diplomacy "growing out of deeper moral values" and a diplomacy of doctrine. The former encourages discriminating choices in foreign policy; the latter too easily becomes a catechism that discourages choice and discrimination. It was the American sociologist and economist William Graham Sumner who warned, "If you want war, nourish a doctrine."

47

THE DANGER OF DOCTRINES

The *American Heritage Dictionary* defines a doctrine, among its other meanings, as a statement of "official government policy, especially in foreign policy and military strategy." Given the sweeping nature of most American doctrines, it is probably fortunate that this is seldom the case. More often, the doctrines, manifestos, and proclamations of American foreign policy express intentions, not official policies. The familiar American aversion to entanglements usually prevents them from serving as blueprints for policy.

Danger can arise if they do. A doctrine taken literally and applied indiscriminately produces policies that are rigid and unrealistic. This is how the Truman Doctrine, effective as a program of military and economic assistance to Greece and Turkey, became a disaster when applied to Vietnam twenty years later. In its effort to justify a doomed policy of massive military intervention, the Johnson administration gave it the label of a successful one. The result was to obscure the fundamental differences between the two situations.

On a flight in 1966 from Honolulu to Saigon at the height of the Vietnam War I saw McGeorge Bundy, then national security adviser to President Lyndon B. Johnson, reading a book on the defeat of the Communist guerrillas in the Greek civil war. Why, I wondered, had Bundy chosen this volume, published the year before, as reading material on an official trip to Vietnam? Though at the time the connection seemed far-fetched, I later decided that there *were* valid lessons to be learned, though not the ones the president seemed to be looking for. The first was that the conditions that had permitted success in Greece simply did not exist in Southeast Asia: unlike the Vietminh and Vietcong, the Greek Communist forces had been unable to present themselves credibly as a nationalist and anticolonialist movement; unlike the North Vietnamese and their Chinese and Soviet allies, the Greek Communists and their East European backers had been weakened and in the end destroyed by internal and external divisions in their ranks. The second lesson was that resisting the temptation to Americanize the military effort in Greece and the equally strong temptation to fight a ground war primarily in the air had been as wise as the opposite strategy had been foolish in Vietnam.

Parenthetically, it should be noted that American military policy in Vietnam was as doctrinaire as the Johnson administration's foreign policy. "Strategic hamlets" and "pacification" were war-fighting theories that no more solved the military problems on the ground than the "domino theory" explained the strategic linkages in the region as a whole. These politico-military doctrines purported to simplify complex problems and make them more manageable. In the end they were overwhelmed by the complexities they had discounted.

Doctrines, whether military or diplomatic, are never solutions in themselves. They are not even signposts to solutions unless based on objective assessments by qualified experts. When this is the case, doctrines can be helpful in clarifying objectives though rarely in identifying the means to achieve them. Policymakers may be the framers of doctrines, but diplomats and soldiers carry them out. They are the ones with the knowledge to judge a doctrine's validity and evaluate its feasibility in specific circumstances. In Vietnam, the United States had few diplomats or soldiers who knew the language and terrain well enough to warn us that Vietnam in the 1960s was not Greece in the 1940s.[10] The warnings of those who did were ignored by political leaders who mistakenly believed that the Truman Doctrine was, as it had proclaimed itself to be, universally applicable.

Even foreign policy doctrines that are rationally conceived, discriminatingly applied, and not shown to be hollow by later events rarely are what they appear to be at the time or eventually become in our imagination. This is another reason to avoid overreliance on them.

The Monroe Doctrine, from which it might be argued all subsequent American foreign policy doctrines derived their respectability, was originally conceived by President Monroe as a strong but nonbinding statement of American support for Greek independence. Monroe's declaration was made in the course of his annual message to Congress in December 1823 and only elevated to the rank of doctrine in the 1850s. Secretary of State John Quincy Adams turned it into a warning to the European powers not to attempt further colonization in the Western Hemisphere. What teeth it had were provided by

George Canning, the British foreign secretary, whose policy was to prevent the continental powers from strengthening their position in the New World. Canning had first proposed a joint warning to the American minister in London. Adams realized that since the British fleet would enforce such a policy whether the Americans joined them in proclaiming it or not, a unilateral declaration would have the same force as a joint one, while conveying a greater impression of independence in the conduct of American foreign policy. The Monroe Doctrine provoked outrage in the capitals of continental Europe, where it was regarded as presumptuous, but embedded itself in the North American imagination as a sign that the United States had come of age as a world power.

Monroe's proclamation was not exactly what it appeared to be, but it met the essential requirements of a good foreign policy doctrine: it stated a broad and high-principled objective without committing the issuing power to take any specific action; the objective was achievable, even if not by the means implied; geographical limits were set; and national pride was gratified at no cost to national resources and with negligible risk to national security. The contrast with the catastrophic application of the Truman Doctrine to Vietnam could not be clearer.

For working diplomats, a well-conceived foreign policy doctrine provides a sense of where their government wants to go. Without a sense of direction, diplomacy becomes aimless or is reduced to small talk. On the other hand, a doctrine primarily conceived to meet internal political requirements with little regard for external realities will provide no sense of direction at all.

John Foster Dulles's repudiation in 1953 of the Truman administration's doctrine of containing Soviet communism, and his declaration of a new doctrine of liberation, provided no policy guidance because, as events in Eastern Europe in 1956 proved, there had been no change of policy. The objective had been to liberate Dulles from the pressures of the Republican right wing, not to liberate the peoples of Eastern Europe from communism. Such "doctrines" do more harm than good because they become substitutes for policy and have a stultifying effect on the conduct of diplomacy. In his Paris mission Franklin resisted the pressure of the Continental Congress to limit his dialogue with the French to how much aid they were prepared to grant and when they would go to war with Great Britain. He correctly reasoned that he could interpret American policy more effectively to the French than could his superiors in Philadelphia. Good diplomats today similarly use their judgment in deciding how best to interpret locally the doctrines handed down to them by Washington.

THE NEED TO INTERPRET DOCTRINES

Political leaders may think themselves well served by diplomats who simply act as the administration's mouthpiece abroad rather than as its eyes and ears. Such a role would also seem (erroneously) to carry fewer hazards for the envoy. In all likelihood, however, the administration is being badly served because it is deprived of objective interpretation of how its policies—its doctrines, if you will—are received and understood by foreign governments and foreign public opinion. Every administration needs an accurate picture of the complexities affecting the reception and implementation of its policies, and informed advice about getting the most from them. Uncritical loyalty to the administration's platform produces indoctrination, not diplomacy. When diplomats become indoctrinated they cease to be diplomats.

This can be costly, to diplomats as well as to policymakers. The number of diplomats who have come to grief because they were too zealous and uncritical in their work probably exceeds the number whose careers suffered because they displayed too much independence of judgment. The Ostend Manifesto of 1854 is an early example of how diplomacy is corrupted by excessive zeal and insufficient judgment.

The election to the presidency of Franklin Pierce in 1852 placed in the White House a leader sympathetic to the views of territorial expansionists whose attention was at this time directed to the south. In his inaugural address the new president declared, "the acquisition of certain possessions not within our jurisdiction [is] eminently important for our protection." It was generally understood that the possession most coveted by the administration was Spanish Cuba.

True to the tradition of the spoils system, President Pierce's sympathies were reflected in his diplomatic appointments. Among them was the French-born Pierre Soulé, a former Louisiana senator who was sent as American minister to Spain. Soulé was so fiery-tempered that after arriving in Madrid he challenged the French ambassador to a duel over a supposed insult to Soulé's wife and wounded him for life with a shot in the thigh.[11] Soulé exerted every form of pressure on the Spanish court to persuade Spain to sell Cuba to the United States. Unsuccessful in these attempts, in 1854 he organized a meeting in Ostend, Belgium, with the American ministers in London and Paris. His intention was to increase pressure on the Spanish to relinquish Cuba. Although the three envoys moved their meeting to Aix-la-Chapelle in France a few days later, the resulting declaration, which was promptly leaked to the press, became known as the "Ostend Manifesto." Among other statements that provoked outrage in Europe, it crucially declared: "After we shall have offered Spain a price for Cuba far beyond its present value, and this shall have been refused, it will then be time to consider the question, does Cuba, in the possession of Spain, seriously endanger our internal peace and the existence of our cherished Union? . . . Should this question be answered in the affirmative, then, by every law, human and divine, we shall be justified in wresting it from Spain if we possess the power."[12]

The phrase "every law, human and divine" may have justified the proposed land-grab in the eyes of American expansionists, but it was totally unconvincing to Europeans. The ensuing furor and the ridicule of Pierce and his envoys by the European press caused the administration to back down. Although Pierce's instructions to Soulé had made clear his desire to "detach" Cuba from Spain (without specifying the means), Soulé himself was made the scapegoat for the episode and resigned. The only participant in the Ostend meeting to gain any benefit from it was the American minister in London, James Buchanan of

Pennsylvania, whose association with the manifesto may have gained him enough southern support to allow him to become the fifteenth president of the United States. As for Soulé, he was neither the first nor the last American diplomat to feel the backlash of an administration he (or she) served too zealously. The experience in Baghdad in 1990 of Ambassador April Glaspie, whom the Bush administration made the scapegoat for its policy on Iraq, brings the story up to date.

The risks of showing independence of judgment can also be considerable, but diplomats who do at least have the possibility of being vindicated by history, as George Kennan was by the peaceful collapse of the Soviet system under the weight of its own contradictions. Vindication, however, is neither automatic nor universal. I once heard the late President Richard Nixon, in the course of a television interview at the beginning of his interminable period of "rehabilitation," warn then President-elect Bush not to trust the views of Foreign Service officers in conducting his administration's foreign policy. "If I had listened to them," he said, "there never would have been a breakthrough to China." Unfortunately, Nixon's interviewer failed to respond, as he should have, "Mr. President, if you had listened to career officials earlier there would have been no need for a breakthrough." Indeed, having denounced the Truman administration for the supposed "loss" of China to communism, and having heralded the new and essentially empty doctrine of "liberation," in 1953 Vice President Nixon was among the Eisenhower administration's most relentless advocates of purging the State Department of the very officials—the old China hands—who argued that the Chinese communists were not simply stooges of the Soviet Union and who maintained that it was in the American interest to preserve lines of communication to them.

Politicization of diplomacy may be superficially gratifying to an administration, but it is rarely healthy for its policies. The majority of mistakes in American foreign policy are the result not of too much resistance by career officials to new policy initiatives but of too little. It is understandable that a new administration comes to power confident of its ability to improve on the performance of its predecessor. It is natural, too, that it will usually be quicker to see opportunities than risks in the situation it inherits. A wise administration, and more often than not an unwise administration in its second term, if it gets one, will realize that there is more continuity than change in the foreign policy of the United States, that risks outnumber opportunities, and that doctrines are less reliable guides to sound policy than values and interests.

The Diplomacy of Process

> *"Negotiation* is out; *process* is in."
> *(William Safire)*

IF THE FOUNDERS of the republic envisioned a diplomacy that would enable the United States to substitute reason for military force, and if their successors increasingly employed diplomacy to pursue national objectives in the guise of moral doctrines, how should we characterize American diplomacy today? Probably by saying that from a diplomacy of reason and of doctrine we have arrived at a diplomacy of process—a diplomacy where the process of reaching agreement determines what agreement is reached. The description applies to both dimensions of diplomatic activity: the shaping of foreign policy and its execution.

To be sure, the tension between our desire to frame policy in universal terms and our instinct to carry it out pragmatically is still very much in evidence. The Clinton administration came into office wrestling with the problem of what the United States should do about the conflict of nationalities in the former Republic of Yugoslavia. Having called for a more robust American role as a candidate, Clinton as president opted for pragmatism. The United States joined the ongoing diplomatic discussions under United Nations auspices seeking a negotiated settlement of the conflict. The United States, in other words, became part of the process.

It is safe to predict that unilateral military initiatives, even in Latin America and the Caribbean where the United States has most often resorted to them, will become steadily less feasible in the years ahead. The economic capacity of the United States for independent action has declined since the glory days after World War II when the United States was responsible for over half of the world's gross national product.[1] The economic strains of unilateral action abroad translate into increased political risks at home. To speak of the United States today as the world's "only remaining superpower," as many commentators do, is to apply the language of the cold war to entirely different international circumstances, and to ignore the fact that we have become more dependent on the rest of the world, not less.

The unique ability of the United States to project military force quickly to distant parts of the globe, so dramatically demonstrated in the Gulf War, is deceptive because so many of the world's most dangerous problems are not susceptible to military solutions. And even this capability is likely to decline as we scale back a military establishment whose size and weaponry were geared to the presumed requirements of superpower parity. In fact, the Gulf War is itself a demonstration of how much things have changed. It was presented by the Bush administration as a bold first stroke in the American design for a new world order. In reality, it was a military police action whose terms of reference were delimited by a series of United Nations resolutions that emerged from intricate multilateral negotiations. The policy and the outcome were determined by the diplomatic process that authorized and then terminated the U.S.-led military campaign.

The contrast is striking between the way strategic objectives were defined in the Gulf War and the way they were defined forty years earlier in the Korean War, also nominally a United Nations military action. Then it was the United States, with General MacArthur in command of military operations, that decided to carry the war to North Korea, and it was the United Nations that acquiesced in the action—which fundamentally changed the objectives and ultimately the outcome of the conflict—only after South Korean troops had already crossed the 38th parallel going north.

CONFERENCE DIPLOMACY

The nature of international problems today is such that conference diplomacy—which is another name for the diplomacy of process—will necessarily become more important than either unilateral action or bilateral diplomacy. As transnational problems come increasingly to dominate the international agenda, they will have to be addressed multilaterally, whether through international organizations or at conferences. The positions of individual states will evolve from discussions usually held first on a regional level and then on a global level.

The European Union (EU) is already showing how this process works and what its problems are. The fifteen members of the EU are in continual consultation on virtually all issues that affect their interests. Indeed, as a Belgian diplomat recently remarked, European diplomacy has become so multilateral that ambassadors in some European capitals are beginning to feel underemployed.[2] Important policy decisions affecting all members are being made in Brussels, the seat of the EU Council of Ministers and the European Commission, and much of the work assigned to embassies in other European capitals is necessarily in the nature of follow-up.

There is, to be sure, a lot to be followed up. Major disagreements on important issues divide EU members, and reaching compromises involves negotiations through bilateral channels in the EU capitals. Nevertheless, an important multilateral dimension has been added to European diplomacy, involving a significant departure from traditional diplomatic practice. The ambassador of one EU member state to another must today keep as well informed about developments in Brussels as he or she is about what is happening in the capital where the envoy works. An ambassador must be concerned as much with multilateral as with the bilateral decisions that affect the relations of the "sending" and "receiving" states. For Europeans, bilateral diplomacy still predominates in Washington, Tokyo, and the capitals of other non-EU states, but even here the policies of individual European governments are significantly influenced by European Union views and the common positions hammered out in EU committees.

In the opinion of many Europeans, the United States will have some catching up to do when it comes to mastering the special skills of conference diplomacy. Europeans believe that the United States became accustomed during the cold war to regarding consultation with our allies as a formality—"the elaboration of American blueprints," as Henry Kissinger once put it—not as a serious attempt to find common positions. This is a fair criticism. Few American ambassadors have been spared the discomfort of hastening, under instructions from Washington, to elicit the views of a friendly government on a proposed "joint" initiative, only to discover that the initiative has already been taken, sometimes already announced. It is of course true that the United States has been participating since 1949 in a form of conference diplomacy as a member of NATO. But NATO is first and foremost a military alliance, and the military preeminence of the United States within the alliance has meant that other members have done more compromising than has Washington. NATO's blueprint has been mainly American.

The current British ambassador to the United Nations, speaking of the skills needed for conference diplomacy, has defined them well.[3] The multilateral diplomatist is seeking to find a consensus that preserves his or her country's essential interests. This requires the government to prioritize its interests and requires the envoy to coax a measure of symmetry out of a welter of positions. Timing becomes extremely important in this process, and the envoy must have the ability to spot openings in an impasse as soon as they appear. Since there is rarely time to consult ministers or ask for new instructions, envoys must be given the authority to react promptly, propose initiatives, and improvise within the broad margins of their instructions.

THE TIGHT REIN ON AMERICAN DIPLOMATS

The British ambassador's analysis suggests why the United States is sometimes at a disadvantage at international conferences. American diplomats often seem to operate on a tighter political rein than their European colleagues. In the case of the United Nations, where the proximity of the United States United Nations Mission in New York (USUN) to policymakers in Washington ought to speed up the American reaction time, the opposite is usually true. United States representatives at the United Nations, whether well-known political personalities or career diplomats, can utter scarcely a word unless it is authorized (and often dictated) by Washington. The State Department's Bureau of International Organization Affairs (IO), the institutional link between policymakers and the delegation in New York, is inevitably as concerned with the domestic political impact of USUN's words and actions as it is with enabling the delegation to reach compromises quickly. When IO takes a broad view of its responsibilities and shields the delegation from nitpicking interventions, the process works reasonably well. If IO's oversight of USUN is overly ideological (as it has a tendency to be) or overly influenced by single-ssue lobbies (which are always active in multilateral settings), USUN's margin for maneuver is correspondingly narrow.

As a result, USUN spends more time arguing and negotiating with Washington than with other delegations. The life of an American ambassador to the United Nations has not proven to be a easy one. In the approximately fifty years of the United Nations's existence there have been twenty heads of the American delegation, of whom seven stayed less than a year. Ambassador Andrew Young's dismissal in 1979 came after he had contact with representatives of the Palestine Liberation Organization that the Carter administration was unwilling to acknowledge having authorized; Ambassador Thomas Pickering was abruptly replaced in 1992, apparently for engaging in too many policy arguments with Secretary of State Baker's inner circle and receiving more favorable publicity than the secretary for his effective diplomacy during the Gulf crisis.

To some extent the limited authority of American officials to adjust positions quickly to meet changing circumstances is inherent in the American system of checks and balances. The instinctive American skepticism about the value of foreign commitments encourages internal debate over policy and therefore complicates policy coordination. The separation of powers that is so precious a safeguard against the imposition of tyranny from within can seriously impede efforts to build a common front against external tyrannies. It took the Japanese attack on Pearl Harbor, for example, to bring the United States into World War II.

"COORDINATION BELOW"

When issues are clear-cut, or can be made to seem so, the machinery of the American foreign policy process can sometimes be speeded up, at least for short periods. This was the purpose and the effect of the 1964 Tonkin Gulf resolution, passed by Congress under intense pressure from President Lyndon Johnson to empower the administration to take stronger military measures against North Vietnam. Most problems in foreign policy are ambiguous, however, and it is risky to oversimplify or misrepresent them, as the Johnson administration found out in Vietnam.

The time spent in achieving internal agreement can be long, as was true for the Strategic Arms Limitation Treaty (SALT II), the Panama Canal Treaty, and NAFTA. Usually it is time spent at the expense of reaching and ratifying *external* agreements. The process is difficult in bilateral negotiations; in multilateral negotiations it can seem endless. In 1988 the former ambassador of the Federal Republic of Germany to the United States, Berndt von Staden, speaking at a symposium at Georgetown University, asked a question about the American diplomatic process that has still to be answered: "Is the American decision-making process, highly concentrated on top but posing challenging problems of coordination below, up to the task of focusing simultaneously on more than one problem at a time?"[4] Von Staden was referring to the need for the United States to engage in negotiations with the Soviet Union in the fields of both nuclear and conventional arms control. He answered his own question tactfully by saying, "We should hope so and have confidence." To have asked it at all, however, betrayed doubts about the way the United States reaches foreign policy decisions.

A world that feels itself threatened by nuclear holocaust is of course a world where certain decisions must be made "on top," though not as many as recent American presidents would have us believe. The world we are entering confronts a different array of threats of which only a few can be deterred by the president's finger on the nuclear button. American diplomacy will have to be conducted at many levels and in many places simultaneously. The process of achieving "coordination below" will become even more complicated.

Faster and more effective coordination of the machinery of foreign policy will require reforms in several areas—better policy planning, clearer (and less politicized) articulation of policy, and greater continuity in carrying it out. These subjects are discussed in more detail in chapter 9. Fundamental to any improvement, however, will be curtailment of the spoils system, which has been steadily creeping back into the foreign policy process, better use of career officials, and a sustained effort to make the American Foreign Service a better instrument of foreign policy, to make it what the United States needs now more than ever, the best and most professional diplomatic service in the world.

THE U.S. FOREIGN SERVICE

This brings us to an examination of the U.S. Foreign Service as it now exists. What kind of service has been produced by the "diplomacy of process"? How do its officers stack up against those of other countries, especially the Europeans who developed the diplomatic method now generally in use?

There are slightly under 13,000 full-time Foreign Service personnel of all grades working in embassies and consulates abroad and for the State Department and other foreign affairs agencies in Washington. This number includes about 4,300 Foreign Service officers (FSOs) whose parent agency is the Department of State; about 6,100 specialist and support personnel (FP)—communicators, security specialists, secretaries, and others; and approximately 2,400 Foreign Service officers from agencies other than the Department of State—the U.S. Information Agency (USIA), the Agency for International Development (AID), and the departments of Commerce and Agriculture.

All of these 13,000 personnel play some useful role in the foreign policy process. Whether in Washington or overseas, they work under the direction of the secretary of state or, in the case of information and cultural officers, the administrator of USIA. The Foreign Commercial Service (FCS) reports to the secretary of commerce. While occasional ambassadorial appointments are made from the ranks of FSOs employed by agencies other than the State Department, the preponderant number of career appointments to senior diplomatic positions comes from State Department personnel. Any evaluation of the overall effectiveness of the American diplomatic service must therefore refer primarily to the 4,300 officers whose parent agency is the State Department.[5] This is the group that defines American diplomacy and is regarded by other governments as the principal instrument of American foreign policy abroad.[6]

AMERICAN AND EUROPEAN DIPLOMATS

A German diplomat and friend recently ventured a comparative evaluation of the foreign services of Great Britain, France, Germany, and the United States. In ranking their overall performance he judged them primarily on four qualities that he considers essential to the success of a modern diplomat: intelligence, including intellectual curiosity; independence of thought, including intellectual courage; ability to relate to others, especially those in a foreign culture; and fluency in the diplomat's own and foreign languages.

The British Foreign Service places first in his rankings. He considers British diplomats highly professional—by which he means that individually they are unlikely to fall below a certain level of excellence—and, though disciplined, capable of probing, independent thought. He has observed that without losing their own distinctive national identity British diplomats are becoming less elitist and better able to relate to foreign cultures. In this he thinks they are better than the French, who tend to be clannish and often convey the impression that they prefer the company of other French to that of foreigners. By the same token, he considers British diplomats superior in their ability (and willingness) to speak foreign languages.

He regards the effectiveness of the French diplomatic service just below that of the British, noting that French diplomats tend to be more intellectually inclined and better educated than their counterparts in other services. They have the French gift for logical analysis and precision in the use of language. In addition, they benefit from the long and brilliant tradition of French diplomacy, which, more than any other, has shaped the forms and conventions of all modern diplomacy. This gives them a self-assurance sometimes lacking in their foreign colleagues, whose importance to their own governments they can rarely take for granted.

Analyzing his own service, my German friend says that it has come a long way since the end of World War II, decades in which Germans, and especially young Germans, have been trying to rediscover their national character. Partly as a result, young German diplomats closely study other cultures, enabling them to mingle more easily with foreigners, speak their languages, and make better professional contacts than rival services. Their main drawback is a tendency to linear thinking, lack of nuance, and heavy-handedness. He thinks, however, that the Germans deserve to rank just below the British and French.

Turning to American Foreign Service officers, my friend cites industry and conscientiousness as among their conspicuous strengths. Americans also display a refreshing lack of pettiness and punctilio—exasperating traits of Old World diplomacy that still crop up today. On the other hand, he often has the feeling that American diplomats are overly programmed. Whatever problem is at the top of Washington's agenda that week is likely to spring to the lips of every American diplomat with whom one converses. Individually, they are likely to have the attractive qualities that foreigners associate with the American character—generosity, openness, and candor. Taken together, they can be humorless and insistent in promoting the U.S. point of view. Finally, although American FSOs take seriously the need to cultivate language skills and to mix with the local population, he regrets that so many are housed in American ghettos and rely so much on imported American conveniences and culture.

FOREIGN SERVICE STRENGTHS AND WEAKNESSES

In general, these observations accord with my own. Some of the weaknesses that my German friend sees in the U.S. Foreign Service are the result of the changed environment in which diplomats operate. The frequency of terrorist attacks on American diplomats and the consequent need to improve their security have accentuated their isolation in some high-risk posts.[7] While it is true that in large posts, or posts where American military facilities exist, Americans can fall into a ghettolike existence, this is much less apparent in smaller embassies

63

and consulates. In the newly established diplomatic missions in states of the former Soviet Union like Armenia, Azerbaijan, and Kazakhstan, diplomats are likely to be living in a rundown hotel and working over the local pub.

In general, it is my impression that American Foreign Service officers are often better informed about current developments than their European colleagues, but not always as incisive in their analysis of them or as prescient about where they may lead. Like Americans generally, many Foreign Service officers are less versed than they should be in history, including the history of the regions where they serve. This deficiency, combined with short tours of duty and frequent changes of post, can deprive American diplomatic reporting of depth and perspective. The training in political science that young American diplomats receive before entering the Foreign Service is no substitute for a knowledge of history, including of course American history.

There is also, in my experience, a proclivity in American missions for quantitative reporting, some of it required by Washington, some not. This results in the transmission of data that are redundant or of marginal importance. Information is often reported with inadequate evaluation and commentary. The former French ambassador in Ankara, Eric Rouleau, has commented that during the Gulf crisis the French and American embassies exchanged a great deal of intelligence. Rouleau was astonished by the sheer volume generated by United States sources but thought the French often made better use of it.[8]

Whatever the weak points of the American diplomatic service, any overall ranking, including those by foreign diplomats, would place it among the best. American Foreign Service officers, with few exceptions, are intelligent, serious, and well-informed. Most American embassies are knowledgeable and productive. If the Foreign Service as a whole appears, notwithstanding, to be less than the sum of its parts, this is not caused by inferior diplomatic training, much less by inferior diplomats.

FSOs are commissioned by the president only after arduous and demanding tests of intelligence and character. Competitive examinations eliminate most unqualified candidates. The State Department's in-service training school, the National Foreign Affairs Training Center (NFATC), installed in 1993 on a handsome new campus a few miles south of Washington, offers good technical training, excellent programs in regional studies, and perhaps the best foreign language training available anywhere in the world.

The paradox to be explained is why the U.S. Foreign Service is such a competent but at the same time such an ineffective instrument of American foreign policy. The reasons lie within the process and within the service.

WHAT DETERMINES EFFECTIVENESS?

The performance of a national foreign service depends on several factors in addition to the quality of its personnel. Good leadership is essential, both in the field and at home. The history of the relationship between the sending and receiving states, and their respective economic and security interests, will have a material effect on the product of an embassy. When I served in the Republic of the Ivory Coast in West Africa in the late 1970s, one of the best-informed embassies was also one of the smallest. The Brazilian embassy, in addition to having an astute, hard-working ambassador, shared with the Ivorians an interest in keeping the price of coffee up. Well positioned and well led or not, an embassy's ultimate effectiveness will be determined by the amount of influence it has on its own government. Allowing for different degrees of influence at different times and places, there is room for disagreement about which country's foreign service is consistently the most influential.

A senior Belgian diplomat concedes the excellence of the British Foreign Service but believes that it has less influence on policy than the French. This was certainly true during the Margaret Thatcher years, when the British prime minister did not conceal her generally low regard for British diplomats. In the American style, she tried to place political loyalists in key positions and when this was impractical either bent the professionals to her will or shunted them aside.

65

Before and after Mrs. Thatcher the influence of British diplomats on government policy has seemed no less, and often more, than that of the Americans and Germans. Even Mrs. Thatcher selected as her last foreign secretary Sir Douglas Hurd, a former British Foreign Service officer.

The influence of French diplomats on government policy is the result of tradition and experience. The French take foreign policy seriously and know that the effectiveness with which it is shaped and carried out will depend in large part on the powers of observation and persuasion of French diplomats. They are, therefore, closer to the center of the policy-making process than are American diplomats. The Quai d'Orsay has seen its power eroded in recent decades, but far less than that of the State Department. This gives French foreign policy, even when it seems wrongheaded to others, a degree of clear-eyed consistency and single-minded devotion to French national interests that few other states can rival.

When the French offend, they rarely do so by miscalculation; their diplomacy is notably realistic in its appreciation of how French national interests will be affected in any given situation. This focus and determination can be maddening to France's antagonists—which often means its allies—and within the European Union they are virtues that are sometimes indistinguishable from faults. This does not detract, however, from the excellence of French diplomacy or its contribution to the policy-making process.

CONTRASTING U.S. AND FRENCH SYSTEMS

The contrast between the French and American systems is especially strong. In the latter, the competing pragmatic and doctrinal impulses behind U.S. foreign policy take the form of competing priorities and goals. Instead of working together to advance agreed-upon American interests, diplomats and their political superiors engage in an endless battle over policy. In the process, it is easy to lose sight of U.S. interests and hard to avoid blurring policies. In the American press in recent years the most prominently reported foreign policy debates have not been between Democrats and Republicans but between the White House and the State Department.

Dean Acheson commented on the baneful effects on U.S. foreign policy at the end of World War II of an unbridgeable split between President Franklin Roosevelt and Secretary of State Cordell Hull:

> President Roosevelt's virtual exclusion of Secretary Hull from high policy decisions during the war had more far-reaching effects than its contribution to the estrangement of the two men. It led directly to the theoretical and unreal nature of the State Department's—*and hence the Government's*—thinking on postwar problems. Largely detached from the practicalities of current problems, the Department under Mr. Hull became absorbed in platonic planning of a Utopia, in a sort of mechanistic idealism.[9]

The State Department, through American diplomats abroad, is the government's institutional link with external reality. Detached from reality, foreign policy turns into "mechanistic idealism," or worse, as in the Reagan administration's nightmarish misadventures in Iran.

Henry Adams described a similar phenomenon in the Grant administration almost one hundred years earlier:

> Secretary [of State] Fish seemed to have vanished. Besides the Department of State over which he nominally presided ... there had been a Department of Foreign Relations over which Senator Sumner ruled with a high hand at the Capitol; and finally, one made out a third Foreign Office in the War Department with President Grant himself for chief. Fish ... as yet asserted no policy of his own. As for Grant's policy, Adams never had a chance to know fully what it was. .... Then he listened with incredulous stupor while Sumner unfolded his plan for concentrating and pressing every possible American claim against England, with a view of compelling the cession of Canada to the United States.[10]

Three administrations—Grant's, Roosevelt's, and Reagan's—widely separated from each other in time, were equally remote from reality on issues of great importance to the United States because divisions of authority in Washington increased the distance between policymakers and diplomats, between Washington and the world,.

Yet my German friend remarked that American Foreign Service

officers seem overly controlled. If they are remote from the well-springs of policy, how can they be programmed to evoke it so literally? In reality, one condition leads naturally to the other. Diplomats who do not feel themselves part of the policy-making process but are sworn to support whatever emerges from it are more apt to rely on diplomacy by rote than those who have a more sophisticated understanding of the administration's thinking and believe that they are contributing to it. Similarly, diplomats who know their subject but not whether their views will reach policymakers have less incentive to do their best work than diplomats who know they participate in an active dialogue with their government.

The barriers erected by the American system between policymakers and diplomats, between appointed and career officials, exist in the European system but are less impenetrable. Sometimes they disappear altogether. In the past twenty years six French foreign ministers have been former Foreign Service officers.

WHERE THE EUROPEANS ARE BEHIND

European diplomacy nevertheless has some catching up of its own to do. When Americans look at the problems the European Union has in reaching decisions—whether on a common agricultural policy or on selection of the next commission president—they can be excused for doubting that the United States lags far behind Europeans in the skills of conference diplomacy. It has yet to be demonstrated that the intensive consultations of the EU are actually producing common policies in the areas where they are most needed. European diplomacy is more skilled in dealing with competing security interests than in dealing with economic ones. Achieving a European balance of power is proving to be easier than achieving a reconciliation of European interests.

It has been apparent for some time that European Commission planners in Brussels are far ahead of European governments in building a true community in which national identities are submerged in a single European identity. This is the case not only with respect to such central objectives as the creation of a common currency, but on less important issues. On a flight to France in 1989 to attend an EU-sponsored conference on the challenge to the U.S. economy posed by a united Europe, I was brought down to earth by an article in a French newspaper reporting a complaint by the European Air Transport Association that the excessive number of air traffic control zones was hindering air travel in Western Europe. An aircraft flying from Frankfurt to Madrid passed through seven zones; in the United States an aircraft traveling from Boston to Chicago, about the same distance, passed through only three.[11]

Despite American checks and balances, and wariness toward foreign engagements, once the United States becomes convinced of the need for action, its ability to act is unquestioned. The American government itself really functions by means of a kind of conference diplomacy. Decisions are reached through a process of permanent negotiation between the executive and the legislative branches of the government, between the Senate and the House, between the federal and state governments, and within all of these bodies. The process of arriving at an internal consensus may be painful, but, once reached, the United States demonstrates leadership and follow-through unmatched by other states. This has been true not only of military security issues but in complex transnational areas where the Europeans have been slow to find a consensus. A case in point is the negotiation of the 1987 Montreal Protocol on depletion of the ozone layer.

THE MONTREAL PROTOCOL

The Montreal Protocol was a pioneering effort to control and cut back, on a world-wide scale, the manufacture of products emitting chlorine gases into the stratosphere.[12] Scientists believed that the thinning out of the ozone layer caused by uncontrolled chlorine emissions would eventually increase ultraviolet radiation in the Earth's atmosphere to life-threatening levels.

The obstacles to reaching agreement were formidable: chlorines were contained in a wide variety of industrial products, ranging from aerosol sprays to computers; scientific evidence of future danger was strong but not conclusive; the chemical companies, especially in Europe, were opposed; in the United States, where Congress had passed the Clean Air Act in 1977, the idea of international controls was controversial; and the industrialized and developing countries had different points of view about how the problem should be addressed.

The successful outcome of the negotiations, which, in their various phases, lasted over two years, was produced by strong American leadership (in the person of an American Foreign Service officer), close collaboration with the United Nations Environmental Programme (UNEP), and an effective partnership between diplomats and scientists. The latter was essential. When the Montreal Protocol was at last agreed to by twenty-four states in September 1987, the executive director of UNEP, Egyptian scientist Mostopha Tolba, hailed it as "a union [of scientists and diplomats] which must guide the affairs of the world into the next century."[13]

The negotiation of the Montreal Protocol under U.S. leadership demonstrates that the American system of decision making, cumbersome though it is, can produce results. Indeed, in this important transnational field it worked better than the European system, which was hamstrung by differences among the European states and tangled lines of communication in Brussels.

New Problems, New Skills

The intricacies of "ozone diplomacy" demonstrate how the scope of foreign policy has broadened and the number of unfamiliar variables has increased. Policy-making and policy implementation in these complex areas will require new kinds of expertise and cooperation across political boundaries and intellectual disciplines. The policies themselves will be harder to package and market under a political label. Credible doctrines will be harder to formulate, and the success or failure of an administration's policies harder to measure in its political lifetime. The new array of threats will only yield to consistent, long-term policies.

Continuous and intensive consultation is required among states exposed to generalized threats like depletion of the ozone layer. These are problems that grow by accretion. Some of them are virtually undetectable without constant monitoring. They lend themselves to preventive diplomacy, not crisis management. It is ironic that before its demise the Soviet Union's deadliest attack against its western neighbors proved to be Chernobyl, and the Warsaw Pact's most destructive secret weapon its obsolete and noxious industrial plants.

Such problems were beyond the reach of traditional diplomacy and beyond the ken of most policymakers. The focus of foreign policy will continue to expand. So will the responsibilities of diplomacy. The questions to be addressed in succeeding chapters are how to make American diplomacy a more effective instrument of foreign policy, and how to educate American policymakers to use it more effectively.

Diplomacy as Representation

"Identity would seem to be the garment with which one covers the nakedness of the self; in which case, it is best that the garment be loose, a little like the robes of the desert."

(James Baldwin)

THE QUESTION of what and whom a diplomat represents is central to his or her functions.[1] To say that diplomats represent their governments does not define the nature of that representation, particularly in the case of the United States, where governments alternate, policies are usually ambiguous, Congress often disagrees with the president, and minority interests cannot be ignored. The inclination of most American administrations is to narrow the area of representation to activities that are official, innocuous, or specifically authorized. The inclination of the best American diplomats is to enlarge the area as much as possible.

On March 10, 1779, Benjamin Franklin in his capacity as United States minister to France issued on behalf of Captain James Cook, the British explorer and navigator who was then on his second voyage to the South Pacific, a passport addressed to American privateers. In it Franklin urged them "to treat the said Captain Cook and his people with all civility and kindness . . . as common friends to mankind." Franklin did not know at the time that Cook was already dead, killed by natives in the Hawaiian Islands, but his action clearly expressed Franklin's view of what he represented as America's senior diplomat in France.

Bearing in mind that Cook was an Englishman, that England was at war with the United States, and that Franklin had no specific authority to issue the passport from the Continental Congress (which was slow to follow his lead in recognizing Cook and his crew as "common friends to mankind"), Franklin's act required a breadth of vision and courage that would get him instantly recalled by the American government today. The issuance of visas and passports by consulates abroad is controlled in meticulous detail by Washington, with a "watch-list" to sound alarms if a visa applicant is ascertained to have belonged to any organization judged subversive by the Justice Department.

As ambassador to Greece in the 1980s I was compelled to seek Washington's approval before issuing a visa to the Greek minister of culture, the much-beloved actress and political activist Melina Mercouri. Although she was the cabinet minister of a NATO ally and married to an American, her name had appeared among the members of a peace organization anathematized by the attorney general as a communist front, and she thus had to be "precleared" before each of her frequent visits. This we managed to do without inconvenience to her, but the procedure reflects a less self-confident image of the United States than Franklin's, and a less generous spirit for American diplomats to represent and rationalize.

Even representatives of the smallest states have at least two personae: their own and that of the state that employs them. It is a fortunate diplomat who finds the two entirely compatible. When former deputy under secretary of state for management L. Dean Brown was cochairing the orientation program for newly appointed chiefs of mission, he would tell them that few ambassadors can afford the luxury of simply "being themselves." They have to choose what official role to play both within the embassy and outside it—the ambassador as micromanager or as custodian of the big picture, the ambassador as confidant of Washington policymakers or as super-expert on the country to which he or she is accredited. "It is your choice," Brown would say, "but whatever image you choose, try not to make it too different from the real one."

Good advice, but hard to follow. Ambassadors who rely too much on themselves and their own experience will find that they cannot speak with the full resonance of their government when they need to; ambassadors who overly identify themselves with their government will mistake its prestige for their own and dissipate their influence in petty squabbles over incidentals. The deadly sins of diplomacy are triviality and portentousness.

In Renaissance Italy ambassadors were nobles of the court who were personally selected by their sovereigns to represent them at the courts of foreign princes. In the United States until after World War II, ambassadors who enjoyed a personal relationship with the president functioned with enhanced effectiveness. Edmund A. Gullion, then dean of the Fletcher School of Law and Diplomacy, wrote in 1964: "Many different lists of ideal qualifications of a Chief of Mission could be compiled and each would be more or less valid. Under the American system, probably the outstanding qualification he can bring to his job is the reputation of having the special confidence of the President of the United States. If the Ambassador is considered to have been a personal selection of the President, he can safely be short a few other specialized qualifications."[2] Gullion himself, a former career diplomat, was known to have been the personal selection of President John F. Kennedy when he was appointed U.S. ambassador to the Republic of the Congo (now Zaire) in 1961. Many well-known noncareer ambassadors in the postwar period, men like Averell Harriman, David Bruce, and Ellsworth Bunker, brought to their diplomatic missions special authority because they were seen as personal envoys of the president.

Today, very few ambassadors have ready access to the president or the secretary of state. Unless an urgent international problem requires the president to receive an ambassador, even friendship and party loyalty will not often open the door to the oval office. Photo opportunities are rarely opportunities for anything else, and a short personal note scribbled across the White House Christmas card provides no policy guidance for the ambassador or the embassy staff.

This is a far cry from the relations of Venetian envoys to their prince, and even from the ties that bound some American ambassadors to their president as late as the administration of Franklin D. Roosevelt. The letters to Roosevelt from William C. Bullitt when he was serving as U.S. ambassador to the Soviet Union and to France in the 1930s fill a long volume,[3] and Lincoln MacVeagh, while serving as ambassador to Greece, addressed about seventy "Dear Franklin"

DIPLOMACY AS REPRESENTATION

letters to his chief,[4], a fellow graduate of Groton and Harvard. In today's much larger, more impersonal, and highly bureaucratized foreign policy establishment, knowledge that an ambassador has personal links to the president may be useful in securing access to senior officials in Washington but not often for getting a direct line to the president. A reputation for having close ties may also be helpful in assuring that a new ambassador is well received by the government to which he or she presents credentials, but it will be a rapidly wasting asset if the ambassador is unable to show that it pays off in policy terms.

By and large an ambassador with a reputation for effectiveness and a demonstrable need to see the president about a real problem in U.S. relations with the country to which the envoy is accredited can usually do so. This was also true of the Harrimans, Bruces, Bunkers, and Gullions. Had their principal claim on the president's time been personal rather than professional, or had they wasted it with trivia and misinformation, their access quickly would have atrophied. As in most other professions, skill, judgment, and seriousness of purpose count for more in modern diplomats than the eminence of their sponsors.

WHAT MAKES A GOOD REPRESENTATIVE?

If ambassadors do not represent the president in a personal way but nevertheless represent something larger than themselves, who or what is it? The definition changes over time. If Benjamin Franklin felt entitled to represent "all mankind" in seeking to facilitate the explorations of Captain Cook, the envoys of the Renaissance deviated at their peril from the most literal interpretation of their prince's instructions. Sad to say, in the age of the imperial presidency, American ambassadors function in a political atmosphere closer in spirit to the Medicis than to the Age of Reason. The physical remoteness of diplomats from policymakers has increased, but new communications technology has made possible ever more detailed and frequent instructions. As a result, it is more difficult than ever for a diplomat to influence

American foreign policy, or to enlarge on it. Self-confidence, and confidence that one knows what one is doing, are essential if an ambassador is to influence policy successfully.

This is why those who offer prescriptions for success in diplomacy—from François de Callières in the eighteenth century to John Kenneth Galbraith in the twentieth—are right to emphasize human qualities as much as diplomatic skills. Harold Nicolson, writing in 1939, identified "moral precision" as the most elusive but most important quality. He meant by this the moral self-discipline to report accurately not only facts that may be unwelcome to the diplomat's superiors but facts that may cast the diplomat in an unflattering light. "Truth, accuracy, calm, patience, good temper, modesty, and loyalty" are other qualities extolled by Nicolson, who added: "'But,' the reader may object, 'you have forgotten intelligence, knowledge, discernment, prudence, hospitality, charm, industry, courage and even tact.' I have not forgotten them. I have taken them for granted."[5] Galbraith, and most other contemporary analysts of diplomacy, stress leadership ability, which in the nature of managing an embassy amounts to an ambassador's ability to compose a coherent and persuasive picture of national policies, and to convey that picture to the government to which he or she is accredited and to his or her own staff. To do this successfully requires leadership ability infused with knowledge and experience. If Nicolson's gentlemanly catalogue of virtues seems inconsistent with this, we must remember that an ambassador is not invested with military powers of command over the embassy staff, three-quarters of whom will not be State Department employees.[6] Even less, of course, does the envoy have such powers over the host government. Leadership ability will be reflected in how well the ambassador utilizes the power of persuasion.

The quality that is probably most essential for ambassadors—and in fact for diplomats of any rank—is judgment, which often means simply the ability to tell what is important from what is unimportant in the relations of the state they represent with the state to which they are accredited. This can be extremely tricky, especially when the two states weigh the importance of a problem differently. At times like these diplomats must ascertain, first, the true importance of the problem to their own government and, second, how their instructions can best be carried out with the government to which they are accredited.

The instructions an embassy receives are all communicated in the name of the secretary of state. If they reflect the secretary's personal wishes, or those of the president, the fact will be made clear. If they do not, which is more often the case, it will be up to the ambassador to determine their true weight. Some will represent real and urgent needs, others will be what is known in the trade as "defensive paper work"—efforts by the administration to show (usually to Congress) that it takes a problem seriously even if it does not. The judgment of the ambassador is crucial in evaluating instructions, based on an understanding of the broad lines of the government's foreign policy and of its priorities at any given time. The ambassador must decide whether the instructions leave latitude for interpretation and, if so, how much; he or she must decide whether they represent the considered views of the government at a senior level (indicating a true consensus) or are cursory views tilted toward the needs of one agency or another.

Once diplomats believe they have assigned the proper weight to their instructions, they must decide how best to carry them out. This involves detailed knowledge of the country in which they serve, and particularly their own relations with its leaders and opinion-makers. The confidence they enjoy is more often the product of their personal reputation than of the standing of their government. If diplomats were, as they are sometimes accused of being, mere "message carriers" reciting their instructions from cue cards, anyone could do it. The process is not so simple, however, and the way a diplomat builds relations, interprets instructions, and follows them up can make the difference between a successful and an unsuccessful démarche.

The complexity of regulating problems between states, where the risk of misunderstanding resulting from different languages, cultures, political systems, and economic needs is always great, explains the reason for Talleyrand's famous maxim for diplomats, "Et surtout, pas trop de zèle." By cautioning against too much zeal, he was pointing to the ever-present danger of confusion and miscalculation in international affairs, and the consequent need for patience, as well as a measure of humility, in dealing with them. These too are qualities of temperament and intellect rather than specific skills, although even a diplomat who has them will need profound knowledge of local conditions to judge the right moves and the right moment to make them.

An ambassador's judgment must even be exercised in diplomatic entertaining, a form of representation abroad that has probably created more misunderstanding in the United States about the nature of diplomacy than any other.[7] Perhaps because funds for official entertaining have so often been criticized in Congress as "whiskey funds" (even by those who have consumed more than their share), much embassy entertaining today is characterized by a certain grim mirth and the fear that someone may actually be having a good time. It is not unusual for ambassadors to warn American personnel not to talk to each other and to concentrate their attentions (welcome or unwelcome) exclusively on foreign guests. This targeting of useful contacts—once a notoriously unsubtle feature of Soviet conviviality—misses the point of the best embassy entertaining, which is to make the guests feel they are the beneficiaries of official hospitality, not its victims. Here too Talleyrand's advice is worth heeding.

Representing Private Interests

An American ambassador looks after not only the official interests of the United States but the interests of its private sector. In addition to American banks and businesses, the private sector may include American-sponsored educational or medical institutions, religious missions, voluntary organizations, and, of course, American citizens living abroad or traveling there in a private capacity. Attending to their routine needs will usually be the business of the consular section of the embassy. Their exceptional needs, including the need to intervene on their behalf with the host government, will become the concern of the ambassador and senior staff.

In the case of American business interests, the commercial and economic sections of the embassy carry the main responsibility, especially in supplying information to foreign firms on American suppliers and markets, but the ambassador and the deputy chief of mission must keep informed of their activities and be prepared to assist them when necessary. The kind of assistance, and the lengths to which the embassy can go in extending it, will depend on circumstances. In the nineteenth century, when trade promotion was the single most important mission of American representatives abroad, no length was too great. Many consuls were salaried by American firms. The precedent had long before been established by European governments, especially the British, for whom world trade was a lifeline. Even today there is a closer identification of European governments with their business interests than exists, or is possible, for the United States.

There are several reasons for this. One is that many British and European firms are nationalized. Being state monopolies, embassy and consular officials can represent them without discriminating against competing firms of the same nationality. This enables them to support tenders submitted to foreign governments with fewer qualifications than United States officials, who may be balancing the competing interests of more than one American company. Another reason is that European governments provide greater flexibility than the United States in enabling their representatives to improve the terms under which a large foreign purchase can be financed. An American embassy cannot secure terms more favorable than those of the Export-Import Bank, which are fixed by Congress. For an important contract, a European ambassador may be able to secure concessionary financing, or at least financing on terms more favorable than those being offered by foreign competitors.

There are frequent calls from Congress and American business for the government and its diplomatic representatives to do more to promote U.S. exports. These are most urgently expressed when the dollar is overvalued and American products, for this or other reasons, are proving less competitive in foreign markets. All governments hear the same complaints. In Britain twenty-five years ago, the Val Duncan Report on British overseas representation stated flatly: "In Britain's present economic situation commercial work is the most useful task of our overseas representatives."[8] The British government soon discovered that the cause for lagging exports was more complicated than ineffective trade promotion by British diplomats. American business representatives, who pride themselves on being independent of government, have usually been more realistic. They do, however, have justified expectations that ambassadors and their staffs will assist them in areas where they are qualified to do so.

These include prompt and effective intervention when they are discriminated against by foreign governments; assistance to their employees when threatened by foreign political upheaval or violence; and recognition that they are important members of the American community entitled to ready access to embassy officers. In addition to these basic services, the American ambassador is often in a position to help American businesses, on an impartial basis, with commercial and political insights useful in protecting their interests. Providing knowledge of who in a foreign government are in a position to make commercial decisions, how to approach them, and if necessary facilitating access will often be among the most effective ways an American ambassador can "represent" American business.

THE NEED TO SCREEN AMBASSADORS

It should go without saying that ability to pass the Foreign Service written and oral examinations and be commissioned in the United States Foreign Service is no guarantee that an officer will demonstrate good judgment when it counts. Foreign Service officers can be as blinded by vanity and ambition as anyone else. Knowledge of the host country and of its language will help avoid some pitfalls, but in the case of ambassadors the State Department itself does not always nominate the most qualified career candidates. Assignments as chief of mission can be used as rewards or, less frequently, as places of exile. There have been occasions when a political candidate put forward by the White House for an ambassadorship had language capability that the State Department's career candidate did not.

There is need for a mechanism that impartially screens both career and noncareer candidates. The Carter administration established a presidential advisory board only for proposed political appointees. It had fifteen members and met once a month for the first six months of the administration. One of its members says it was ineffective because only three members had significant foreign affairs experience and because it was clear from the outset that any candidate the administration really wanted to have approved would be approved.

Panels that reflect too faithfully either the political interests of the administration or, conversely, the professional interests of the Foreign Service will not do the job. The Senate Foreign Relations Committee can recommend that the full Senate disapprove a candidate it considers unqualified, and if the members of the committee were sufficiently impartial and had time to scrutinize the qualifications of candidates more carefully, no other mechanism would be necessary. In general, however, the confirmation process has been perfunctory. At its worst, in highly politicized cases, it can be arbitrary and unfair. A screening of *all* ambassadorial candidates, career and noncareer, by a panel of foreign affairs experts, some reflecting the outlook of the administration, others the experience of professional diplomats, would almost certainly be an improvement over the present system, in which the State Department and the White House haggle over which embassy will go to a political nominee and which to a career, and in the process of making trade-offs the actual qualifications of the candidates can become of secondary importance.

Impartial screening would also make it harder to play the game of percentages that now dominates discussion of how chiefs of mission posts are distributed. By making a rough calculation of the average percentage of ambassadorships filled by political appointees in the last twenty-five years, the Foreign Service has concluded that a figure of about 28 percent is "normal." Administration officials usually try to show that their ambassadorial appointments are consistent with this figure.

The percentage of ambassadors who are political or career, however, has nothing to do with their qualifications or whether they are filling the right posts. It also distracts attention from the creeping escalation of political appointees in State Department positions, a trend that reduces the number of openings for senior Foreign Service officers and contributes to excessive politicization of the foreign policy process.

POLITICAL REPRESENTATION

Some observers have questioned whether a diplomat is capable of faithfully implementing the foreign policies of successive governments of different political complexions. Former ambassador to Yugoslavia Laurence H. Silberman, a political appointee of the Ford administration, has recommended that all career officers nominated to become ambassadors be obliged to resign from the Foreign Service before being sworn into office. His reasoning is that a chief of mission whose diplomatic career will end with an ambassadorship is committed to the priorities of the administration, not those of the Foreign Service; a chief of mission who will retain a Foreign Service rank (and salary) may not be.

Silberman exaggerates both the willingness of career ambassadors to frustrate the policies of administrations they serve and that of noncareer ambassadors to promote policies they consider wrongheaded. The fundamental obligation of an ambassador is not blind loyalty to an administration and its policies but informed loyalty. The latter assumes two things: first, that there will be more continuity than discontinuity in the foreign policy of the United States from one administration to another; second, that the capacity of ambassadors for "moral precision," in Nicolson's phrase, will compel them to speak honestly to their government when they disagree with it, but not allow them to obstruct its central purposes.

A corollary assumption is that loyalty operates in two directions. However inconvenient an ambassador's disagreement with proposed policy initiatives may seem at a given moment, any government that suppresses or penalizes dissent courts disaster. This should be self-evident to a generation of Americans old enough to remember the domestic conflicts that paralyzed the Johnson and Nixon administrations, whose Vietnam policies, different though they were, polarized the country between forces of engagement and disengagement that had in common only their intolerance of nuance and dissent.

In fact, it is customary for all American ambassadors, career and noncareer, to submit their resignations before a new administration is sworn into office, even if it is headed by a reelected president. The opportunity is thus available to begin with a clean slate and, if the administration chooses to reassess its priorities, to make new appointments. When elections result in changes of party as well as administration, outgoing secretaries of state will ordinarily provide their successors with a list of chiefs of mission, usually career officers, who for one reason or another are recommended to be retained in their posts.

PROFESSIONAL REPRESENTATION

The Silberman proposal is a fairly typical expression of the distrust political loyalists feel for those who, like diplomats, profess to be, if not "above" politics—intellectually and morally a precarious position to take in a democracy—at least adjacent to the political process. A completely apolitical American diplomat would be an envoy so pale and chaste as to be wholly ineffective. But one's commitment to implement faithfully the foreign policy of the incumbent administration is not contingent on how one voted. If it were, diplomacy would become a ceaselessly shifting parade of political personalities, less concerned with international affairs than with the fortunes of the administration that appointed them.

The reason professional diplomats can function in a democracy without becoming either politically neutered or politically disloyal is that foreign policy differences between parties in the United States, or any other democratically governed state, are usually smaller than the parties themselves are prepared to admit. They tend to be differences of emphasis rather than direction. This does not mean that they are completely without significance, particularly over time. But it does mean that they are less significant than party activists pretend, and that, in practice, moving from the foreign policy of one party to that of another involves less reorientation than a bare reading of the plat-

83

forms would suggest. When a British diplomat was asked how he could serve governments of opposing political parties with equal loyalty, he replied, "By doing so one at a time."

This kind of response is infuriating to the appointed officials of incoming administrations who believe that they are keepers of the political flame and must ignite a sodden bureaucracy with new vitality and different values. Consequently, they tend to treat the career Foreign Service as holdovers from the previous administration rather than recruits to the new administration with useful knowledge of the situation it is inheriting.

The fact that policy adjustments between one administration and another will invariably be fewer than promised and less dramatic than prophesied only adds to the administration's desire to provide visible evidence of change. The easiest way to do so is to change people. Career officers know and accept this almost as readily as political appointees, even though the reshuffling of senior State Department personnel that accompanies a change of administration rarely contributes to efficiency in the internal management of foreign affairs or a better understanding of basic U.S. aims by other governments.

CHANGE AND CONTINUITY

When a new administration takes office, career officers do feel entitled to be judged individually on their professional merits, not exclusively on their association with policies of the previous government. If such policies were legitimate and aboveboard, career officers were sworn to implement them. In their minds, having done so is the new team's best assurance of their professionalism. Few incoming administrations see it that way. Before the Eisenhower administration succeeded the Truman administration in 1953, for example, an almost wholly artificial but immensely destructive debate over foreign policy had envenomed the election campaign. The issues of "who lost China," alleged Communists and Communist sympathizers in the State Department, and containment versus "liberation" in Eastern Europe dominated the postelection atmosphere. Secretary of State John Foster Dulles, whose broad views on foreign policy were in most respects indistinguishable from those of his predecessor, Dean Acheson, created the illusion of fundamental change by rhetorical flourishes and callous opportunism in his handling of personnel. He presided over the purging of the State Department's China experts as his way of answering the question of who lost China; he appointed a collaborator of the witch-hunting Senator Joseph McCarthy to head the department's internal security service as his way of demonstrating that career officers whose political reliability had been questioned, however irresponsibly, would be dismissed or placed in limbo; and to dramatize his contention that the previous administration's policy of "containing" the Soviet Union was too passive, he conspicuously refrained from offering a new post to its author, George F. Kennan.[9]

As noted earlier, when the Hungarian revolt against communism erupted in 1956, the Eisenhower/Dulles administration opted for containment, not liberation. The administration's foreign policy, worldwide, differed little from that of its predecessor. So it has been with most new administrations since World War II, not because Foreign Service mandarins entrenched in the system and impervious to political direction prevent change, but because great states, like ocean liners, shift course almost imperceptibly and achieve their destination in an interval of time determined by inertial forces more powerful and fundamental than any controlled by their Foreign Service crews.

WHO CONTROLS FOREIGN POLICY?

Dulles began his stewardship of the State Department by having placed on the desk of every officer a memorandum stating that he would expect from them not merely loyalty to the policies of the new administration but "positive loyalty." The term was never precisely defined, but the assumption behind it was clear. Like the Silberman proposal, it assumed that diplomats were, by the nature of diplomacy, resistant to democratic controls.

European governments have traditionally found fewer problems in diplomatic professionalism, perhaps because the system was devised by them, perhaps because a parliamentary government, as we have seen, pays for its foreign policy mistakes more promptly than does a presidential government. This encourages greater diplomatic continuity and greater reliance on the advice of professional diplomats. Even European governments, however, are beginning to feel more pressure from public opinion on their foreign policy decisions.

In Europe as well as the United States, the line between foreign and domestic affairs is becoming harder to distinguish. This leads to growing public awareness that people's lives are affected by foreign affairs. As interdependence is brought home to the average citizen— through television, immigration, foreign investment, imported goods, and more extensive tourism—the need for governments to justify foreign policy decisions promptly and publicly becomes both more imperative and more difficult.

Alexis de Tocqueville believed this to be an inherent weakness in the ability of democracies to conduct foreign affairs: "a democracy can only with great difficulty regulate the details of an important undertaking, persevere in a fixed design, and work out its execution in spite of serious obstacles. It cannot combine its measures with secrecy or await their consequences with patience. These are qualities which more especially belong to an individual or to an aristocracy."[10] The notion of a foreign affairs "aristocracy" is exactly what American presidents most distrust about the Foreign Service and is the reason both Democratic and Republican administrations install political loyalists in key posts at home and abroad. The psychological gulf between administrations and the Foreign Service has been aggravated by the tendency of politically appointed officials with limited direct experience in working with foreign governments to believe that when Washington's views are not shared in foreign capitals, it is either because they have not been robustly promoted by career officials or because career officials have actively obstructed them. The problem was well stated by Dean Acheson:

> All presidents I have known have had uneasy doubts about the State Department. They extend to the White House staff, and in fact often originate there. They are strongest at the beginning of presidential terms, when the incumbent and his new associates in the White House believe that foreign affairs are simpler than they in fact are and that they can be confi-

dently approached under the guidance of principles (liberal, conservative, idealistic, or moral) even without much knowledge or experience. Foreign Service officers seem to them cynical, unimaginative, and negative.[11]

In a similar vein Arthur Schlesinger, Jr., has observed that the Kennedy White House regarded Foreign Service officers as people "for whom the risks always outweighed the opportunities." Kennedy took risks—at the Bay of Pigs, for example—and paid for them. Nevertheless, the prevailing winds for American foreign policy were still favorable during the Kennedy presidency. The United States in the first two decades after World War II was incontestably the strongest military and economic power in the world. The opportunities were almost always greater than the risks, and if the risks turned into foreign policy failures the United States was strong enough to recover from them. It was the Johnson administration that felt the winds begin to shift; however belatedly, it learned that even the United States was not strong enough to ignore risks and bounce back instantly from failures.

New administrations have continued to be reluctant fully to employ the resources of the State Department and Foreign Service in political risk assessment, the job for which they are best qualified. To the extent that it is shared in some degree by all democratic governments, this is a healthy reluctance. Princes and oligarchies may be able to orchestrate foreign policy more effectively than democracies—may be able, in Tocqueville's words, "to persevere in a design"—but their designs are likely to be flawed and their ability to correct them nonexistent. To the extent, however, that reluctance to use the Foreign Service effectively is motivated by fear that diplomats will become foreign policy "mandarins," beyond the control of a democratically elected government, it is misguided.

DEMOCRATIC DIPLOMACY

Tocqueville's comments on the incapacity of democracies in conducting foreign policy referred to the effect of public opinion on policymakers, not diplomats. Diplomacy requires patience, as noted earlier, but nothing in its nature resists political control. On the contrary, from the time of Machiavelli to the present, diplomats have regarded their primary duty to be one of helping political leaders reach their foreign policy objectives. They have more often, and more justly, been criticized for political conformity than for insubordination.

Equally unwarranted are attacks on the Foreign Service as an elite corps of specialists, unrepresentative of the American people as a whole. Today the wealthiest American diplomats are likely to be political appointees. The first paragraph of the Foreign Service Act of 1980 states that the service must be "representative of the American people." There has been a sustained recruiting effort since that time to make it so. The process has created management problems that will be considered in the next chapter, but it has also created a more representative Foreign Service. As of November 1993 (the most recent date for which figures are available), white males still represented 56 percent of the Foreign Service workforce, but white females had increased to 24 percent, minority males to 7 percent, and minority females to 4 percent.[12] Between 1987 and 1993, rates of promotion for eligible female and minority employees exceeded those of white males.

In the American system, foreign policy mandarins are easier to find in the White House than in the State Department or the Foreign Service. Ironically, these politically appointed officials are less politically accountable than career officials. Staff members of the National Security Council are not subject to confirmation hearings and do not testify before congressional committees. Their increased influence on the foreign policy process is a reflection of the more direct leadership role played by the president. Greater public awareness of the impact of foreign on domestic affairs has accelerated the trend toward concentration of foreign policy decision making in the White House.

DECENTRALIZATION OF FOREIGN AFFAIRS

There are two reasons for believing, however, that the trend is not irreversible. The first is that foreign affairs have become too complicated, and the problems too numerous, to permit a small group of

White House managers to exercise effective control without the data and informed advice of thousands of experts and observers. The second is that too conspicuous a preoccupation with foreign affairs on the part of the president, which probably contributes more than any other factor to excessive centralization of control, can, as George Bush discovered, become politically costly when domestic problems look more immediately threatening than do problems abroad. Going forth to slay dragons enhances the president's prestige only if he goes where the dragons are; if he is abroad and the dragons are at home, valor begins to look like negligence. President Carter lost the 1980 election abroad, President Bush the 1992 election at home.

In this sense the increasing pressure of public opinion on policymakers may actually encourage them to depoliticize and decentralize the management of foreign policy. The United States will not soon again, if ever, occupy the dominant position in the world that it did after World War II. Foreign affairs for many years to come will have as many risks as opportunities, and presidents will be more than willing to share them with career officials. This can be a healthy development, for there has been something incongruous about the impression cultivated by too many administrations that the president's personal mastery of foreign affairs keeps the peace. The panoply attending summit meetings—a pretentious phrase that the founding fathers would have detested—has rarely been justified by the often meager results, most of which, in any case, were earlier negotiated by experts. Who today remembers the accomplishments of Geneva in 1955, Glassboro in 1967, or of Malta in 1989?

Professional diplomats can anticipate problems before they require the attention of senior officials at home or at the summit; they can make certain that American positions are understood by policymakers abroad; and they can accomplish quietly what special emissaries can do only with a blare of trumpets.

After the tragedy of Tiananmen Square in 1989, how much easier it would have been for the Bush administration to convey its position through the embassy in Beijing rather than to send the deputy secretary of state and the national security adviser to China on secret missions that were revealed in the press only after the administration had clumsily denied they had taken place. The fact that President Bush was a former American ambassador to China probably encouraged him to believe that messages through diplomatic channels would have lacked immediacy or been too impersonal. He may have been right, but he would have been better served by a degree of impersonality. The Nixon administration preferred to communicate with the Soviet Union through the Soviet embassy in Washington rather than the American embassy in Moscow. It gave senior American officials the illusion that they were dealing directly with the Kremlin, and the press and public the illusion that superpower diplomacy could only be entrusted to the president and secretary of state. One of the effects was to make the Soviet ambassador in Washington a major personality and the American ambassador in Moscow a hotelier. Another, costlier effect was to reduce our relations with the Soviet Union to a series of negotiations over technical problems that took place at a time of vast societal changes of which American policymakers seemed barely to be aware.

Our chief executives and their secretaries of state have much to gain and little to lose by relying more on professional diplomats to conduct the permanent international conversation we call diplomacy. The personal relations formed at summit meetings are a two-edged sword. Political leaders may conclude that serious government-to-government problems can be cleared up through personal charm and charisma. They may attach more importance to their (good or bad) relations with another leader than to relations with his or her country. The personal bonds that successive American presidents formed with the shah of Iran and President Marcos of the Philippines are only two examples of the dangers of overly personalized diplomacy at the summit.

Trained Foreign Service officers are inherently less likely to mistake good rapport for agreement; they have learned to distinguish between the personal and official dimensions of diplomacy. The most successful among them will also be the most objective. To employ them more effectively and more authoritatively in foreign capitals would not weaken the president's control over foreign policy. It would simply recognize that the foreign relations of the United States are not pulled up by the roots and replanted every time we change presidents. It would reaffirm Franklin's belief that an ambassador of the United States and his staff represent large ideals, permanent interests, and nonpartisan values. As emissaries of a democratic leader, in the words of our first diplomatic historian, they represent "nothing but the nation."

Diplomacy as Management

> "In a sweeping overhaul of the way it does business,
> I.B.M., long one of the world's most admired and suc-
> cessful companies, said yesterday that it would become
> a federation of smaller, nimbler companies able to re-
> spond more quickly to demands of the marketplace."
> *(New York Times, Nov. 27, 1991)*

THE LEADERS of the State Department and the Foreign Service in recent administrations have not been good managers of the foreign affairs bureaucracy. Neither have they shown much understanding of the special nature of the diplomatic profession, the proper contribution diplomacy can make to American foreign policy, or the best ways to facilitate the work of diplomats.

Better management is clearly needed, and better management will almost certainly mean less management. The State Department and its services abroad have for decades been overmanaged and underled.[1] The State Department in terms of its payroll is a pygmy among federal giants: in Fiscal Year 1993 its budget was slightly over two billion dollars and its workforce about 12,000 Foreign and Civil Service employees, of which, it will be recalled, only 4,300 were Foreign Service officers. The entire U.S. Foreign Service, including specialists, secretarial staff, and Foreign Service officers from other agencies, numbers only 13,000. By contrast, the FY 1993 Defense Department budget was 280 billion dollars and its civilian workforce 844,000 employees. Even the much smaller Commerce Department has a payroll about four times that of the State Department.

FREQUENT REFORM, LITTLE PROGRESS

Yet the organization, responsibilities, and terms of employment of the U.S. Foreign Service have been the subject of almost continual controversy and upheaval since the end of World War II. Its operations, and those of the State Department, have undergone three major reorganizations and countless minor ones. The first major reorganization occurred in 1946 when the State Department was required to absorb many of the 10,000 employees of defunct wartime agencies that had carried out activities abroad; the second, the so-called Wriston reforms, took place in 1954 and resulted in compulsory integration of most State Department Civil Service personnel into the Foreign Service; the third came with the Foreign Service Act of 1980, which restructured the selection, assignment, and promotion processes of the Foreign Service to reflect the priorities of a new generation of Foreign Service officers. It was designed to create a more "open," less disciplined service that gave officers a larger voice in their assignments and the prospect of faster promotions into the senior ranks.

Throughout the period leading up to passage of the Foreign Service Act of 1980 there were a series of high-level studies and congressional hearings that focused on the management of foreign affairs. Pervasive awareness that the existing system would not meet the future foreign policy needs of the United States was reflected in the titles of reports like *Toward a Modern Diplomacy*, published in 1968 by the American Foreign Service Association,[2] and *Diplomacy for the 70s*, released by the State Department in 1970.[3] From an organizational standpoint, these reports envisaged a central, coordinating role for the State Department in the Washington foreign affairs system; from a personnel standpoint, they advocated greater flexibility, less emphasis on traditional diplomatic skills, and the development of what the State Department report called "a new breed of diplomat-manager."

Despite the extensive discussion, and the active participation of Foreign Service officers in its drafting, the 1980 Act has produced disappointing results. The coordinating role of the State Department is less significant than it was before 1980, and the personnel structures of the Foreign Service are more rigid and bureaucratic. Further reforms to make the system work better were recommended in the 1989 Bremer and Thomas reports and the 1992 Veliotes report. The Institute for the Study of Diplomacy at Georgetown University added to the body of expert advice in a 1992 study entitled *The For-

eign Service in 2001,[4] setting forth a series of recommendations to improve the Foreign Service's ability to address the new order of international problems emerging after the cold war. The State Department's contribution to the 1993 Gore report on "Reinventing Government" is called *Change at State*.[5]

NEW WINDS OF CHANGE

Clearly, change is again in the air. Flaws in the 1980 act are one reason; another is that the Foreign Service has always posed special problems for the federal government. The sense of apartness conveyed by a service whose essential mission is outside the borders of the United States inevitably results in a degree of bureaucratic isolation. It can result in grotesque misconceptions of who career diplomats are and what they do, cultivated not only by ideologues of the right and left but by others who should know better. A former National Security Council staffer some years ago contended that Foreign Service officers became so rootless that the foreign policy of the United States would be better carried out by citizens randomly picked off the street. The experience of most FSOs and their families is just the opposite. There is usually nothing like service abroad to increase one's appreciation for the privileges and comforts of life at home.

Despite (or because of) its small size and high standards and its record of loyal service to the nation, often in difficult and dangerous circumstances,[6] charges of elitism, effeteness, and worse have dogged the Foreign Service almost from its inception. Few FSOs join the service for fame or fortune, but most would welcome greater recognition of the quality and value of their work. American diplomats are not alone in feeling that their profession is misunderstood. Even in countries where the diplomatic tradition is well established, concern exists that diplomacy has become too serious a factor in domestic affairs to be left to the diplomats: the Berrill Report on the British Foreign Service in 1977 postulated that service abroad for Britons was "intellectually blunting," and the Viot report on the French Foreign Service in 1987 spoke of a general "malaise" among French diplomats who feared a gradual loss of status within the French government.

Whatever their nationality, the unique position of diplomats and their distinctive mission pose special management problems for the government that employs them. In the case of the American government, these problems are compounded by the instinctive mutual distrust that exists between political and career officials. Unless strong leadership is exercised to protect it, the professional integrity of the State Department and the Foreign Service in the Washington foreign policy community is easily challenged—more easily than that of the Department of Defense or the Central Intelligence Agency, which also have numerous personnel serving abroad in American embassies. Both of these agencies have bureaucratic advantages denied to the State Department: in the case of CIA, the secrecy of its operations and funding; in the case of Defense, its enormous domestic political clout. Abuse of the State Department's consular authority in the 1992 election campaign by officials of the Bush administration, rummaging for material that could damage the Clinton candidacy, is only the latest evidence of the department's vulnerability to political manipulation.

JURISDICTIONAL PROBLEMS

The first and most obvious management problem posed by the Foreign Service is that its leader, the secretary of state, is based in Washington while most of the Foreign Service staff is employed abroad. The secretary has, at best, limited contact with even the most senior of them. It is the conventional wisdom of FSOs that they need periodic tours of duty in Washington if they are to be noticed by the secretary and other senior officials—-the so-called seventh-floor principals who occupy offices on the policy-making seventh floor of the State Department, and whose recommendations go a long way in assuring timely promotions and desirable assignments.

But the problem of distant centers of operations is not the critical management issue. Dozens of multinational corporations deal with this successfully every day. Rather, the most important obstacles to rational management of the State Department's overseas operations are, first, the fragmented and contested nature of the secretary of state's authority over foreign policy within the U.S. government and, second, the overcentralized, domestically oriented nature of the secretary's authority within the State Department itself. The second condition is aggravated by the first.

An ambassador's authority over embassy personnel, including those who are not employed by the State Department, was first formalized in President Kennedy's 1961 letter to all U.S. ambassadors: "You are in charge of the entire United States Diplomatic Mission and I shall expect you to supervise all of its operations. The Mission includes not only personnel of the State Department, but also the representatives of all other United States agencies which have programs and activities in [the ambassador's country of assignment]. I shall give you full support and backing in carrying out your assignment."[7] No such mandate has been issued or enforced by any president on behalf of a secretary of state. All cabinet departments were created by Congress, not the Constitution, and the State Department was the first, tracing its origins back to a 1789 act of Congress. The wording of that act explains many of the Secretary's jurisdictional problems:

> The Secretary of State shall perform such duties as shall from time to time be enjoined on or entrusted to him by the President relative to correspondences, commissions, or instructions to or with public ministers or consuls from the United States, or to negotiations with public ministers from foreign states or princes, or to memorials or other applications from foreign public ministers or other foreigners, or to such other matters respecting foreign affairs as the President of the United States shall assign to the Department, and he shall conduct the business of the Department in such manner as the President shall direct.[8]

The secretary, in other words, has no duties or responsibilities not specifically assigned by the president, and no recourse to constitutional safeguards should the president choose to delegate power in the field of foreign affairs to others, or should others appropriate powers that the president does not choose to reserve for the secretary of state. This is why the relationship between presidents and secretaries of state is so crucial to the management of U.S. foreign policy and why Dean Acheson wrote in 1969: "The President cannot be Secretary of State; it is inherently impossible in the nature of both positions. What he can do, and has often done, is to prevent anyone else from being Secretary of State."[9]

In the nineteenth century the ambiguous division of duties between the president and the secretary sometimes worked to the advantage of the latter, especially when a strong secretary was reporting to a weak or overburdened president. Lord Bryce, in his classic study of the United States published in 1888, placed the secretary in the driver's seat: "The conduct of foreign affairs is the chief duty of the State department: its head has therefore a larger stage to play on than any other minister and more chances for fame. His personal importance is all the greater because the President is usually so much absorbed by questions of patronage to be forced to leave the secretary to his own devices. Hence the foreign policy of the administration is practically that of the secretary, except so far as the latter is controlled by the Senate."[10] Such has rarely been the case in this century, and only once, under the special circumstances of the Ford administration, since World War II. Even when relations of trust and confidence exist between the president and the secretary of state, as they did between Truman and Acheson, Eisenhower and Dulles, and Bush and Baker, the secretary must spend an inordinate amount of time fending off bureaucratic challenges from other agencies. Often the most difficult to parry come from the White House staff. The attention of the secretary and his advisers, therefore, has a tendency to become focused on the struggle for power in Washington instead of on the world of foreign affairs.

In the Reagan administration, Secretary of State George Shultz sometimes gave the impression of a feudal lord fighting to preserve his domain from rival barons. To make matters worse, the struggle seemed to take place under the blank gaze of an uncomprehending sovereign. As a result, the secretary became increasingly inaccessible to his ambassadors abroad. During part of this period I was posted to Athens and therefore responsible for the day-to-day conduct of very uneasy relations between the socialist Greek government and the conservative Reagan administration—relations as important to the United States as they were uncomfortable, due to the existence of American military facilities there. Yet when I was in Washington it was easier to see the secretary of defense, the chairman of the Joint Chiefs, the national security adviser, or even, on one occasion, the president than the secretary of state. This was not because Secretary Shultz failed to recognize the importance of U.S.-Greek relations, but because he was extremely preoccupied, as we now know from his memoirs, with the plots and counterplots that plagued the conduct of foreign policy in the Reagan administration.

The situation is in some degree similar in all administrations: when senior State Department officials lower their voices over lunch in the executive dining room they are probably talking about the secretary's current fortunes in the bureaucratic wars in Washington, not the prospects for peace in Ruritania. The moral is that as long as the president does not provide the secretary of state with lines of authority as clear to the Washington foreign affairs community as those of the ambassador are to his or her country team, the secretary will be obliged to devote more time to the balance of power at home than abroad.

EFFECTS ON FOREIGN POLICY

The result of this domestic focus is that the distance between the secretary and the ambassadors becomes not only geographical but operational as well. The vacuum of leadership is rapidly filled by others— unofficial delegations, special emissaries, and "back channel"[11] instructions that diverge from or contradict those the ambassador has received from the State Department. When the secretary and senior staff are looking inward instead of outward, the ambassador has to spend even more time than usual in determining which communications are legitimate, which solicitations from other agencies are valid, and which requests are just make-work projects that with better management could be curtailed or eliminated.

The time that the secretary spends on domestic infighting inevitably reduces the time that can be devoted to the foreign problems that are, or will be, on the agenda. By reducing the time he has for his ambassadors he limits his most important source of direct information. Cables and despatches are poor substitutes for the give-and-take of dialogue with a trained observer who has just come from a foreign post. Ambassadors and embassies are not only the secretary's best source of information about foreign problems but, in some areas, his privileged source. Without them, he is no better off than his rivals in the Washington foreign affairs community. An ambassador serving in a country where there are U.S. military facilities can almost always brief the Joint Chiefs of Staff on developments affecting U.S. forces and security interests. There is no comparable opportunity to brief "seventh-floor principals." The Department of State has much to learn from the Department of Defense in this regard.

In terms of its vital functions—its product, if you will—no agency of government has more reason to decentralize its command structure and open up its lines of communication than the State Department. Unfortunately, the trend has been steadily in the opposite direction. Under Secretary of State Baker, operations were so tightly centralized, and channels of information so constricted, that when he left the department in 1992 to take over the Bush reelection campaign virtually everyone who was privy to his thinking on the most sensitive issues confronting the United States went with him. The *Boston Globe* was not alone in predicting that Baker's departure would leave "policy-making voids in almost every area."[12]

DEFINING (AND REDEFINING) DIPLOMACY

Under the circumstances, it is unsurprising that the U.S. Foreign Service goes through periodic identity crises. Who are American diplomats and what do they really do that others, especially the administration's political operatives, could not do better? The Foreign Service's answer varies with the mood of the country. The brochures it issues to attract recruits are an accurate reflection of the priorities and values the service wishes to project. The application booklet for the 1992 written examination, for example, depicts the Foreign Service as a "truly representative" organization whose new recruits will address the key technical and transnational issues of the day. Under the familiar caption "The New Diplomacy" it declares: "The challenges to today's Foreign Service extend well beyond the confines of traditional diplomacy. To deal effectively in the foreign affairs environment of the 1990's, the Foreign Service must develop new skills and possess greater knowledge in such areas as computer science and technology, narcotics, international terrorism, refugee affairs, corporate management, and industrial marketing."[13] In the 1970s, when Washington had become a magnet of attraction, the Foreign Service recruiting literature featured a young FSO serving as staff aide to the secretary of state ("I'm sorry, Senator, but Secretary Kissinger is not available at the moment. May I take a message?"). In 1990, when the Una Chapman Cox Foundation commissioned a made-for-television film on the Foreign Service, *Profiles in Diplomacy*, it emphasized the activist, people-oriented aspects of modern American diplomacy: an ambassador visiting victims of civil war in Mozambique, a vice consul in Peru visiting a U.S. citizen in a local prison, and an attaché in Central America participating in a narcotics raid, along with more traditional diplomatic activities.

The changes in Foreign Service literature over the years do, in fact, correspond to the changing priorities of modern diplomacy. But the core skills that define the diplomatic profession are constant—the skill of living and working among foreigners, of communicating with them, of understanding their motives and intentions, and finally, on this basis, of being able to make American foreign policy more effective by making it more supple and realistic. None of the "new" technical skills will be of value without the ability to perform them in a foreign context.

The central reason for joining the Foreign Service today is exactly what it has always been: to serve the United States abroad. Recruits whose primary interest is computer science, corporate management, or industrial marketing may or may not find their talents adequately employed in a Foreign Service career. Their success or failure, in any event, will depend less on their technical expertise than on the skill with which they can translate it into terms comprehensible to a foreign culture.

LEADING THE FOREIGN SERVICE

The Foreign Service's difficulty in defining its own identity is to an important extent the by-product of ineffective leadership. If the secretary's failure to lead is in part caused by deficiencies inherent in his bureaucratic mandate, what can be done to supply strengthened or alternative leadership? The French and British rely on the heads of their foreign service, the secretary general of the Quai d'Orsay and the permanent under secretary of the British Foreign Office. Both have far more authority to maintain professional standards than does their American counterpart, the director general (DGP) of the Foreign Service.

For twenty years after World War II the director general's authority was bolstered by a nonpartisan Board of the Foreign Service. The board was created by the Foreign Service Act of 1946 and invested by the act with statutory powers to protect the service against political manipulation. In 1965 a Presidential Reorganization Order abolished the statutory powers of the board and transferred them to the secretary of state. Operating since that time as an "advisory" body, the board has seen its powers, and those of the DGP, steadily eroded.

Another challenge to the director general's authority has come from the professional associations of American diplomats, the American Foreign Service Association (AFSA) and the American Federation of Government Employees (AFGE). The Foreign Service Act of 1980 formally recognized the right of Foreign Service personnel, including FSOs, to "exclusive representation, adversarial bargaining, and referral of disputes and unfair labor pratice charges to neutral outside bodies." Since any management decision affecting conditions of employment is negotiable, as is "the impact on employees of the implementation of management decisions in areas that are otherwise excluded from the bargaining process," the director general's powers of independent action are severely circumscribed.[14]

Professional and political pressures thus converge on the director general. They do not, however, cancel each other out. Sometimes they are even complementary. The professionals pay lip service to the principle of integrity in the appointment process, over which they have little control, and expend their main energy on issues related to improving working conditions. The politicians pay lip service to holding down costs, over which their control is limited, and fix their attention mainly on the next ambassadorial openings in Western Europe or the Caribbean. Caught between these powerful forces, the director general of the Foreign Service is often reduced to reassuring the administration of the Foreign Service's loyalty to its policies, and the Foreign Service of the administration's respect for its abilities. Neither group is convinced. It is not surprising, therefore, that, unlike the comparable positions in France and Britain, the director generalship of the U.S. Foreign Service is not an eagerly sought after post.

HENDERSON AND CROCKETT

The only U.S. Foreign Service officer since World War II to exercise powers equivalent to those of a permanent under secretary was Loy W. Henderson, who served not as director general of the Foreign Service but as deputy under secretary of state for administration from 1955 to 1961. Henderson was an early specialist in Soviet affairs whose independence of judgment in opposing the Roosevelt administration's policies toward the Soviet Union in the 1930s and 1940s (he considered them naive) got him transferred into Middle Eastern affairs. There he ran into trouble again for disagreeing with the Truman administration's decision to recognize Israel. He went on to serve as ambassador to Iraq, India, and Iran. Even those who disagreed with Henderson's stand on policy questions conceded his intellectual integrity. As deputy under secretary for six years he became known as "Mr. Foreign Service" and gave American diplomats professional leadership they have not had since.[15]

It may have been Henderson's justified reputation for independent (and not necessarily politically correct) thinking that caused the Kennedy administration to transform his position into a primarily administrative one. Henderson's successors have included officers with equally broad substantive experience, but none has been permitted to wield his influence, which, like that of his European counterparts, extended both to personnel and to policy questions.

Henderson's most influential successor was appointed by the Kennedy administration for the express purpose of modernizing the management of the State Department and Foreign Service. His name was William J. Crockett and, unlike Henderson, his experience had been exclusively administrative. As a State Department budget officer, he had been integrated into the Foreign Service under the Wriston reforms. Crockett served as deputy under secretary for administration from June 1963 to January 1967. Although his ambitious plans to put the State Department in charge of American foreign policy through modern management techniques failed, the Crockett approach has had lasting effects.[16]

Crockett had been given a mandate by the president's brother, Attorney General Robert F. Kennedy, who summoned him to his office in the early days of the administration. According to Crockett, Robert Kennedy said to him: "First of all, get your loyalties straight. No matter whom you think you work for, the President appointed you and he is your boss. He will expect your absolute loyalty. Second, get your job straight. The State Department must be made to be loyal and responsive to the President. It must become more positive and proactive. It must be made to assume a leadership position in the Foreign Affairs Community. Your job is to make this happen."[17] The tone and content of the attorney general's message, as recalled by Crockett, show how the presidential role in foreign affairs had changed since Lord Bryce assessed it in the 1880s. Although Crockett never met the president, never again met with Robert Kennedy, and, he says, was given no implementing instructions by Secretary of State Dean Rusk, he was confident that he knew what the problems were and how to solve them.

As a maverick who had risen through the ranks, Crockett had a healthy distrust for mainstream Foreign Service officers, describing them as people who "considered themselves an elite group . . . jealous of their privileges, rank, and perquisites."[18] One of his first actions was to commission a study by a Yale social psychologist[19] to construct, on the basis of questionnaires and interviews, the profile of a typical FSO. The study concluded that among the "norms" of State Department personnel were such characteristics as "Withdrawal from interpersonal difficulties, conflict, and aggressiveness; minimal interpersonal openness, leveling, and trust; distrust of the aggressive behavior of others; disguise of emotional responses and feelings; emphasis on the substantive, not administrative, activities; loyalty to others in the system." These conclusions might have been predicted without the study. They were simply an unflattering translation of traits that characterize the profession of diplomacy—without which, in fact, it would cease to be diplomacy. One would not expect questionnaires and interviews to reveal the same qualities in a group of military officers, but neither would one be wise to conclude from their differently biased responses that all military personnel were spoiling for a fight. The study provoked great indignation among Foreign Service officers, who angrily protested that their professional attitudes toward conflict resolution were being confused with their psychological makeup. Crockett was undeterred, however, and turned his attention to the question of how to "rationalize" the work of the Foreign Service.

It was his conviction that the so-called substantive work of embassies—political and economic reporting and analysis, representation, establishment of professional contacts, and so forth—needed to be restructured to provide tangible tasks and goals. In each country where the United States had diplomatic representation there should be a master plan defining American objectives and the policies to be employed in attaining them. The State Department's Policy Planning Council was given the job of preparing the plans, working with the regional bureaus and country desks. In due course, a complete set of master plans was developed. Crockett believed that he now had the tool he needed to evaluate the work of the embassies.

His diagrammatic approach to Foreign Service work was called the "Comprehensive Country Programming System," or "CCPS." Individual Foreign Service officers analyzed their own work in terms of specific objectives in the master plan under such headings as "Limiting Soviet Influence" or "Preserving and Strengthening U.S. Influence."[20] The officer then estimated the percentage of time spent in reporting or representation that was dedicated to these objectives; senior State Department officials and embassy staff could in theory use the estimates to measure the FSO's effectiveness against a tangible set of goals.

CCPS did not work. As Crockett noted: "it was distressing to find that our departments and officers considered the process a useless paperwork operation. Most of the plans simply were not used by the regional bureaus in their pursuit of U.S. goals abroad. Despite Secretary Rusk's active participation, the plans were actually only nice desk-drawer documents."[21] The failure of CCPS did not end Crockett's efforts to improve the management of the State Department. However, his other programs—including "Management by Objectives," "Action for Organizational Development" (known as ACORD), and a program to eliminate bureaucratic layering—were concentrated in an area over which he had greater control, the Management or "O" section of the department. Even here success was elusive. Crockett attributed his failure to the resistance of Foreign Service personnel and their cynical approach to the concept of management. His own, unwavering conviction that management techniques could have saved the State Department from itself is revealed in a later comment: "ACORD was dead and with it died the chance of the State Department to seize the reins of leadership in foreign affairs."[22]

THE MANAGER-DIPLOMATS

In a sense, Crockett lost the battle but won the war. Whether it is better or worse managed since his departure, the State Department can no longer be criticized for taking management for granted. Even the furor aroused by the psychological profile of the Foreign Service commissioned by Crockett had an effect. "Management experience" has become so vital a prerequisite for promotion into the senior ranks of the Foreign Service that assignments promising management experience are often in greater demand than posts of much greater significance to U.S. foreign policy.[23]

Crockett's initiative also altered the image of the "typical" Foreign Service officer. Rather than the reflective and intellectual student of foreign languages and cultures, the ideal FSO was increasingly seen as an aggressive, take-charge type who was likely to have made his reputation in Washington rather than abroad. While the two models are stereotypes, and the majority of FSOs today have a mix of both sets of characteristics, there is no doubt of the change that has occurred, or that it began in the Crockett period.

To a degree, this change was undoubtedly necessary. The "diplomacy of process" means a heavily bureaucratized diplomacy, with more personnel, larger missions, and less collegiality among Foreign Service officers. But what has been seriously skewed by Crockett's emphasis on management is revealed in his concept of diplomacy as a set of fixed objectives to be achieved rather than a continuing process of inquiry, analysis, discussion, and negotiation. This "management by objective" is, of course, a very American attitude. Problems without solutions are inconceivable to us. Foreign affairs, however, do not necessarily have a beginning and an end. They flow like water and are not easily compartmentalized. Crockett's master plans, like his CCPS grids, misconceive what diplomacy is all about. Conducting diplomacy became, for Crockett, incidental to managing it.

Management, for diplomats, means managing the foreign relations of the United States. The care, feeding, and protection of the staff and physical equipment of the embassy or consulate, while important, are administrative, not management, concerns. This is why embassies have counselors for administration, not management. Political ambassadors from the private sector always ask how it is possible to manage a diplomatic mission effectively if you do not control resources and personnel and if the budget is largely out of your hands. The answer is that these are not the things diplomats manage. If they were, managers from the private sector would always be preferable to Foreign Service officers because it would always be possible to find executives with experience in managing much larger enterprises than the most important embassy. The tendency to treat management as an end in itself, oblivious to the nature and purpose of diplomacy, contributed to the flaws of the Foreign Service Act of 1980, which continues to set the priorities for today's Foreign Service.

THE FOREIGN SERVICE ACT OF 1980

The most significant reforms in the Foreign Service Act of 1980 affected the advancement of officers into the most senior ranks and the influence given to them in determining working conditions and resolving grievances. Aligning the structure of the Foreign Service more closely with that of the Civil Service, a Senior Foreign Service (SFS) was created, including four top ranks, to correspond to the Senior Executive Service (SES) in domestic departments. At the same time, taking a page from the military, entry into the Senior Foreign Service (which was conceived as the equivalent of general- or flag-officer rank in the uniformed services) was made more difficult and bureaucratically exacting.

In the Foreign Service before 1980, officers who arrived with good records at the top of the middle ranks of the service could expect—whether or not they were appointed to the position of ambassador or deputy chief of mission—to remain on active service, often as the senior officer at consular posts or in State Department positions where area experience was needed, until they reached the age of retirement. The 1980 act limited sharply the length of time for an officer to cross the threshold into the Senior Foreign Service. From the time an officer's probationary status ended, within five years of entry, he or she had twenty-two years (covering five promotions) to be admitted into the Senior Foreign Service or face mandatory retirement. The maximum time allowed in each SFS grade before promotion to the next higher grade was also reduced. The purpose and the effect of these reforms was to make it more difficult for senior FSOs to remain on active duty if they were no longer considered "competitive." This was intended to open up more promotion possibilities for the impatient middle-ranking officers and reduce the number of "corridor walkers"—senior officers who did not have jobs. Consequently, since 1980 the Foreign Service has been warning new recruits that "in a small service with relatively few openings at the top, many will not reach the Senior Foreign Service."[24]

Despite earlier retirement of senior officers and a more rapid turnover of midcareer officers, the job placement problems of the former and the frustrations of the latter have not been relieved by the 1980 legislation. The reason is that congestion at the top is caused less by burnt-out senior FSOs than by political appointees performing duties that could more logically, economically, and (usually) efficiently be performed by career personnel. Mandatory early retirement is, meanwhile, depriving the Foreign Service of specialized skills, especially hard language skills, that it badly needs. To compensate for the loss, the State Department and the Foreign Service offer retiring officers "limited career extensions" (LCEs), which allow them to continue working without being eligible for promotion. It is hard to conceive of a bureaucratic expedient more likely than this to create genuinely burnt-out cases.

The basic flaw in the 1980 act is philosophical. By introducing the up-or-out principle into senior promotions and retirements, the framers of the act seemed to envisage a Foreign Service organized along military lines and infused with military discipline. The desires of the individual officer (for a longer career) would be subordinated to the needs of the service (for fresh blood in the system). But the collective bargaining, grievance, and performance pay provisions of the act, inspired by the Civil Service, ran counter to this concept of a disciplined Foreign Service. So did many of the administrative regulations that grew out of the act, notably the "open assignments" system under which Foreign Service positions are advertised a year before they are expected to become available and officers are invited to bid on them. The 1989 Thomas report criticized the system and recommended that it be replaced: "[the "open assignments" system] . . . gives less weight to Service needs and career development imperatives than to individual perceptions of what constitute 'fast track' assignments or desirable posts."[25]

A former inspector general of the State Department, Sherman M. Funk, speaking to the American Foreign Service Association in 1994, also criticized the service for failing to maintain a disciplined assignment process: "a recent inspection of ours called for an urgently needed GSO [General Services officer] in Bratislava. We were told, however, that no FSO would bid on the position. . . . What kind of Fortune 500 company, what kind of military service, would manage its business that way?"[26]

REPRESENTIVITY AND MERIT

The ambivalence of the 1980 act about "discipline" also characterizes its attitude toward "merit" and "representivity." Both principles are emphasized in chapter I of the act: "(4) . . . the members of the Foreign Service shall be representative of the American people. . . . (5) the Foreign Service should be operated on the basis of merit principles."[27]

There should be no conflict between these principles. If the political and professional leaders of the Foreign Service worked together better, there would not be. Confusion arises when they are unable to agree on criteria or stick by them. This leads to fears that representivity will be achieved at the expense of merit or, conversely, that merit will be used to impede progress toward representivity. Evident uncertainty about testing procedures, delays in assignments, inconsistent statements by senior officials, and, more than anything else, lack of confidence in the integrity of the personnel system have combined to create discontent among officers of all ranks. The elaborate grievance machinery of the 1980 act is working overtime to handle the workload. The State Department's under secretary for management, Richard M. Moose, was quoted as saying with tongue in cheek: "We've done quite well. We are being sued by women charging discrimination; we are being sued by blacks charging discrimination, and now we are on the verge of being sued by a white male charging reverse discrimination."[28]

They are doing quite well politically, not so well professionally. The turmoil will continue until those in charge of the State Department and the Foreign Service define clearly their criteria for merit and their goals for representivity and convince their Foreign Service colleagues that they mean what they say. Since merit is a more subjective, and therefore less self-evident, principle than representivity, it behooves them to be as specific as possible. Consensus may not be attainable, but greater clarity certainly is. More leadership, and less management, is needed.

For the longer term, the Foreign Service needs to become more representative at the base of its personnel pyramid before it can hope to be more meritorious at the apex. It needs a larger and younger recruiting pool. According to the Bremer report,[29] the average age of incoming junior officers is now over thirty-two. This is too old for the Foreign Service and for the recruits, whether minority officers or not. So is the average age of those who take the Foreign Service examinations, which is twenty-seven. The service needs to get the attention of potential FSOs while they are still students. A former ambassador to the Soviet Union, Jack Matlock, has suggested creating a diplomatic ROTC program. Students who passed the written Foreign Service examination in their junior year of university would qualify for a scholarship covering their fourth year. The Foreign Service would be able to influence what they studied in their senior year, and the scholarship recipients would be committed to serving as junior Foreign Service officers for a specified period. Young Americans spending their junior college year abroad would provide an excellent pool of talent among students with a demonstrated interest in foreign affairs. From this group it would not be difficult to recruit junior officers—perhaps 25 percent of those entering the Foreign Service in a given year—who were both representative and meritorious.

Up-or-Out

Obviously, the framers of the Foreign Service Act of 1980 cannot be blamed for the issue of merit versus representivity. One of their purposes was to shake American diplomats out of old habits of thought and make American diplomacy more democratic. However, like those who devised the system of "open assignments," they did not consider carefully enough what diplomacy really is and what diplomats actually do. The principle of up-or-out, borrowed from the military, is not well suited to diplomacy without critical adjustments. Diplomatic skills are not primarily technical and are only acquired over time. Hard languages like Chinese, Japanese, Arabic, or Russian cannot be learned well in less than two or three years of intensive study. The State Department's investment in such long-term training cannot possibly be amortized if the officers who learn hard languages are involuntarily retired because they are not competitive for positions of senior management. The gaps left behind them in the Foreign Service's inventory of language skills when they depart will take years to fill. Similarly, in-depth knowledge of a foreign country and a foreign culture takes years to acquire and years to replace.

Up-or-out is incompatible with the diplomatic profession in another way. The career of any successful officer will span several presidential administrations. As the officer arrives at senior positions of responsibility, he or she will inevitably serve at posts in countries where the issues are unclear and policies become controversial at home. These are usually the most interesting posts, but also professionally the most dangerous. Some of our best Foreign Service officers have testified before Congress in defense of unpopular policies or implemented U.S. foreign policy in unpopular countries. They therefore find themselves identified with policies that incoming administrations are committed to change. As hostages left by the previous administration to its successor, they will customarily be the first to be banished to the sidelines by the new administration. The only way to preserve the skills and usefulness to the nation of such officers is to enable them to endure periods of political eclipse—which invariably mean periods of professional noncompetitiveness—and wait it out until the climate clears. The 1980 Foreign Service Act makes no allowance for this contingency.

George Kennan was by no means alone in being consigned to political limbo until the Kennedy administration brought him out of retirement to become ambassador to Yugoslavia. Charles E. Bohlen and many others had similar experiences. Up-or-out would have deprived them of their safety net and the government of their continued service. It is not for nothing that a former FSO, David Aaron, who served as deputy to the national security adviser in the Carter White House, proposed, only half in jest, that the two plaques in the State Department lobby commemorating Foreign Service personnel killed in the line of duty be joined by a third, "dedicated to those Foreign Service officers cut down in their prime by a change of administration."[30]

Diplomacy as Communication

> "Our inventions are wont to be pretty toys, which
> distract our attention from serious things. They are
> but improved means to an unimproved end."
> *(Henry David Thoreau,* Walden)

COMMUNICATION is the essence of diplomacy. There has never been a good diplomat who was a bad communicator. Ancient Greek words that were used to describe types of envoys, like *angelos*, meaning messenger, and *kiryx*, meaning herald, convey the unchanging concept of diplomacy as communication. The central object of diplomatic communication is likewise unchanged—persuasion through nonviolent means. Only when reasoned persuasion proves impossible do civilized states resort to compulsion, although the ability and willingness of a state to compel agreement by force remains the spine of adversarial diplomacy—the *ultima ratio regum*, the final argument of kings.

Through most of diplomatic history, from classical Greece to the France of Talleyrand, communication was primarily oral, at least up to the point where oral understandings were committed to writing in the form of treaties. The focus was on threats to the sovereign. Today, the scope of diplomacy is much broader than when diplomats acted as intermediaries between princes, but also much more plodding and piecemeal than when Franklin and Jefferson were practicing diplomacy in the spirit of the Enlightenment. Written communications outnumber oral exchanges. Ever greater amounts of data and information are transmitted with ever less insight and synthesis. To understand why this is so, one needs to understand that modern American diplomats communicate as much with themselves—the State Department bureaucracy—and with other official and unofficial Americans as they do with foreigners.

COMMUNICATING WITHIN THE SYSTEM

Traditional forms of diplomatic correspondence, in which the reporting officer presumed to be addressing the secretary of state and began his despatches with the words "Sir, I have the honor to report . . . ," for all their formality, had the virtue of encouraging the reporting officer to weigh his words. This was easier to do when diplomacy proceeded at a more leisurely pace; seaborne despatches were the only form of diplomatic correspondence between Europe and the United States until the inauguration of transatlantic cable service in 1867. Even then the bulk of American diplomatic reporting was by despatch. At the time of the Franco-Prussian War in 1870, the American minister in Paris chose to communicate with Washington by despatch for reasons of economy. As a result, the Grant administration received its first warning of the imminence of war two days after war had been declared.[1] Not until the 1930s were the first diplomatic pouches conveyed by air, and most communications were still traveling by sea as late as the end of World War II.

Writing despatches in the first person—a privilege today reserved only for the chief of a diplomatic mission—contributed to a sense of personal accountability on the part of the diplomat; the author was never anonymous, and one's professional reputation was indelibly linked to the quality of one's reporting.[2] Well-reasoned, well-expressed despatches quickly became known beyond the circle of their designated recipients. A despatch from Moscow by George Kennan in 1952, analyzing Soviet views of the North Atlantic Pact and warning against excessive militarization of American policy,[3] attracted so many readers in other offices (including myself) that the Soviet Desk had to prepare a check-out sheet for borrowers. While Kennan was by then a prominent figure whose messages could be expected to arouse widespread interest, other, less well-known officers succeeded in building professional reputations mainly through their reporting skills, as indeed Kennan himself had done in 1946 with his famous "long telegram" from Moscow, which laid the foundation for the American containment policy.

113

Today's "diplomacy of process" is far more impersonal. Since the State Department in a twelve-month period sends or receives thirty million messages, including two million cables,[4] the task of distribution—making sure the right officials receive the right messages—becomes as difficult and demanding as preparation of the communications themselves. Prioritizing what is communicated, unavoidable when the drafting officer and his or her superiors had to decide whether a message should go by cable or by pouch, and, if the latter, whether by air or sea, is no longer strictly necessary. Prioritizing today takes the form of affixing captions to the cables—"priority," "immediate," "flash." Because they are imprecise and in many cases arbitrarily chosen, these designations are often meaningless. Since *everything* is conveyed electronically, the communications gap between Washington and the field is created not by too few messages arriving too late, but by too many arriving too soon.

Gresham's law applies to the coin of diplomatic correspondence as surely as it does to that of the marketplace. In the debased currency of bureaucratically oriented communications, trifling administrative problems are invested with undeserved importance by being given "immediate" precedence, and their stature can be elevated further by adding the caption, "For the Ambassador." Genuinely important messages risk being buried under trivia as easily as a check sent by domestic mail can be lost in advertising circulars. By the time I departed from Athens at the end of 1985 I was receiving almost as much junk mail at the embassy as I do at home in the United States.

The increase in official junk mail results in part from the increasing bureaucratization of the Foreign Service. It is also a product of the more narcissistic innovations of the Foreign Service Act of 1980. The need to worry about "career curves," to file and settle grievances, and for officers to lobby for their next assignment contributes to the proliferation of messages that have little to do with the foreign affairs of the United States. It is indicative that between July 1973 and February 1993, according to a State Department survey, 72.85 percent of the documents processed (16,319,606 messages) were unclassified. It can be assumed that at least half of these were administrative.[5]

But the fault lies not only with the nervous preoccupation of officers with their careers. There is also considerable abuse of the rules of precedence, germaneness, and utility by diplomats, including chiefs of mission, who are conscious that the worst sin an embassy can commit is to fail to report some item of information that the American government subsequently learns from another source—usually from the press or another government. Since the penalties for excessive or redundant reporting are negligible, ambassadors and their deputies are far more likely to encourage than to discourage reporting that is marginal or repetitious.

Inherent in the makeup of an embassy, and by no means undesirable, is the competition between different reporting elements of the mission. Embassy officers whose parent agencies are the State Department, the Central Intelligence Agency, and the Defense Department have areas of responsibility that inevitably overlap. The competition to report a significant development first and best can either be wisely managed, leading to information that is accurately reported and sensibly interpreted, or be allowed to degenerate into a race for diplomatic or intelligence scoops, leading to misinformation and faulty or nonexistent evaluation. The cause for the latter is usually an inexperienced ambassador, who simply does not know enough about the situation being reported to exercise effective supervision of the embassy's treatment of it. Unaware of what is significant and credible, the chief of mission places the burden on Washington to decide whether a given piece of information is accurate and useful.

Information whose significance is carelessly evaluated is also likely to be improperly classified. Overclassification is a common fault of American diplomatic reporting. Its effect is to burden channels of communication, processing systems, and archives with classified material that could just as easily and safely have been transmitted en clair. A German Foreign Service officer estimates that only 6 to 7 percent of the documents in the German Foreign Ministry are classified confidential or higher.[6] This contrasts with a State Department figure of almost 17 percent. Not only does overclassification create processing and filing problems, it adds to the mountain of official documents that must be subjected to the laborious process of *de*classification before they can be released in twenty-five years.

115

Embassies, in other words, produce their own "defensive paper-work." When combined with that of Washington, it has a multiplier effect of mind-numbing proportions. Foreign affairs agencies in the capital demand data they may or may not need for fear that something, however arcane, may be missed. Embassies grind out data both to fill these Washington-generated reporting requirements and to forestall the levying of new ones. Furthermore, since officers' career prospects are heavily influenced by their superiors' evaluations of how comprehensively they have covered their areas of responsibility, ambitious officers are usually prolific authors of reporting cables.

Electronic Excesses

The logorrhea is compounded by technical improvements in the means of communication that make it possible for embassies to disseminate their messages laterally. With the appropriate caption, an embassy report can be transmitted as a "collective" message—that is, sent simultaneously to multiple addressees en bloc, such as those in all NATO or EU countries. While in Athens I received a long cable from the newly arrived American ambassador in Rabat, who sought closer military ties between Morocco and the United States and thought a step in that direction would be to send all American embassies in NATO countries the text of his welcoming speech to a task force of the Sixth Fleet after their first exercises in Moroccan waters. It did not occur to him that his words wasted time better dedicated to more relevant business. Communication was simply too easy to forgo.

This suggests that one way to solve the problem of excess message traffic would be to make it harder to send routine messages. If cables only tangentially related to the making of foreign policy were consigned to sea pouches, it is safe to say that the majority of problems they addressed would have solved themselves by the time the messages arrived. This runs against the grain of our technocratic age and mentality, but considering how much worthless, or at least perishable, information is conveyed electronically, the virtues of slower, more painstaking means of communication seem unmistakable.

David D. Newsom, former under secretary of state for political affairs, was surely correct when he wrote: "Given the amount of information received by the United States, a case can be made that almost any event [in foreign affairs] was foreshadowed by someone. That, however, is not the important question. What is meaningful is whether accurate information was sifted, assessed, received in time, and believed by those with a capacity to act."[7] He might have added that the likelihood of this happening decreases in direct proportion to the extent the system is choked with information that has been carelessly evaluated and prioritized at the point of origin, reported for essentially "defensive" reasons, or sent to serve purely bureaucratic ends.

Reforms in Diplomatic Reporting

The State Department is aware that reforms in diplomatic reporting are needed. Its response to the Clinton administration's "Reinventing Government" initiative in 1993 recommended that marginal reporting be reduced and the processing of classified message traffic be simplified.[8] The important "new" area of science and technology (S&T) reporting is beginning to get the department's attention, but not enough funding. There are only about thirty full-time S&T officers assigned to American embassies. S&T officers assigned to foreign embassies in Washington have increased at a faster rate.[9] Other reforms are also needed.

The conventional focus of embassy political and economic reporting is on personalities, policies, and prevailing trends, the same areas covered by the press, though usually in more detail and with less bounce. Both at home and abroad the press has the power to alter official priorities and fix deadlines. When U.S. government spokespersons in Washington are questioned on foreign developments, U.S. diplomatic missions are immediately asked to comment. When correspondents report or speculate about events in a foreign country, the embassy comments without waiting for a query from Washington. As a result, much official reporting is focused on short-term, newsworthy developments at the expense of longer-term trends that may be of greater significance to the United States.

A wider and deeper focus is needed to include the underlying societal forces that produce political and economic change. Neglected areas require greater attention. Religious affairs, for example, when reported at all, are customarily assigned to the most junior political officer. "Cultural" affairs are interpreted to mean the performing arts, and reporting on them is left to the cultural attaché. In economic affairs, the embassy's periodic (unclassified) "trends" report is likely to be its most valuable product. Much of the embassy's other economic reporting is devoted to "required" interrogatories, some of them mandated by Congress, many of them providing information available to Washington in other forms or no longer needed.[10]

Another category of congressionally mandated reporting is on human rights. In unfriendly, closed societies much of the information comes from discreet contacts with dissidents or is covertly acquired by the embassy's intelligence arm; in friendly states the problem is harder. Congress requires human rights reports to be published annually on all states receiving American military or economic aid. This includes states that provide services or facilities of value to the United States in exchange for the aid they receive. Reports critical of human rights abuses in these countries can damage other American interests and, if the embassy is held responsible, impair its ability to conduct other business.

Better reporting on both human rights and long-range political and economic trends will probably necessitate closer collaboration with foreign embassies and nongovernmental organizations (NGOs) than the United States has practiced in the past. Given the number of shared interests and concerns in the world today, this is a logical direction to take. Seconding more Foreign Service officers to NGOs and United Nations offices would facilitate reporting on transnational issues, including human rights. Sources of information would be broadened, and slowly developing issues could be studied systematically with other diplomats who were examining them from a different perspective. Great Britain is reported to be considering "shared" embassies for budgetary reasons.[11] There are good reasons for allied countries to share more than costs in improving the scope and quality of their diplomatic reporting.

TALKING TO STRANGERS AT HOME

When we turn from diplomatic channels of communication between the State Department and American embassies abroad—the internal communications network of American diplomacy—to communications between diplomats and the political echelons of the government, especially those in the White House concerned with foreign policy, we immediately encounter effects of the mutual skepticism with which these two groups regard each other. Political appointees tend to believe that professional diplomats are incapable of carrying out their instructions in the spirit in which the administration intends them. This leads to overly detailed and inelastic instructions and a tendency to be more interested in what the American diplomat says in making a démarche than what the foreign official says in response to it.

When Henry Kissinger was secretary of state, it was not unusual for an ambassador, after reporting a meeting, to receive word from the State Department that "the secretary wants more of what you said to the foreign minister."[12] Some chiefs of mission began to prepare verbatim accounts of their exchanges, or approximate them as closely as possible. Yet even this kind of control cannot assure absolute fidelity to instructions. Tone of voice, and what precedes and follows an official démarche, will always (fortunately) be beyond regimentation.

The same skepticism about the reliability of professional intermediaries, reinforced by questionable faith in the value of voice contact, has contributed to the increase noted earlier in "telephone diplomacy" by American presidents. This is a method of conducting foreign affairs that is as inefficient as it is imprecise. Harold Nicolson correctly said, "Diplomacy is the art of negotiating documents. . . . It is by no means the art of conversation."[13] The telephone is a conversational instrument. When presidents use it, the dangers of misunderstanding, ever present in foreign affairs, are greatly increased. A precise record is rarely kept and, if it is, almost never circulated in a timely fashion to those with a need to know and act on agreements reached or assumed to have been reached.

Competent ambassadors have the authority to coordinate reporting and analytical responsibilities within their missions to assure that all interested agencies in Washington receive an intelligible account of significant developments. While the tendency to overreport needs constantly to be restrained, the chief of mission rarely finds among competing elements within the mission the kind of mutual incomprehension so common between Washington and the field. To members of a country team, "them" almost invariably refers to Washington and "us" to the mission as a whole.

INFORMATION AND INTELLIGENCE

A word needs to be said here about how well the State Department communicates with the Central Intelligence Agency, whose reporting responsibilities have the largest overlap with other agencies and hence the largest potential for conflict. To complicate the relationship, the CIA manages worldwide communications for the State Department and is therefore responsible for transmitting all electronic communications between diplomatic missions and Washington, regardless of the originating agency.

The intelligence generated by U.S. government agencies includes data obtained by technical means, such as signals intelligence (SIGINT), and gained by human intelligence (HUMINT). The latter are collected abroad by means of controlled foreign agents and communicated to Washington through American embassies.[14] Both SIGINT and HUMINT need to be fitted together and assessed by Washington analysts before they can become the basis for policy decisions. Viewed strictly as a management question, State Department and CIA reports are coordinated by several interagency groups at different levels in the Washington bureaucracy. If significant action is to be taken, the ultimate coordination will be in the hands of the president's national security adviser and the president himself; at diplomatic missions the responsibility is that of the ambassador. No organizational chart or wiring diagram can adequately explain the intricacies of the relationship between diplomacy and intelligence in the conduct of foreign affairs. There are, however, few occasions when differing estimates on the part of diplomatic and intelligence officers in the field cannot be reconciled within an embassy. In the case of individual intelligence reports that run counter to accepted thinking, the rule is always to transmit them, sometimes with a cautionary comment or word of explanation from the chief of mission.

Secret information is probably less vital to the normal conduct of foreign relations than is common sense. It can be valuable, even essential, in looking behind the mask of totalitarian states and in countering the activities of terrorist organizations; it can reveal military plans and capabilities that unfriendly governments try to conceal; it is sometimes a useful check on overtly acquired information; and it can point to areas where further inquiry and reporting through normal diplomatic channels is needed. These are, to be sure, significant missions. When the target is terrorism or the proliferation of nuclear weapons, military and civilian intelligence agencies provide services to national security beyond the capabilities of conventional diplomacy. But for most purposes the sources of foreign conduct are not deduced from secret files or decoded messages. They are both more readily available and more elusive, being, as they are, rooted in the history, makeup, and values of individual nation-states. Much secret information has relatively little bearing on the conduct of foreign policy. In some cases the reliability of the source is impossible to verify; in other cases the source may qualify information so heavily that it becomes useless; and in a few cases the information may be accurate but unusable for other reasons. I was, for example, once involved in negotiations with a foreign official about whom unflattering secret information of a personal nature existed in embassy files. Not only was there no credible way to use this information, it had no bearing on the business at hand. The matter being negotiated concerned two governments, not two individuals, and any concessions made on personal grounds by the foreign negotiator would have been instantly disallowed by his superiors.

In matching the covertly acquired image of a subject with the image produced by overt diplomatic means, there is no substitute for the experienced eyes of senior officials in the embassy and in Washington who have enough independent knowledge to make a sensible judgment on the accuracy of the picture being presented. This is why an ambassador's comment on an intelligence report provides Washington with such an important perspective. Scraps of raw intelligence, unevaluated at the source, can be dangerously misleading in Washington, especially if partisans of one policy option or another seize them, or leak them, to bolster positions that are basically unsound. The ambassador's comments are, therefore, a valuable opportunity and a significant safeguard. It is an opportunity not afforded to ambassadors from all countries. A former Soviet ambassador told me that KGB reports were never shown to him before they were sent to Moscow. If the information they contained was inconsistent with the reporting of the embassy, Moscow would make further inquiries with the ambassador and the KGB *rezident*. By keeping reporting channels separate, the Soviet government believed that it avoided homogenizing the intelligence received from its agents. But the risk of a discrete intelligence channel is that it encourages end-users to assess external reality primarily on the basis of the covertly constructed image and to give too much weight to it in framing policy—a weakness characteristic of the foreign policy of totalitarian states, including the Soviet Union.

It is a weakness to which democratic governments regrettably are not immune. Virtually every American administration will have senior officials who favor covertly acquired information over what is obtained through normal diplomatic channels. A similar preference will be found in some members of Congress and in certain journalists. This may be because they share the misconception that most United States diplomats suffer from "localitis" or that they are easily gulled or cowed by foreigners; it may simply be a bent for conspiracy theory; it is most likely to exist in those who have had the least contact with foreign governments and foreign cultures. Whatever the cause, when policymakers fail to subject intelligence reports to critical scrutiny, the result can be bad mistakes in foreign policy.

Two U.S. blunders in Cuba, eighteen years apart, show that the lesson is hard to learn. The Kennedy administration's assessment of Cuban public opinion before the Bay of Pigs, and the Carter administration's belief that it had identified a new Soviet "combat" brigade there, were both caused by overreliance on faulty intelligence assessments. An excess of zeal, wishful thinking, and a disinclination to apply common sense to the situations being assessed were mainly responsible for the fiascos. These are the very flaws that diplomacy is designed to mitigate in the conduct of foreign policy.

COMMUNICATIONS WITH CONGRESS AND THE PRESS

How effectively do American diplomats communicate with two groups that exercise such decisive influence on American foreign affairs—Congress and the press? The answer depends of course on how "communicable" American foreign policy is at any given time. More generally, communications with both groups have improved, although the executive branch as a whole has increasingly come to regard Congress and the press as natural adversaries. Some diplomats share this distrust, considering members of Congress and journalists to be in the business of revealing the secrets that diplomats are supposed to guard. This is a fallacy based on the same unworldly assumptions that underlie the school of thought that considers foreign policy a kind of secret code rather than a dialogue. Congress and the press have changed as much as diplomats have since World War II.

The days are long gone when George Kennan in Moscow worried whether one member of a congressional delegation would actually carry out his threat to punch Stalin in the nose during a Kremlin audience.[15] The sophistication of most members of Congress who have an interest in foreign affairs, and that of their staffs, has increased to a point where they may display more understanding of foreign problems than their interlocutors in the executive branch, including the State Department. As ambassador to Greece, accredited to a socialist government often outspoken and not infrequently wrongheaded in its criticism of the United States, I found that visiting congressional delegations were often better briefed on Greek affairs than senior State Department officials and better able to communicate the American point of view.

Based on my own experience, I would venture the opinion that in the past thirty years the overall quality of thinking about foreign affairs on Capitol Hill has been ascending almost as steadily as that of the executive branch has been declining. It is hard to agree with the conventional wisdom of policymakers in the executive branch who contend that everything would be all right in foreign policy if Congress stopped interfering. Congressional attitudes on foreign affairs can still be parochial, in the sense of reflecting constituency interests or of being unduly influenced by pressure groups; individual members of Congress with political axes to grind, or personal hang-ups on individual issues, can be unduly obstructive. But the real contribution that Congress makes to foreign policy is to bring it down to earth. The fact that debate now takes place on a better-informed basis diminishes the danger feared by Tocqueville that foreign policy in a democracy would become the province of know-nothings and chauvinists.

The change in climate on Capitol Hill makes the challenge of defending American foreign policy before congressional committees more difficult. Diplomats may have to work harder to satisfy congressional inquiries, but they can be sure that most essential questions will be asked. In fact, if basic questions about policy are raised at all, it is likely to be by members of Congress, however unwelcome this may be to an administration's policymakers and the diplomats who advise them.

In the years of the cold war, American foreign policy became firmly identified in the public mind as "the president's" foreign policy. It is still popularly regarded as a crucial test of presidential leadership. As they became more closely identified with the president, foreign policy decisions, as noted earlier, became more difficult to influence or question. (It is not by chance that American foreign policy "doctrines" are usually adorned with the names of presidents.) Whatever benefits for presidential image-making are derived from this personalization of foreign policy, it has a stultifying effect on debate among policymakers. Far too many interagency meetings deal preponderantly with how initiatives favored by the administration will be implemented; the initiatives themselves, and the reasons for them, are likely to receive less scrutiny. In this context, foreign policy becomes the responsibility of political rather than diplomatic advisers. The bad habits of the cold war persist, and even in today's more complex world too many things in the executive branch "go without saying" because the president has already spoken.

When exchanges between congressional committees and diplomats turn into confrontations it is usually because, in perfect understanding of each other, legislators ask questions they know cannot be answered and diplomats answer questions they know have not been asked. Genuine misunderstandings and deliberate deceptions are more frequent between the political echelons of an administration and career officials than between career officials and Congress. In the Iran-Contra affair Foreign Service officers were lied to as often as members of the House and Senate.

Communications between diplomats and the press in a sense represent communications between diplomats and American public opinion. Although the increased travel of Americans abroad brings more direct contact, especially through consular services, than was possible or necessary before World War II, the direct influence of Foreign Service officers on the popular view of diplomats is small compared to that of the press and television.

Since both diplomacy and journalism require a great deal of legwork, interrogation, and the piecing together of details to form a picture of events that conforms to reality, journalists and diplomats more often help than hinder each other's efforts to report accurately. This is especially true outside Washington, where they function in a less politicized environment and are not under such close scrutiny from their political overlords and managing editors.

The French speak of *journalistes de terrain* when they refer to newspaper correspondents who know foreign cultures and languages, who have local friends and trusted contacts, and who are accustomed to seeing things for themselves before reporting them. They are distinguished from journalists, including most columnists, who deal primarily in opinions and rely primarily on secondhand sources. In diplomacy there is a corresponding category of *diplomates de terrain* who serve in difficult and dangerous corners of the world, speak little-known languages, and spend more time out of the embassy or the consulate than buried in their in-boxes. They are distinguishable from the staff aides and foreign affairs functionaries who feel most at home in Washington and for whom proximity to power is the ultimate reward of government service. It is a misfortune shared by diplomacy and the press that columnists and staff aides enjoy more prestige than their hardworking brethren in the field and, probably as a result, have become the new role models for their professions.

As in the case of their relations with Congress, when American diplomats fail to communicate effectively with the press it is more likely to be because they are under orders to deny the obvious than because they are protecting official secrets. In Laos (then a kingdom, now a peoples' republic), where I served between 1969 and 1972, years when the Vietnam War was at its height, relations between the American press and the American embassy in Vientiane ranged from poorly concealed distrust to open hostility. The reason was not that the so-called secret war in Laos was a secret. Anyone on the outskirts of Vientiane who looked skyward could spot American Air Force Phantom jets going to and from their bases in northern Thailand on bombing sorties against North Vietnamese forces near the Plain of Jars. The city's bars, thronging with Air America and Continental crew members back from the day's battles and eager to recount them, were virtual military operations centers open to all comers. The war, and the part in it being played by the United States, were, in other words, an open secret. The anger and frustration of the journalists was basically caused by the fact that embassy officials were under instructions from Washington not to jeopardize the status of Laos as the only "neutral" state in Indochina by confirming officially what they and the journalists already knew perfectly well.

So-called gotcha journalism, where reporters "catch" diplomats who are not telling the truth, or the whole truth, thrives in conditions like these, where policies are known but not avowed and where diplomats are in the position of denying the undeniable. When this happens it is the policy that needs to be questioned—not only by journalists but also by diplomats. A sound policy is rarely a secret policy, and in a democracy never a politically safe one. Terrain journalists and terrain diplomats are usually the first to realize it. Their differences lie not so much in what they report as in their deadlines and perspectives.

Diplomats need to be patient; journalists cannot afford to be. Diplomats tend to think that nothing in the world is new; journalists are purveyors of novelty. Diplomacy is a cool profession; journalism is hot. This is why the influence of the press on diplomacy is to shorten deadlines and rearrange priorities. It can be a headache for diplomats, forcing them to shift their focus from long- to short-term problems, but it can also compel them to address problems they would prefer to ignore. Like Congress, the press asks fundamental questions and almost nothing goes without saying.

TALKING TO STRANGERS ABROAD

As professional intermediaries, diplomats have always had to communicate effectively in at least two directions: with their own government and with the government to which they are accredited. It is a measure of the many layers added to traditional diplomacy by the diplomacy of process that communicating with foreigners—the only reason for diplomats to exist—should be discussed last.

Effective communication with foreigners requires, as it always has, the ability to speak other languages, to understand other cultures, to see the world through other eyes. Although distinct from it, comprehension of a foreign culture is virtually impossible to achieve without proficiency in the language. Communicating in his or her own tongue, the diplomat will always be on the outside of the culture, looking in. Only by knowing what the world looks like from inside will diplomats be able to provide political superiors with a realistic interpretation of the motives of other governments and a reasonably accurate forecast of their future conduct. There is nothing else that a diplomat does that could not be done by lawyers, businesspeople, or academics, all of whom do, in fact, serve frequently as nonprofessional diplomats. When nonprofessionals fail in diplomacy, the failure is usually one of communication, not of technical aptitude.

It is sometimes suggested that English is becoming the world's lingua franca and therefore that proficiency in other languages is less important than it used to be. This may be true of tourism, but not of

127

diplomacy. Diplomats not only will learn a foreign culture best through its language, the personal rapport they establish when they speak the language cannot be established in any other way. Most diplomats find that there are occasions when even foreigners fluent in English prefer to speak their own language or express a nuance of meaning in it.

While the language proficiency of American Foreign Service personnel has improved across-the-board, mainly through excellent instruction at State Department schools, there are some weaknesses for which the Foreign Service itself bears primary responsibility.

LANGUAGE TRAINING

In 1986, after leaving Athens and before leaving the State Department, I was asked by the under secretary for management to undertake a study of hard language proficiency in the Foreign Service. His request was prompted by complaints from the American ambassadors in Moscow and Beijing that newly assigned officers who had received language training in Russian and Chinese and had been certified to speak at a "professional" level of competence were unable to do so. The assumption was that Foreign Service language instructors were becoming too lenient in their certification of proficiency. The under secretary suggested that I look into the Japanese and Arabic training programs as well, since there was also a chronic shortage of officers fluent in these languages.

I spent six months interviewing experts—language specialists in and out of government, Foreign Service officers being trained in the hard languages, foreign diplomats knowledgeable about the training methods of their own diplomatic services, and personnel specialists in the State Department. I visited the Foreign Service Institute's Arabic Language School in Tunis, its Chinese Language School in Taipei, and its Japanese Language School in Yokohama. To gain an insight into what the competition was doing, I paid visits as well to the Beijing Language Institute and to the Moscow State Institute for International Relations.

This research revealed that many experts in foreign language instruction acknowledged the Foreign Service Institute (FSI) to be a leader in the field and to have pioneered some of the training techniques that are now in general use. In terms of its teachers and texts, FSI's courses and methods were at least as good as the training programs of other diplomatic services, including the Soviet and Chinese. Nor could I find any evidence that faulty certification accounted for the apparent decline in fluency.

The problem, I concluded, lay in the disincentives to language study that had been gradually built into the Foreign Service promotion and assignment process; it also grew out of a well-intentioned but misguided effort to emphasize horizontal training at the expense of vertical. A great many Foreign Service personnel were being encouraged to acquire enough familiarity with a language to ask directions, go shopping, and so forth. Very few were being allowed to undertake the intensive, longer-term study needed to achieve anything approaching bilingual fluency.

Here, it seemed to me, the innovations of the Foreign Service Act of 1980, and various administrative decisions that grew out of it, were decidedly unhelpful. In particular, the six-year window for officers to be promoted into the Senior Foreign Service or, failing that, be involuntarily retired served to make most officers hesitate before agreeing to enter hard language training. In the period of up to two years they would devote to training, they would effectively be out of competition for promotion but would hear the clock ticking as their permissible time-in-grade elapsed. Furthermore, for officers who accepted the risk and entered hard language training, the system offered few rewards and no apparent edge in getting promoted when their training was completed.[16]

If the Foreign Service Institute was conducting programs of instruction superior to those of most other schools, why were Foreign Service language skills not better? The answer was clearly because FSI was not authorized to train students beyond the minimum professional level of fluency.[17] The reason for limiting instruction to a level of proficiency inadequate to the needs of an embassy or consulate was presumably budgetary. Language fluency improves in stages. The student climbs from plateau to plateau; the higher the plateau, the greater the amount of individual instruction required to move to the next one. With a relatively small budget, and limited teachers and classroom space, it was more economical for FSI to group students together, even though this often put naturally gifted and highly motivated students together with those less gifted who were content to achieve "survival" proficiency.

These deficiencies might have been compensated for had the State Department been taking better advantage of the language skills that newly recruited officers were bringing with them into the Foreign Service. Unfortunately, this was not the case. I analyzed the hard language skills of the class of fifty officers who entered the Foreign Service in early 1986 and came to the following conclusion:

> Of [the class] . . . no less than sixteen had some proficiency in a total of twenty hard languages by the time they entered on duty in the Foreign Service. . . . The Foreign Service, however, was only able to capitalize on those skills in the case of three officers. The other thirteen, including four Chinese speakers, three Russian speakers, one Japanese speaker, and one Arabic speaker, are being given twenty weeks of training in either Spanish or French and will be posted [in the consular assignments obligatory for first tour officers] in areas where these are second languages.[18]

This was an abysmal record, made worse by the tenuring policies of the Foreign Service—the procedures under which officers in their first four years of service progress from probationary to permanent status. Since State Department regulations require entering officers to help relieve the chronic overload in visa work abroad by serving at least one year in a consular assignment, and because of other personnel regulations, they could not be placed in hard language training until they had completed their probationary period. Analyzing the prospects of those same fifty officers, I commented, "Under present tenuring procedures, the youngest member of the class could not be enrolled in hard language training (for longer than six months) until he was 27 and the oldest would be 52."

When my report was finished and its recommendations reviewed by the under secretary and the director general of the Foreign Service, both of whom were favorable to the idea of reforming the system, some of the recommended changes were actually implemented. Periods of time spent in hard language training were no longer counted against time-in-grade; Secretary Shultz earmarked funds in the State Department budget for advanced training in hard languages; attempts were made to enable more junior officers to enter such training. Following the collapse of the Soviet Union and Yugoslavia, programs of instruction in fifteen languages spoken by newly independent nationalities were added to the FSI curriculum. But in many other respects the system remained impervious to change.

The moral of this story is that in improving its ability to communicate with foreigners, the Foreign Service needs to start communicating better with itself as well as with its political superiors. Some of the same bureaucratic problems emerge when one evaluates American diplomacy's command of another diplomatic core skill—negotiation.

Diplomacy as Negotiation

> "Behold a republic gradually but surely becoming
> . . . the accepted arbiter of the world's disputes."
> *(William Jennings Bryan)*

NEGOTIATION is the ultimate form of diplomatic communication. In the classic seventeenth-century work by François de Callières, *The Art of Diplomacy*, the terms "negotiator" and "diplomat" are used interchangeably.[1] All diplomacy implies some degree of negotiation—in exchanging information or withholding it, in settling a problem informally or referring it to higher authority, in agreeing to cooperate or agreeing to disagree. But it is more practical and precise in a contemporary context to treat the practice of negotiation in the narrower and more formal sense of discussions designed to resolve differences by treaty or other written agreement.

The less structured talks, meetings, and memos that diplomats engage in or exchange on a daily basis with their foreign counterparts and, in the case especially of American diplomats, with fellow participants in the foreign affairs bureaucracy are more accurately described as communications. They are important to American negotiating methods mainly for the light they cast on the strengths, weaknesses, and peculiarities of the process.

Military history chronicles battles; diplomatic history chronicles treaties. The United States is currently a party to 13,427 international agreements, of which the State Department estimates that about 8,000 are still in effect.[2] The earliest record of diplomatic activity, the Tell el Amarna tablets of the fourteenth and thirteenth centuries B.C., preserves a treaty between the great king of the Hittites, Hattusilis III, and the Egyptian pharaoh, Rameses II. British diplomat and author Adam Watson tells us that their correspondence, in cuneiform Aramaic, the diplomatic language of the period, exhibits characteristics and employs conventions that would not seem out of place in modern diplomatic correspondence—specifically, in the way it cultivates the impression that a community of interest exists even when the evidence points unmistakably in the other direction. Thus, when the king of the Hittites discovered that the pharaoh in payment of a debt had sent him gilded instead of solid gold bricks, rather than taking the pharaoh to task for the deception, he wrote a message, in Watson's words, "very tactfully warning his fellow ruler that there was a dishonest steward in the Pharaoh's household [who] . . . was cheating them both."[3]

This is what modern experts in the field of conflict resolution call a "yesable proposition," that is, a proposition that invites an affirmative response. It is not so much a technique of diplomacy as it is the assumption underlying diplomacy, namely, that in a successful negotiation none of the parties will be obliged to lose face. In somewhat different form, it is the assumption that underlay the Kennedy administration's tactics in the Cuban missile crisis. Following U.S. discovery that the Soviet Union was preparing to install offensive missiles in Cuba, and Kennedy's announcement of a naval blockade of the island, the president received two letters from the Soviet leader, Nikita Khrushchev, both dated October 26, 1962. The first letter was conciliatory and offered a face-saving way out of the deadlock. The second took a hard line and demanded American concessions. The administration chose to ignore the second message and to respond to the first. By choosing to answer the message that invited an affirmative response, Kennedy moved the crisis toward a peaceful resolution.[4]

CONFLICT RESOLUTION SPECIALISTS

The effort to find "yesable" ways to resolve differences between states is not always successful. Some disputes involve irreconcilable national objectives; some disputants are prepared to risk (or wage) war to achieve them. States, like individuals, come to blows despite the best efforts of intermediaries to harmonize their interests. Indeed, states can often be less willing to compromise than individuals. According to one conflict resolution expert, states habitually "operate at a primitive level of emotions," and psychologists have found that groups of twelve people—whether coincidentally or not, the usual size of juries in Anglo-Saxon courts of law—interact most reasonably. In general, the larger the group the greater its susceptibility to undifferentiated passion and impulse.[5]

The irrational element in the behavior of some states, and the easily offended national pride of virtually all states, has led to a school of thought that places psychological factors on a par with, or even above, economic, political, and military power factors as a source of international tension. Academic interest in this dimension of foreign affairs has steadily grown. There is a large volume of scholarly literature on the subject[6] and numerous university programs that seek to apply psychological insights to diplomatic problems. One of the most active is the Conflict Resolution Program of the Carter Center at Emory University in Atlanta, founded by former president Jimmy Carter.

Institutions involved in conflict resolution act like marriage counselors, whose influence derives not from their power over the parties but from their lack of it. Having no personal stake in the outcome of a dispute, they are presumed to be objective in their assessment of it. The role played by officials of the United Nations and small neutral states is not dissimilar. The Carter Center has established an "International Negotiation Network" (INN), which is described as "a flexible, informal network that coordinates third-party assistance, expert analysis and advice, media attention, and funding to bring about the peaceful resolution of conflict."[7] Its first conference was held in January 1992, under the cochairmanship of Carter and former Soviet foreign minister Eduard Shevardnadze, and included a galaxy of Nobel Prize winners and former chiefs of state.

TWO TRACKS OF DIPLOMACY

The techniques of nongovernmental diplomacy—or, in conflict resolution terminology, "Track Two" diplomacy—are the techniques employed at the Carter Center. The 1992 conference dealt with eight problem areas, ranging alphabetically from Afghanistan to Sudan and geographically from Angola to Korea. The conference unintentionally highlighted the uncertainties of Track Two diplomacy, and the harsh realities of Track *One* diplomacy, when cochairman Shevard-nadze at the last minute was unable to participate due to civil war in his native Republic of Georgia. The cochairmen were obliged to communicate by satellite hookup.

The Carter Center and similar institutions are doing valuable work in bringing opinion leaders, experts, and government officials together to assure that specific international problems, some too enduring and impacted to be headline news, others at too early a stage of development, are not forgotten or neglected. And by assembling individuals who might refuse to meet face to face under official auspices, private institutions can perform diplomatic services beyond the capability of governments. The secret meetings between Israelis and PLO representatives in Norway in 1992 and 1993 were a notable example of peace negotiations initiated through intermediaries acting in a nongovernmental capacity.

The importance of this facilitative role should not, however, be interpreted to mean that privately arranged talks can take the place of negotiations among governments. For better or worse, power still counts for almost as much in conflict resolution as it does in conflict. The fact that Yitzhak Rabin and Yasser Arafat met for the first time in Washington, not Oslo, signifies as much. Nongovernmental intermediaries, including those associated with academic programs, can be useful adjuncts to official diplomacy; they cannot be substitutes for it.

The essential difference between Track Two and Track One diplomacy is in their approach to conflict resolution. Track Two practitioners see conflicts as basically the result of misunderstandings that can be resolved when clashing perceptions are brought into focus. The underlying assumption of Track One diplomacy, on the other hand, and of the professional diplomats who practice it, is that while international disputes often involve conflicts of perception, they invariably involve conflicts of interest. For the diplomat, misunderstandings can aggravate conflicts of interest but rarely create them. His first step in negotiating a settlement is, therefore, to identify divergent interests; only when the diplomat is confident that he has done so will he proceed to examine the ways in which misperceptions, due to psychological or historical or other factors, impede the process of bridging differences.

TECHNICAL VS. DIPLOMATIC EXPERTISE

Both Track One and Track Two diplomacy have their limitations. Political psychology, while it exercises a powerful appeal, especially in the United States, is still too conjectural and untested to apply confidently to the behavior of nations. Professional diplomats, on the other hand, may underestimate psychological factors and conduct negotiations as though they were purely technical exercises, trying to quantify the unquantifiable and, as a result, flattening out diplomacy and making it brittle where it should be flexible. Perhaps because the preponderance of agreements negotiated by the United States in the cold war period *were* technical—arms, bases, and trade agreements, as well as some nominally cultural agreements, like those covering overseas broadcast and relay facilities of the Voice of America—there has been a tendency to exaggerate the amount of technical expertise required to perform modern diplomatic work. (This misconception is not confined to the United States. In 1976 the Berrill Report on improving the management of British foreign affairs recommended that in negotiating certain technical agreements abroad, representatives of the Home Civil Service should replace British diplomats, on the grounds that the former were more likely to be experts in their field.[8])

This perspective distorts the nature of diplomatic negotiation, which, even when it deals with technical problems, is at the seam, not the cutting edge of the subject. The successful negotiator of a trade agreement need not be a trade economist; nuclear arms control agreements are rarely negotiated by nuclear scientists. With some advance preparation, and with expert advice available to the delegation, a competent diplomat will be able to handle most varieties of technical negotiation. The key to the diplomat's effectiveness as a negotiator will be, as in other areas of diplomatic activity, the ability to distinguish between what is important and what is unimportant. From what is important the diplomat must then extract what is essential, and finally compose an agreement that reconciles the essential conflicts of interest and perception in language that all parties understand and accept—not least the home government. Allowing for exceptions on both sides, it is usually easier to make a technician of a diplomat than a diplomat of a technician.

If a diplomat is doing the job right, he or she will utilize both the data of the technical expert and the insights of the political psychologist. Even technical agreements are affected by nontechnical considerations, often crucially so. Military base and arms control agreements, for example, are rarely, if ever, purely about hardware. It was the American perception of Soviet military capabilities, influenced as much by psychological as by military factors, that determined U.S. priorities in arms control negotiations.

Perceptions of reality, that is to say, are more powerful than reality itself. Experts in Track Two diplomacy are right in not letting us forget them. When a United States negotiating team in 1983 sat down with representatives of a newly elected Greek government that had come to power on a platform calling for the removal of American military bases from Greece, the Americans were taken aback to discover that technical concessions they were prepared to make to secure an agreement—joint military production projects, greater intelligence sharing, and training in advanced weapons systems—did not interest the Greek side. When a draft agreement was finally concluded, the Greek government removed from the text any provisions suggesting that a close U.S.-Greek military relationship still existed, including the very "sweeteners" that the American side had persuaded Washington to offer only with the greatest difficulty,. Although the agreement extended the life of American bases for another five years and left open the prospect of a further extension,[9] the Americans were astonished to find the document described triumphantly by the Greek government press as an agreement to terminate the bases.

MULTIPLE AGENDAS

In this negotiation, as in many, there was a political agenda that was more important than the formal negotiating agenda—not hidden, but certainly one that required some knowledge of modern Greek politics and psychology to appreciate and reconcile with the technical objectives of the negotiation. This is what the professional diplomat should be able to provide. Lacking it, he or she can contribute little of value to the negotiating process.

To become overly preoccupied, however, with the political and psychological aspects of a negotiation, to search for hidden motives, double meanings, and innuendoes, is to fall into another kind of trap. It can result in the negotiator reading significance into changes of mood and atmosphere that the facts do not warrant. This is a mistake most often made when the success or failure of the negotiator becomes more important than that of the negotiation. The risk is inherent in summit diplomacy and occurs more often in Track Two than in Track One negotiations because the Track Two negotiator's only stake in the conflict is his or her ability to resolve it.

The best international negotiator is someone with a firm but not necessarily exhaustive knowledge of the subject matter under discussion, who is sufficiently well acquainted with the history and culture of foreign counterparts to understand their approach to the negotiation, and who can maintain sufficient credibility with the home government to bring it along when the course of the negotiation departs, as it inevitably will, from that charted in advance by policymakers at home.

It is the latter requirement that constitutes one of the strongest arguments against appointing incumbent ambassadors to head delegations charged with negotiating special accords, such as military base agreements, with the countries to which they are accredited. While resident ambassadors will know the main government and opposition leaders of the host country, the political climate, who makes the decisions, and what local factors will most significantly influence the outcome of the negotiation, there are also two liabilities that in most instances will disqualify them from being effective chief negotiators. The first grows out of their relationship with the home government, the second from their relationship with the host government. An example from two different sets of military base negotiations in Greece will illustrate both problems.[10]

AMBASSADORS AS CHIEF NEGOTIATORS

The 1975–1977 negotiations to extend the life of United States military facilities in Greece began at a difficult time in Greek-American relations. The military junta that had ruled Greece for seven years had fallen in the summer of 1974, a victim of the Cyprus crisis that the junta itself had provoked. While in the years immediately after the 1967 coup that brought the Greek colonels to power the Johnson administration had shown its opposition to them by suspending shipments of heavy military equipment to Greece, U.S. policy had moved gradually toward acceptance, as reflected by the visit of Vice President Spiro T. Agnew to Athens in October 1971. For the vast majority of Greeks, if the United States had not actually been responsible for installing the junta, Washington had certainly done nothing effective to oppose it. In late 1974, as the United States prepared for the first round of base negotiations, anti-American feelings in Greece were running high.

In these circumstances the American ambassador, Jack B. Kubisch, and I, as his deputy chief of mission, agreed that it would be impossible for an American negotiator unfamiliar with Greek public opinion and the pressures being faced by the Greek government to handle the upcoming talks successfully. At the request of the ambassador and with the agreement of the Greek side, I was appointed American negotiator while remaining deputy chief of mission at the American embassy. As I later described the experience at a symposium in Washington:

> No negotiator can be in Washington and the host country at the same time. In actuality my delegation had much closer links to Washington and a much stronger power base there than I did. While I was perfectly confident that I could work out agreements with the Greeks that would serve U.S. interests, I was not confident I could sell the agreements in Washington. . . . The understandings reached with the chief Greek negotiator had nuances which were either not understood or not accepted in Washington.

There was always a dichotomy between what we were trying to do in Athens . . . and what we could convince Washington to go along with.[11]

In short, my experience as a chief negotiator whose institutional base was in the embassy rather than in Washington led me to conclude that this arrangement prevented the negotiator from spending enough time at home to make sure that concerned agencies in Washington remained in step with the negotiator. The ambassador and I had not been wrong in believing, in the conditions then prevailing in Greece, that the embassy should have primary responsibility for conducting the negotiations. We had simply not discovered the best way to do it.

When I returned to Athens five years later as ambassador, the United States was still confronted by the bases problem. Although an agreement had been initialed in 1977, it had never been signed and ratified. The elections of October 1981 turned out the Greek conservatives and brought to power a socialist government pledged to close the bases. It was clear that we were entering a new and difficult phase of Greek-American relations and that the base negotiations would be only one of a series of problems likely to arise, albeit a particularly thorny and politically sensitive one.

Shortly after the new Greek government was sworn into office, I received a letter from the assistant secretary of state for European affairs, Lawrence S. Eagleburger (later to become the only secretary of state to have been a career Foreign Service officer[12]), soliciting my advice on how the base negotiations should be handled. The State Department favored designating a special negotiator but did not wish to proceed without obtaining the ambassador's views and approval. My reaction was mixed. On the one hand, I had not forgotten the difficulties I had encountered in the earlier negotiation, dealing with Washington by remote control. On the other hand, I feared that the overall American relationship with the new Greek government might be indelibly stamped by the outcome of the base negotiations and I was reluctant to entrust them to someone else, even a negotiator whose abilities I knew. Once again, I described the denouement in the Washington symposium referred to above:

Out of sheer intellectual curiosity, I talked to some of my diplomatic colleagues in Athens: the French ambassador, the British ambassador, and
the Dutch ambassador—three of the most experienced in Athens. I asked
them what they would do if they were in my position—just starting negotiations on military facilities with [a government pledged to close them].
Would they keep negotiations in the embassy or would they seek a separate negotiator? Without exception my colleagues advised me not to take
on the negotiations. They pointed out that talks would be extremely difficult, an adversarial negotiation from the very beginning. If I wanted to
maintain any ability to conduct a dialogue on other subjects with the
[Greek] government, they said, I should urge Washington to appoint a
separate negotiator.[13]

This accorded with my own, somewhat uneasy, instinct and was
what I said in my reply to Eagleburger, adding that to assure an or-
ganic connection between the embassy and the delegation, my deputy
chief of mission, Alan T. Berlind, should also serve as deputy to
the special negotiator. Eagleburger and the negotiator agreed to this
arrangement.

The nine months needed to complete the accord were hard on my
deputy, but his direct participation in the negotiations kept the embassy and the delegation in step and was indispensable to their ultimate success. The separation of the delegation from the embassy was
also advantageous. When deadlocks occurred it was possible for the
ambassador to discuss directly with the prime minister ways to break
them, something that would have been impossible if he had also been
the chief negotiator. In the end, negotiations on the final sticking
points were conducted in Washington by the chief negotiator and in
Athens by the ambassador.

THE MODERN NEGOTIATOR

Effective negotiation depends of course on a great deal more than the
ability of individual negotiators. We are no longer in an age of diplomacy when the one-on-one relationship of an ambassador with a mon-

arch was all that was necessary to advance the purposes of the negotiation. The Flemish painter Peter Paul Rubens accomplished several successful diplomatic missions during royal portrait sittings because they provided excellent opportunities for him to use his intelligence and charm to conduct other business. Harold Nicolson tells us that the British ambassador to the court of Catherine the Great beseeched the empress so passionately to join forces with Britain against France that in turning him down, she said, "Were I a younger woman, I might be less prudent."[14] Charm, good looks, and charisma are still valuable assets in diplomacy, as in most professions, but diplomats fortunate enough to possess them will need more mundane talents as well, and will use them as much with their own government as with the government to which they are accredited.

In American diplomacy today, effective negotiation depends first on effective preparation and organization. This means collecting the right data and assembling the right negotiating team, preferably one whose members have the confidence of their parent agencies but can see beyond bureaucratic horizons. Before the first round begins, the chief negotiator will need to have prioritized attainable objectives, ironed out interagency disagreements, and achieved a general consensus on what constitutes a successful negotiation. Furthermore, none of these preparations will be adequate if the negotiator has not also obtained firm assurances that concerned agencies will provide prompt and effective backstopping once the negotiations have begun. This is all much easier said than done.

DISADVANTAGES OF U.S. NEGOTIATORS

It is sometimes argued that balkanization of the management of foreign affairs within the federal bureaucracy—including the contested nature of the secretary of state's authority—poses as many problems in the negotiation of treaties as the constitutional separation of powers poses for their ratification. In support of this argument can be adduced the habit of American delegations to spend a great deal of time negotiating among themselves—in extreme cases, nearly as much as they spend negotiating with the delegation across the table. It is also true that in piecing together a negotiating position that incorporates the positions of different interest groups, tradeoffs may be made that are irrelevant or even damaging to the main objectives of the negotiation. Military cooperation agreements were notoriously vulnerable to interservice tradeoffs before the strengthened authority of the Joint Staff in the Pentagon reduced the autonomy of the services and harnessed interservice rivalry. In the 1975 military base negotiations with Greece, for example, the Navy Department's desire to announce publicly its prior decision to terminate the home-porting of American warships and their crews and families in the Athens-Piraeus area almost prevented the U.S. delegation from using home-porting as a bargaining counter.

Trade negotiations, which since 1962 have been, by act of Congress, the responsibility not of the State Department but of the United States trade representative, also present difficult problems of coordination. These arise partly because the interests of so many domestic groups are affected by trade agreements, partly because the office of the U.S. trade representative mixes a large number of political appointees with career officials and, when administrations change, there is usually a greater turnover of personnel and even less continuity than in other agencies. It is especially in the area of trade policy and trade negotiations that congressional pressures are most insistent, though almost any field of negotiation can and does attract congressional interest. The foreign policy expertise of members of Congress and their staffs, so valuable when constructively used, can also turn obstructive when deployed to serve ideological or excessively short-term and partisan ends.

ADVANTAGES OF U.S. NEGOTIATORS

Democratic diplomacy has some of the messiness of democracy itself because it shares some of the virtues. The negotiating positions adopted by the United States may be laboriously arrived at, but they usually represent an attempt to balance diverse political, economic, and social interests that a more authoritarian government could afford to ignore or subordinate to *raison d'état*.

Fortunately for American diplomacy, the actual process of negotiation is more manageable than the problems of administering foreign policy in Washington might suggest. The head of a delegation will almost always have sufficient authority, if it is exercised, to control his or her side of the table. This does not immunize the negotiator from being overruled, undercut, or circumvented. But if this happens, the source of trouble will usually be the White House and the reason will usually be political considerations, not bureaucratic gridlock.

Certainly the number and durability of the agreements reached and ratified by the United States since World War II suggest that the complexity of the foreign affairs machinery has not been an insuperable handicap to American negotiators. Indeed, it may sometimes be an advantage. Sergei Tarasenko, a former senior Soviet diplomat, remarked that he and his colleagues often envied the ability of their U.S. counterparts to say that they would like to consider such and such a compromise proposed by the Soviets but that Congress or public opinion or some other influential power center "would never accept it."[15] On the Soviet side of the table, of course, no such plea was possible.

How Diplomatic Agreements Differ from Others

The negotiator's ultimate concern is to find "yesable" propositions that adequately protect American interests. Diplomatic agreements differ from agreements reached in politics or business. In politics, deals are informal and unwritten; their terms are not necessarily binding and, in any case, will be affected by events over which the parties have little control, such as elections. These conditions do not apply to the formally negotiated, meticulously worded written commitments made by states to each other in the form of treaties. In business, it is assumed that a negotiation will produce winners and losers: someone gets "the better of the deal." Although deals that benefit both parties equally are better than those that do not, equal advantage is not assumed to be intrinsic to deal-making, as it is to treaty-making. The sole exception to this rule in diplomacy is the negotiation of peace treaties by winners with losers. Yet even here, the best treaties are the least one-sided. The punitive Versailles Treaty imposed on Germany after World War I led only to World War II, which produced settlements with the defeated Axis powers, Germany, Japan, and Italy, that were not punitive and have endured.

Nor are business deals equivalent to diplomatic compacts in the penalties of failure. In business, a broken contract can result in a lawsuit; in diplomacy, a broken contract can lead to a war. This is the dimension of treaty negotiation that imbues it with solemnity; this is why elaborate ceremonials customarily surround the signing of treaties, even between democratic states. This is also why trained diplomats are apt to approach negotiations from a standpoint different from that of business representatives or politicians, even though, as Americans, all have American interests at heart and exhibit an American style of negotiation.

NEGOTIATING WITH EQUALS

P. M. S. Blackett, the British Nobel laureate in physics and a strong critic of American policy toward the Soviet Union during the cold war, once expressed the view that the negotiating styles of the two countries could be deduced from the fact that the national game of the United States was poker and of the Soviet Union chess. This gloss on game theory turned out to be spectacularly wrong. It was the Soviet Union that was doing most of the bluffing and the United States that ended up controlling the geostrategic chessboard with an ever more powerful array of ballistic rooks, knights, and bishops.

In its dealings with the Soviet Union, we now know that the United States was negotiating from strength—a favorable position for negotiators, to be sure, but not the most exacting test of negotiating skills. Although American intelligence consistently exaggerated Soviet military strength, it was, in fact, almost impossible for the United States to "lose" an arms control negotiation, despite the fears of many Americans that we were constantly doing so. The more complex and intangible issues that dominate the diplomatic agenda today, and that must be negotiated multilaterally, pose a different kind of challenge.

The real test for American diplomacy lies ahead, when the military and economic power of the United States are less decisive factors in determining the agenda and the outcome of negotiations than they have been for the past fifty years, and when accurate appraisal of the capabilities and intentions of other states will be more essential. Successes like the Montreal ozone agreements are encouraging, but the American record in GATT is less so. The ability of American diplomacy to conduct sustained negotiations on more than one politically important issue simultaneously has yet to be seriously tested. When this happens, two things will become clear: first, that American diplomacy is weak in its expertise in foreign cultures, languages, politics, and peoples; and second, that it is strong in its technical and specialized expertise.

The deficiencies that exist in the language skills of Foreign Service officers and their in-depth knowledge of foreign cultures cannot be corrected by training alone. The entire Foreign Service needs to be refocused to make service in remote, difficult, and potentially explosive foreign posts as professionally rewarding as service in Washington. More attention must also be paid to cultivating the special skills involved in multilateral diplomacy, a field neglected in the past by the Foreign Service.

American diplomacy's strength in technical expertise, though it has on occasion blinded policymakers to the importance of nontechnical factors, especially in bilateral negotiations, is potentially an enormous advantage in conference diplomacy. It derives from the extreme porousness of the American system—the ease with which data can be transmitted laterally; the accessibility of specialized information and specialized expertise. Increasingly, as problems common to mankind come to dominate the world's diplomatic agenda, whether they are the proliferation of threats to the environment or proliferation of weapons of mass destruction, experts, especially scientists, and diplomats will have to work side by side. Fortunately, the United States is in a better position to combine technology with diplomacy than is any other nation. However, to do so effectively will require not only reforms in American diplomacy but reforms in the way the U.S. government directs and uses it.

Improving the Reach of American Foreign Policy

> "Sir, Sunday morning, although recurring at regular and well foreseen intervals, always seems to take this railway by surprise."
> *(W.S. Gilbert, Letter to Station Master)*

THE CONTRIBUTION that professional diplomats can make to the creation of a more successful foreign policy depends not only on individual skills but also on the institutional and political context in which the skills are used. How the Foreign Service is administered, how foreign policy is formulated, and how priorities are defined all contribute to (or detract from) the effectiveness of diplomacy.

To improve its effectiveness, three areas in particular are ripe for reform: policy planning needs to be based on a more accurate appreciation of problems before they reach crisis proportions; there needs to be greater continuity and predictability in policy-making, based on a clearer definition of long-term American interests; and there needs to be more detailed, sophisticated, and readily available regional expertise in order to fine-tune global policies. An American foreign policy strengthened in these three areas would enable the United States to correct the single most serious flaw in its approach to international affairs—more conspicuous than ever since the end of the cold war—namely, the inability to distinguish what is significant from what is marginal to American security interests and what is doable from what is not. These are precisely the functions professional diplomats can perform better than others in the foreign affairs bureaucracy because their vision is less likely to be clouded by the need to defend ongoing programs or by political considerations incompatible with a well-conceived and realistic foreign policy.

DEMYSTIFYING FOREIGN POLICY

A realistic foreign policy means a policy conducted not at the "summit" or by a peripatetic secretary of state but through embassies and consulates. These are the daily workplaces of diplomacy where representatives of the American government engage in a continuous exchange of views with the states with which the United States maintains diplomatic relations. It is a more logical and efficient role than the one they are too frequently called on to play, as diplomatic fast-food outlets for traveling officials from Washington.

Diplomacy, as Cardinal Richelieu perceived in seventeenth-century France, should be a permanent dialogue conducted in the service of a permanent set of negotiations. This assumption still underlies European diplomacy and finds its logical expression in the unending consultations of the European Union. The American appetite for problem-solving, however, finds little nourishment in a convention of statecraft whose purpose is to eliminate or round off the edges of problems whether it solves them or not. For European policymakers an international problem requiring a solution is usually a problem that has remained too long unattended; for American policymakers a problem not ripe for solution is usually a problem not worth bothering with.[1]

DECENTRALIZING FOREIGN POLICY

Treating foreign policy as a natural, indeed inescapable, exercise of sovereignty in an interdependent world, not primarily as a gauge of America's global prestige, would have the conceptual virtue of conforming to reality; treating diplomacy as a permanent dialogue conducted on a daily basis by American representatives with their foreign counterparts, not as a test of presidential leadership, would have the practical virtue of decentralizing a process that has become increasingly oligarchic.

149

Decentralization of the American foreign affairs bureaucracy might dispel some of the confusion between means and ends that bedevils the foreign policy process. Policy is primarily concerned with ends, but planning it is fruitless in the absence of means; diplomacy is primarily concerned with means, but cannot function effectively in the absence of clearly articulated ends. It is a peculiarity of the American approach to foreign policy—the result perhaps of our technical bent or of the assumption, explicitly stated in the preamble to the constitution, that the purposes of the American republic are by definition virtuous[2]—that American governments tend to become so absorbed in the means of implementing a policy that the ends become of secondary importance and cease to be critically reexamined.

This may explain the attractiveness of the cold war containment policy for successive American governments. The ends to be achieved having received the political benediction of both major parties, government agencies did not need to concern themselves further with this aspect of policy and could get on with doing what they preferred to do, and did better, which was to improve the means of containment. This preoccupation with detailed means in the service of broad and often vaguely defined ends is an American idiosyncrasy that foreign observers have often commented on. It may have been what Tocqueville had in mind when he wrote: "[The American's] ideas are all either extremely minute and clear or extremely general and vague; what lies between is a void."[3] If one extreme is preferable to the other, wise policymakers should err on the side of the general over the minute. When Secretary of State George Marshall in April 1947 instructed George Kennan, the director of his policy planning staff, to come up with a set of recommendations to avert economic and political chaos in Europe, Marshall had one piece of advice: "Avoid trivia."[4] The advice is still good.

Another French observer, the journalist Eve Curie, visiting a civilian American air base in West Africa in 1941, was struck by the fact that only a few months before the United States was to enter the war, the American foreman "was obsessed, not exactly by the foreign policy of the United States, but by mere practicalities, by the 'job that had to be done'": "It was remarkable how little was said in the American camp about the war. Nobody seemed to read papers or listen to the radio. There was no excitement about headlines, no hysterics. The only news that put the men of the American service almost out of their minds concerned American production."[5]

Mlle. Curie was a somewhat bemused witness to the admirable American trait of "getting on with the job." That trait, when reflected in American foreign policy, is equally admirable, provided that the job is worth doing and its larger purpose is regularly reevaluated. It is in the latter regard that American policymakers tend to fall short. It is why reform is badly needed in the broad area of policy planning.

THE POLICY PROCESS

The variables in foreign affairs always outnumber the constants. Demosthenes said of a statesman that his duty was to "foresee and foretell," but no statesman ever has enough information to project his policies confidently into the future. Political and economic conditions change; personalities appear and disappear; opportunities come and go. The timing of a policy is as important as the accuracy of the information on which it is based. This was first brought home to me by a despatch from the American embassy in Tehran sometime in the mid-1950s, after the flight and subsequent restoration of the shah. The author commented that Iran reminded him of a disintegrating building that he passed on his way to work. Every morning he wondered whether it would still be standing, and every morning, so far, it still was. He knew that one day it would collapse, but not how soon the day would come. In the case of the shah's Iran, it stood another twenty-five years. Any U.S. policy predicated on an earlier collapse of the shah's regime would have been as problematic as the policy actually adopted, which appeared to assume that imperial, Western-oriented Iran would last forever.

Two prerequisites exist for sound policy planning: the first is that policymakers know where they want to go; the second is that they know where they are. The latter is usually harder to determine than the former, as shown by muddled American policies in historically complex, culturally compacted regions like the Balkans and the horn of Africa. When policymakers know little or nothing about the tribal politics of Somalia, for example, and have little feel for the personalities of clan leaders or their traditional codes of conduct, it is unwise and potentially dangerous to aim policy at an almost certainly unattainable target, like disarming the warlords and turning them into statesmen. Similarly, a policy of precipitate recognition of the former Yugoslav republics as independent states, with the justification that the principle of self-determination demanded it, revealed scant appreciation of the historic or contemporary causes of tension among the republics. Policymakers seemed oblivious to the fact that it was precisely to serve the principle of self-determination that Yugoslavia—"land of the South Slavs"—was created in the first place by the victorious Entente powers after World War I.[6]

It may, of course, be pointed out that neither the introduction of U.S. forces into Somalia nor the prompt recognition of the former Yugoslav republics was a considered policy, much less a planned policy. Much of what passes for policy planning in American foreign affairs is reactive and short-term, prompted by domestic political factors, not foresight. Having no clear idea of what it wishes to accomplish beyond enhancing its image at home, the administration seizes whatever means are available to demonstrate that it "has a policy" to cover whatever foreign crisis has aroused the concern of Congress or the moral indignation of the media. In the case of Somalia, there was criticism of the European and American governments for appearing to take the plight of the (European) ex-Yugoslavs more seriously than that of the (African) Somalis. The United Nations secretary general had himself voiced it. In the case of the ex-Yugoslav republics, a combination of German pressure and disinclination to appear unsympathetic to the Wilsonian principle of self-determination overcame the initial hesitations of the Bush administration. In both cases it might be argued that the administration was motivated by nothing more profound than a desire to silence its critics. Foreign policy improvised on this basis causes policymakers and diplomats to spend less time asking "Where am I and where do I want to go?" than "How did I get here and what is the best way out?"

The reason why it is better to plan policies than to improvise them is that improvised policies are more likely to be influenced by events than to influence them. The very act of planning a policy requires consideration of the external resistance it will encounter, the resources that will be needed to implement it, and the ways in which it can be adapted to unforeseen circumstances. Even badly planned policies cause policymakers to consider consequences.

Looking to the future does not come naturally to government officials. They live in daily fear of being overwhelmed by current events. Here the influence of the media—so valuable when it forces the administration and the bureaucracy to reexamine the rationale for entrenched policies—tends to reinforce the policymaker's preoccupation with short-term issues. No problem, especially no foreign problem, can be assured of the attention of the media, and hence of the most senior echelons of the American government, until it reaches crisis proportions, until, that is, it may be beyond solution at an acceptable price.

The need for governments to see beyond the headlines and to address problems before they are "ripe" and while the price for solving them is still affordable was well expressed by Machiavelli: "When trouble is sensed well in advance it can easily be remedied; if you wait for it to show itself any medicine will be too late because the disease will have become incurable. As the doctors say of a wasting disease, to start with it is easy to cure but difficult to diagnose; after a time, unless it has been diagnosed and treated at the outset, it becomes easy to diagnose but difficult to cure. So it is in politics."[7]

POLICYMAKERS AND DIPLOMATS

Policymakers are usually political functionaries; policy implementers are usually professional diplomats. This distinction defines the differing attitudes and priorities of the officials mainly responsible for conducting American foreign policy but does not explain either the degree to which they are interdependent or the antagonism inherent in their roles. The latter arises not only from the commitment of political appointees to "change" and of diplomats to "continuity" but, just as fundamentally, from the fact that each has information the other needs but does not readily accept: policy guidance from the political appointee to the diplomat, restraints on policy from the diplomat to the political appointee.

There is no organizational chart that will eliminate the friction between the two groups, out of which, in any case, creative sparks are occasionally struck. Ideally, the National Security Council staff, operating in the shadow or, perhaps more accurately, the glare of the presidency, should take charge of policy planning in addition to its responsibility for policy coordination. This would give the planners greater political credibility and NSC staffers less time to venture into operations. Many recent problems in the management of American foreign policy—the Iran-Contra affair, for example—have arisen from excessive involvement of the NSC staff in intricate situations abroad that should have been left in the hands of operating agencies. State Department planning, on the other hand, can seem to political functionaries more sensitive to foreign than to domestic pressures and for that reason inexpedient on domestic political grounds.

The State Department as Policy Planner

The effectiveness of the State Department's policy planning staff since its inception in 1947 has always depended in large part on the personal chemistry between the secretary of state and the director of policy planning. George Kennan was able to work well with Secretary Marshall but not with Secretary Acheson, who, on the other hand, had a productive relationship with Kennan's successor, Paul Nitze. The staff seems to have been most influential under Marshall, who used it as he had used the Division of Plans and Operations in the War Department; Acheson, whose collaboration with Nitze, produced NSC-68, the defining policy directive of the cold war; Dulles, who relished discussion of foreign policy and had in Robert R. Bowie, his director of policy planning, an adviser trained in the law with whom he was comfortable discussing policy options; and Kissinger, whose director of policy planning, Winston Lord, was trusted by the secretary and steeped in his thinking from years of close association at the NSC.

The primacy of Marshall, Acheson, Dulles, and Kissinger in the formulation and management of foreign policy in their respective administrations enabled the director of policy planning to exercise leadership and exert a unifying influence within the foreign affairs bureaucracy. This is indispensable to the policy process. In a government as complex and sprawling as that of the United States, how policies are to be carried out is negotiated at the working level, not promulgated from above. The need for "coordination below" is greater after a policy has been formulated than before.

In contrast to its unifying role, the policy planning staff has sometimes been used to question options and raise alternatives to existing policy. This can be productive if the secretary takes it seriously. If not, fruitful debate on established policy and serious consideration of alternatives are unlikely. The reluctance of career officials to appear "obstructive," and the tendency of policies, once launched, to develop their own momentum, discourages meaningful discussion. More often the director and his staff have functioned as a pool of speech writers for the secretary, which is a better way to embellish policy than to plan or evaluate it.

The NSC as Policy Planner

Moving policy planning from the State Department to the NSC would bring those responsible for setting foreign policy goals closer to those who control the resources needed to attain them. It would encourage better coordination of foreign with domestic policy, something notably lacking in most administrations, where foreign and domestic policy advisers work opposite sides of the street with little contact and less collaboration.

The main objection to making the NSC responsible for policy planning is that it would widen the already significant gap between White House and State Department perceptions of foreign affairs. Policy planners need not concern themselves with the daily give-and-take of

155

foreign affairs, but it is important for them to stay in touch with those who do. Foreign policy decisions need to be fueled by a constant flow through the system of accurate information from abroad on events, personalities, and developing trends. The further decisionmakers are removed from actual events the greater the likelihood that their decisions will be wrong.

The proximity of State Department policy planners to the bureaus, offices, and desks that deal with foreign affairs at the working level provides a useful reality check for the planners and reassures the desks that their views are not being ignored. Similarly, U.S. embassy personnel around the world, who are likely to be among the first to spot danger signs abroad, can report directly to policymakers. The views of foreign governments are also more easily elicited by the State Department, which has established lines of communication with them, than by other agencies of the Washington bureaucracy. Lodged in the White House, policy planning would risk being shaped preemptively by domestic political considerations. Proposed policies would be more insulated from critical discussion and, as the NSC is now organized, less easily projected beyond the term of the administration. Clashes over foreign policy within the executive branch and with Congress would almost certainly become more bruising than ever.

REGIONAL VS. GLOBAL PLANNING

There are ways to improve the system, however, that would reduce these risks. The differing strengths and weaknesses of the NSC and the State Department suggest how to do so. The division of responsibility should be determined by the nature of the problem. When a potentially troublesome trend or event is identified in a particular region, the responsibility logically belongs to the State Department. The director of policy planning obtains an intelligence estimate from the CIA on the seriousness of the problem. The judgment of other agencies is also sought. The director and staff then set forth the various policy options, and a meeting of officials from directly concerned agencies is chaired by the national security adviser to decide what should be done. This was the approach adopted by the Clinton administration on the problem of South Asian nuclear capabilities.[8]

The initiative for this kind of policy planning remains with the State Department because the problems being addressed are regional and the planners must stay as close to them as possible. A different approach is needed to global problems, where the goal of planning is to prevent threatening conditions rather than crises.

As long as the ultimate objectives of American security policy were nuclear deterrence and the defense of our allies against conventional military attack, crisis management was the ultimate test for policy-makers because any crisis was presumed capable of leading to conflict between the superpowers. Tiny geographic entities as obscure as Grenada and as remote as Diego Garcia were invested with strategic significance by the cold war. The president himself was credited with supervising policy toward them when they were cast in supporting roles on one side or the other of the superpower confrontation. In these circumstances the priorities of the NSC were foreordained. To facilitate the NSC staff's ability to monitor operations it was organized along geographic and functional lines that made it resemble, depending on the problem being addressed, a mini–State Department or a mini-Pentagon. By being geared so directly to crisis management the NSC's structure precluded it from a significant policy planning role even in areas where the State Department was itself deficient.

The State Department's deficiencies were usually in the transnational areas that today are assuming new importance. These are the department's stepchildren because mainstream diplomacy is still uncertain how to deal with them. They are the responsibility of the so-called functional bureaus and offices that deal with human rights, environmental affairs, refugees, and other problems that cannot be confined within one geographic region.

Functional bureaus have traditionally been less powerful than geographic bureaus in the State Department. Decision-making authority must be shared with many other agencies, including domestic agencies. Because they tend to be long-range, the problems of the functional bureaus normally get less of the secretary of state's time than do those of the geographic bureaus. They will yield, if at all, to carefully planned and coordinated policies rather than to crisis management. In addition, the functional bureaus deal primarily in conference diplomacy, whose special requirements and skills have been neglected by the U.S. Foreign Service.

In transnational areas the NSC could play a policy planning role that is not being done systematically or well by anyone else. But a more innovative NSC structure is needed. As currently organized, the NSC staff tends to deal with regions that correspond to the geographic bureaus of the State Department. It also has special assistants for nonproliferation, arms control, and Russian, Ukrainian, and Eurasian affairs. As their titles suggest, these officials are dealing more with the detritus of the cold war—admittedly a dangerous mountain of radioactive rubble—than with policy-making in areas unrelated, or only tangentially related, to the cold war.

Reorganizing the NSC to strengthen it in functional areas and to give it a global planning capability would improve policy planning where it is now weakest. Today's transnational problems all have an important domestic dimension. No administration can be expected to "solve" them unilaterally. A greater premium must be placed on conducting a continuous dialogue with other states than on managing crises. In shaping its approach to long-term issues, each administration will continue to have its own priorities, but global policies will need to be planned with a view to continuity as well as change. Organizational reform of the NSC to emphasize longer-term, global planning will clearly not place foreign policy outside the political arena, nor would that be desirable. Politics do not need to be eliminated from the foreign policy process, only politicization.

CHANGE AND CONTINUITY

Obviously, new administrations staff government agencies with new political appointees and set new priorities. However, the amount of reshuffling that takes place when administrations change in the United States has become excessive, time-consuming, and wasteful.

Screening, selecting, and clearing new appointees in the Bush and Clinton administrations was so tedious a process that two years after they entered office, important policy-making positions were still unfilled. The effect on foreign policy is to disrupt continuity without introducing change. The pervasive atmosphere becomes one not of innovation but of uncertainty.

In a highly politicized agency like the Office of the Special Trade Representative, the number of political jobs is so numerous that when administrations change virtually all of the staff also change and ongoing negotiations are left in a state of limbo. Not only are the negotiating partners of the United States kept in suspense, so are domestic groups with an interest in the outcome. Ratification of the North American Free Trade Agreement (NAFTA) was almost certainly complicated for the Clinton administration by the fact that verbal understandings that had been reached by the Bush administration's negotiators with environmental groups and labor unions did not survive the turnover of the staff that followed the elections.[9]

But the special trade representative's office is not the only foreign affairs agency to lose continuity when administrations change. The staff of the NSC is almost completely reshuffled, and at the State Department all senior officers, down to and often including deputy assistant secretaries, career and noncareer, are customarily replaced. Even when Republican President Bush took over from Republican President Reagan in 1989, there were top-to-bottom changes in the State Department and the NSC with incumbent assistant secretaries kept at arm's length by the transition team of Secretary of State-designate Baker.

While diplomatic and consular missions abroad are largely spared the discombobulation-in-depth of domestic agencies, there have been many occasions when political chiefs of mission were removed by incoming administrations with unnecessary and undignified haste and when career officers suffered a similar fate merely to make room for an impatient political appointee.

Assuming that a sufficient degree of continuity between administrations would be assured if one-third of the NSC staff remained in place and roughly the same fraction of career assistant and deputy assistant secretaries of state, who should the carryovers be? In the post–cold war security environment foreign policy professionals will include scientists, both physical and social, capable of analyzing the new generation of international problems and explaining them to the political leadership and their advisers; they will include military experts knowledgeable in the more familiar problems of weapons control and nuclear nonproliferation but able to identify new capabilities and vulnerabilities before they reach dangerous proportions; and they will include Foreign Service officers who have the regional knowledge the new administration will need if its foreign policy goals are to be realized.

Carrying over one-third of the NSC and State Department policy-makers from one administration to another will not assure predictability but will reduce unpredictability. It will discourage new administrations from thinking that American interests change every four or eight years. Articulating an agreed-upon definition of long-term interests will still be difficult in many areas. There are deep philosophical differences between liberals and conservatives on how far the United States should go in making "justice" as important an objective of American foreign policy as "security." But by improving its institutional memory, the American government will at least increase its awareness of how much in American foreign policy must remain constant and what can change.

WHY REGIONAL EXPERTS ARE NEEDED

The last area where American foreign policy most needs to be strengthened is in developing sophisticated and readily available regional expertise. The question may be raised whether such expertise is still needed when the end of the cold war has reduced the strategic significance of regional conflicts. It may be argued that specialists can always be trained as the need arises. This is what the United States did in Vietnam when the government created in fairly short order a group of military and civilian Vietnamese language and area specialists to guide it through the conflict.

The American experience in Vietnam is in fact a good example of how crisis-driven diplomacy fails to provide policymakers with the expertise needed to situate themselves accurately in an unfamiliar political terrain. Prior to the defeat and withdrawal of the French in 1954, Indochina was regarded in Washington as a French colonial backwater and its importance evaluated in strictly cold war terms. Could the non-Communist Vietnamese, supported by the French, defeat the Communist Vietnamese, supported by the Soviets and Chinese? The American chiefs of mission assigned to Saigon between 1950, when the post was accorded the status of a legation,[10] and 1975, when it was closed shortly before South Vietnam surrendered to the North Vietnamese, were almost all European specialists. None had served before in Indochina and, until the mid-1960s, few members of their country teams spoke Vietnamese or knew the area much better than their chiefs. Starting with the decision in 1965 to introduce American military forces massively on the ground, it was belatedly recognized that there was a huge gap in regional expertise that had to be filled, and quickly. A crash program of Vietnamese language training was instituted for younger officers, and the Foreign Service's most promising officers of all ranks began to be assigned to Vietnam.

It was much too late. The time when the U.S. government needed informed advice from officers who had direct experience of Indochina and knew where the French had made their mistakes was much earlier, long before Vietnam became an "American" problem. Both the military and civilian services of the American government developed a number of area specialists reasonably fluent in the Vietnamese language, and a great deal of first-rate diplomatic talent was invested in the losing effort in Vietnam, but there was never enough time to develop the depth of knowledge or the historical perspective that the situation required. By ignoring the "wasting disease" in Vietnam for too long, the United States began to treat it only after it had become incurable.

Preoccupation with superpower rivalry did encourage training in the languages of regions that figured prominently in cold war strategy—Russian, Chinese, Japanese, and Arabic-—although, as noted in chapter 7, the results were mixed. In other regions policymakers tended to divide and subdivide the world into theaters of potential military conflict. Blocs were considered more important than regions, and problems internal to regions like Eastern Europe, however deep-rooted, were assessed not on their merits but in terms of their cold war implications. It is easy to see now that the American government spent too much time pondering the external relations of Yugoslavia and too little the internal; the same is true of the Soviet Union, Iran, Somalia, and any number of other countries that we saw as pieces on a strategic chessboard rather than as products of their own historical experience.

Today, the bloodshed and instability of these regions are not "part of the problem," as we might have said before 1990. They *are* the problem, and we know less about them than we should to formulate realistic and effective policies. How much better our understanding of Yugoslavia would have been, for example, had the American government given a higher priority to the kind of close-up reporting that Thomas Jefferson despatched from the prerevolutionary French countryside. What he learned in villages about internal conditions in France was just as important as anything he learned in court about high French policy.

This kind of expertise cannot be created in crash training programs. In fact, it cannot be created in most people at all. It requires passionate interest in a foreign culture, great intellectual discipline, and an extended period of time living among the people of the region and speaking their language. Not all diplomats are willing to plunge into another culture so deeply. Furthermore, the professional ethic that has been cultivated in the service since 1980 discourages it.

Intensive language and area study is not compatible with short tours of duty at highly visible foreign posts; periodic longer tours of duty in Washington, preferably as staff aide to one of the "seventh-floor principals"; and not too much time in training programs in order to remain competitive, especially in the middle and senior ranks. The existing professional culture is not likely to equip the Foreign Service to guide the American government safely through the perils of future Somalias, Yugoslavias, or Vietnams, much less map out policies to relieve the tensions of entire regions and avert the perils in advance.

This raises the question of whether the United States government needs long-term regional policies. Bloodshed and instability in Eastern Europe and the Caucasus may have become serious problems, but are they *our* problems? Surely, having carried heavier military and diplomatic burdens than its allies during the cold war, the United States is now entitled to shift the responsibility for regional peacemaking to others closer to the afflicted regions.

Every period of frustration in American foreign policy produces a mood of disengagement—which in any case is never far from the surface of American thinking about foreign affairs. After Vietnam, the Nixon Doctrine was born, surviving for only three years until the overthrow of the shah of Iran, who had been cast as a leading regional surrogate. After the frustrations of Somalia and ex-Yugoslavia, some observers advocate a "Clinton Doctrine" along similar lines.[11] Under this approach, ending bloodshed in Bosnia would be a Western European responsibility and in the Caucasus a Russian one. Other powers would assume the responsibility to maintain order in other regions, except perhaps Latin America where the United States would continue to play its traditional role.

The problem with regional surrogates is that they usually have regional axes to grind and do not make disinterested peacemakers. States outside the region are often more trusted and have a better chance of producing viable settlements of regional disputes. From the standpoint of damage control, long-term regional policies are more necessary for the United States today than when the destructive effect of regional explosions was contained by the alignments of the cold war.

If there must be a new doctrine to guide U.S. foreign policy, let it be a doctrine that encourages the United States to see the world not as a post–cold war strategic equation but as the infinitely complex cultural and political mosaic that it is, a doctrine based on the recognition that global policies will only be as effective as the regional policies needed to implement them.

Improving the Grasp of American Diplomacy

> "Diplomatic expertise is inevitably adulterated in a
> democracy, as it often is with other forms of govern-
> ment, but the expertise itself is not anti-democratic,
> any more than are military, medical or other catego-
> ries of expertise offered to governments. However,
> in practice, the advice of professional diplomats
> tends to be anti-populist and anti-ideological."
> *(Adam Watson,* Diplomacy)

AMERICAN FOREIGN POLICY reflects the largeness of the American
view of things, the inclination to invest foreign policy with moral
content, and the incessant search for uniform categories and universally applicable codes of behavior. American diplomacy, on the other
hand, is skeptical of generalizations and inclined to address problems
on a case by case basis. In practice, the moral stance that proclaims
universal ends for American foreign policy has not prevented our diplomacy from becoming obsessively preoccupied with means; nor
has the search for overarching foreign policy doctrines prevented the
United States from regarding itself as exceptional among nations and
practicing a diplomacy inspired more by a desire for separation than
engagement.

The inconsistency of these characteristics is partially explained by
the fact that American foreign policy is defined primarily by political
leaders, who prefer it to be writ large, and implemented primarily by
diplomats, who prefer it in small print. Despite the inconsistencies, or
perhaps even because of them, American diplomacy may lend itself
more readily to global diplomacy than it has to national diplomacy.
Foreign policy that aims to make the world less noxious and more
law-abiding is likely to be more appealing to Americans than foreign
policy that aims simply at a balance of power.

Balance-of-power diplomacy requires a degree of engagement in the process, and a willingness to empty it of moral content, that is inconsistent with American historical experience and uncongenial to the American temperament. The ethical and scientific components of global diplomacy make it seem less cynical and self-serving than traditional diplomacy. It conforms more to the spirit in which Franklin addressed American privateers when he asked them to look on Captain Cook and his crew as "common friends to mankind."

This global bent is suited to problems confronting the international community that seem to challenge nation-state sovereignty and hence the legitimacy and relevance of diplomacy itself. The distinction between internal and external affairs so clearly drawn in 1961 by the Vienna Convention on Diplomatic Relations is little help in addressing problems that may be internal at birth but can have dangerous external repercussions if they are permitted to grow unattended. It is a paradox of diplomacy that international law is hardest to apply when problems are still within national borders where they would be easiest to contain. It is as though a doctor were precluded legally from treating Machiavelli's "wasting disease" until it had become incurable.

INTERNATIONAL LAW AND THE NATION-STATE

The international community has responded indecisively to the dilemma. In 1975 it recognized in the Helsinki Final Act that the way states treat their own citizens (or rulers their own subjects) has international implications, but it withheld from other states the right of corrective action by warning them against intervention, "direct or indirect, individual or collective, in the internal or external affairs falling within the domestic jurisdiction of another participating state."[1] Similarly, in 1987 the Montreal Protocol on depletion of the ozone layer treated the subject of non-compliance with obvious caution: "The Parties, at their first meeting, shall consider and approve procedures and institutional mechanisms for determining non-compliance with the provisions of this Protocol and for treatment of Parties found to be in non-compliance."[2] Penalties for noncompliance to which the parties subsequently agreed were confined to a ban on the import of products containing uncontrolled substances from noncomplying states. The reason the penalties could not be made stronger was that both monitoring compliance and effectively enforcing it required the cooperation of the participating states themselves. If the protocol was not self-enforcing it could not be enforced.

On the occasions when the international community has used military force to regulate the internal affairs of a sovereign state, it has delegated the responsibility for enforcement to other sovereign states. It may be, as the present deputy secretary of state, Strobe Talbott, has written, that a "turning point" was reached in world affairs "when the U.N. Security Council authorized allied troops to assist starving Kurds in northern Iraq,"[3] but the wording of the Security Council resolution was negotiated by diplomats of the member states and it continues to be monitored and enforced by their military forces (primarily by American military aircraft flying out of bases in eastern Turkey).

The nation-state, in other words, is far from dead. Diplomacy is still its preferred instrument of external policy and military force its ultimate sanction. United Nations Secretary General Boutros Boutros-Ghali was undoubtedly correct in stating, "The centuries-old doctrine of absolute and exclusive sovereignty no longer stands,"[4] but what has taken its place? When the doctrine falls, it falls before the sovereign power of another state or group of states. The attachment of governments (and those they govern) to the doctrine of absolute sovereignty remains strong. What has weakened is their confidence that it can assure absolute security. Military threats are still problems to worry about, and defend against, but not the only problems and perhaps not even the most dangerous.

EQUALITY UNDER INTERNATIONAL LAW

The rights of nation-states under international law can be compared to the rights of citizens in a democracy. Though the world is not governed by democracies, all states are theoretically equal under international law. In a democratic state, the distinction between individual and community rights is continually being redrawn as the community learns more about what is good and bad for it. Not so many years ago the right of the individual to smoke cigarettes in a public place was taken for granted. Today, as scientific knowledge increases about the lung damage caused by casual inhalation of smoke, it is taken for granted that the individual's right to smoke can be subordinated to the community's right to be spared from inhaling it.

Average American citizens may continue to worry about their physical safety in cities where there are too many firearms, but they have also been taught to worry about other threats to their well-being. As shown by the acid rain controversy, caused by potentially dangerous pollutants drifting across the U.S.-Canadian border, the principle applies as well to the international community. The difference is in the mechanisms of enforcement. If an American citizen feels threatened he or she can call the police; if a nation-state feels threatened it can only call for negotiations or a meeting of the Security Council or the General Assembly.

The loopholes in international law, and the absence of reliable mechanisms to enforce it, explain why states are less careful than individuals about taking actions stigmatized as antisocial by their communities. The divergence between personal and state morality, which Americans from the origins of the republic have believed it was the business of foreign policy to redress, remain appreciable, even though the ability of one state to isolate itself from the antisocial behavior of others has been greatly reduced. Diplomacy, therefore, in addition to its traditional role of preventing armed conflict or negotiating peace if conflict has broken out, must in the future assume a new range of responsibilities. Among the most important will be achieving consensus among members of the international community on what "internal" actions of nation-states should be considered dangerous beyond their borders, finding ways to mobilize the power of the international community to end such antisocial actions, and preventing their repetition.

The United States will have a leading role to play, both because of its importance in world affairs and because American diplomacy, unlike its European counterpart, has never pretended to be value-free.

167

The United States was a skeptical participant in the Helsinki accords, underestimating their impact in Eastern Europe. The accords represent a first step toward genuine modification of the doctrine of "absolute and exclusive" sovereignty, but they are not a treaty and are neither binding nor enforceable.

The real job of defining the points at which the internal behavior of states becomes the legitimate concern of other states remains to be accomplished. So does the task of setting up workable procedures to enforce what Jefferson in the Declaration of Independence called "a decent respect for the opinions of mankind." The United States should take the initiative to convene an international conference to reexamine the rules of diplomatic conduct set forth in the Vienna Convention. Indeed, there could be no better demonstration of the moral leadership to which the United States aspires in world affairs.

DISORIENTATION OF OTHER STATES

Other states are also suffering from confusion in the face of problems unfamiliar to traditional diplomacy. The 1987 report on the management of French diplomacy, prepared by a special commission presided over by the then French ambassador in London, Jacques Viot,[5] cites problems that are readily apparent in the conduct of U.S. diplomacy: proliferation of foreign policy centers, or "mini-Quais d'Orsay"; the attempt to manage an aggregation of foreign affairs programs without adequate coordination; lack of coherence in articulating French foreign policy ("The media and the public must know who speaks with the 'voice of France,' especially in periods of crisis"); lack of continuity; successive and contradictory reforms of administration; too rapid rotation of personnel "in the American style"; and failure to recognize the need to adapt to changing conditions of diplomacy.

All of which suggests that the Quai d'Orsay has also had a fight on its hands to retain a dominant role in the conduct of foreign policy. The same is true of the British Foreign and Commonwealth Office and of the foreign offices of most of the other major powers. What distinguishes their situation from that of the State Department is the extent to which their governments value the contribution professional diplomacy makes to the foreign policy process when its vantage point is distinct from that of political policymakers. Understanding that professional diplomats can provide a valuable perspective on foreign policy and bring to it special skills and expertise means greater willingness to allow them a margin of independence comparable to that of the military services in establishing criteria for performance, assignment, and promotion, and resisting political intervention in the personnel process.

How can this be restored to the American system? The most effective way would be to create the position of permanent under secretary in the State Department and back it up with a Board of the Foreign Service whose statutory powers were revalidated. A permanent under secretary would assure not only more rational personnel policies but greater continuity in policy-making. If concern about foreign affairs "mandarins" makes this course of action unfeasible, the secretary of state will have to assume the responsibility for revitalizing U.S. diplomacy, improving its core skills, and restoring its professional integrity. It will take a strong secretary to do so, but also a *strengthened* secretary.

STRENGTHENING THE SECRETARY OF STATE

There was a time, before the Kennedy administration placed American ambassadors unequivocally in charge of their country teams, when diplomatic missions, especially large ones in countries significant to United States interests, were torn apart by almost as much internecine warfare as Washington is today. The heads of American aid missions, often American political figures or prominent business leaders, squabbled with the ambassador over everything from political and economic trends in the host country to who was entitled to leave a social function before the other. The differences were often petty, but no more so than those of the foreign policy barons in Washington today about who will be accommodated nearest the President on trips abroad and similar points of protocol.

Such disputes over precedence were common among diplomats until the matter was settled in 1815 at the Congress of Vienna by the simple expedient of agreeing that ambassadors would be ranked, not by the "importance" of the rulers they represented, but in order of their arrival at a foreign post and the date on which their credentials were accepted by the host government. Before that time, the jostling for position by the ambassadors of the leading powers had been rancorous and sometimes bloody. In a notorious clash that occurred in London in 1661 between the carriages of the Spanish and French ambassadors, each seeking to get ahead of the other in a diplomatic procession, several attendants were killed, France broke relations with Spain, and war was narrowly averted.[6]

Thus far, in the Washington wars of precedence, no secretary of state, so far as we know, has actually come to blows with a national security adviser or the head of some other foreign affairs agency, but the effect of their incessant feuding on the conduct of American foreign policy has always been disruptive and usually unnecessary. Although there have been exceptions to the rule, it is surely time for an American president to forestall unhappy recurrences by arming the secretary of state with the explicit authority to coordinate the administration's foreign policy. The secretary would still be in a weaker position with respect to his cabinet colleagues than an ambassador is with members of the country team, since they rely on the ambassador for logistic and other support that a secretary of state is more likely to require than to furnish. He or she would however, under the president's leadership, be better able to assure that the mosaic of American foreign policy presented to the world is a coherent picture of our interests, values, and objectives.

The secretary of state sits to the right of the president at cabinet meetings. His precedence over his cabinet colleagues is due to seniority, his department having been created by Congress before the others. He may thus be first among equals, but the power of the cabinet itself has long since been eclipsed by that of the White House, and much of the secretary's turf has either been appropriated by, or ceded to, his cabinet colleagues. Without strengthened authority the secretary of state will continue to expend more energy on domestic than on foreign affairs. He will be unable to provide the focus that American foreign policy lacks and the leadership his department needs.

DECENTRALIZING THE STATE DEPARTMENT

A clearer mandate from the president to the secretary of state might encourage him to begin decentralizing his department which, given its relatively small size, has become enormously top-heavy. When the secretary is not out of the country conducting negotiations that, in many cases, could more systematically be undertaken by his ambassadors, he sits barricaded on the seventh floor of the State Department behind phalanxes of staff aides and security personnel. Decentralization of decision-making authority would enable the secretary to concentrate on more than one problem at a time. In so doing it would bring him closer to his bureaus, offices, and desks and therefore closer to his posts abroad.

Like the secretary of state, the State Department has also become too inward-looking. The concern Foreign Service officers feel for their careers if posted for prolonged periods far from Washington, especially in the remote and difficult regions that are the truest tests of character and ability, is an indication of where they think the attention of the secretary and his senior advisers is directed. So is the competition for positions of staff aide to the department's senior officers, jobs that require more zeal than judgment and a greater talent for making the master's words visible than for independent thought.

The absorption of the secretary and his top echelon in the Washington bureaucratic wars, coupled with the encroachments of political patronage on senior assignments, sets the personnel system adrift and deprives it of logic and coherence. The State Department, as virtually every secretary of state finds occasion to say, has only one resource, its people. Yet it is precisely the "people" of the Foreign Service whose talents are squandered when they are asked to serve under unqualified political appointees, placed in positions that do not suit their talents, or retire before their potential has been realized or even tested. Here, as in other areas, the State Department has much to learn from the Defense Department, where the uniformed military services have been more successful than professional diplomats in preserving the integrity of the career service. The skills of these officers are more respected and better employed than are those of professional diplomats.

In this connection, it should not be forgotten that professional military officers also had a long struggle before they gained acceptance in the United States. The tradition of the minutemen gave amateurism in the military services the same cachet it continues to have in diplomacy. Politically appointed generals in the Civil War contributed to the slaughter by their mistakes. Theodore Roosevelt's celebrated "Rough Riders" were one of three federal volunteer cavalry units that participated in the Spanish-American War. They reflected Roosevelt's distrust of the regular army, a sentiment shared by many Americans. As one expert states, "To many Americans, it was essential that the career Army take a secondary role in the war to volunteers organized in National Guard units representing the states and localities."[7]

The same suspicion of professionalism colors political (and popular) attitudes toward diplomacy and confounds efforts to manage and employ it more logically. Twenty years ago, an observer of American diplomacy said the Foreign Service was composed of "first-rate people in a third-rate system."[8] The situation today is even worse. Let me briefly summarize the most significant problems identified in earlier chapters and the most logical approaches to solving them.

PROMOTING DIPLOMATIC PROFESSIONALISM

A key lesson to be learned from the diplomacy of reason is that the best diplomats are those who understand foreign affairs, are capable of making themselves experts in the affairs of the country where they serve, but have intellects versatile enough to look beyond its frontiers. They can see the forest as clearly as the trees—an essential attribute of a diplomat—because they are able to transcend political or professional partisanship.[9]

It follows that the American practice of bestowing senior diplomatic posts as rewards, either for services to the party or for services to the profession, should be abandoned.

The mismanagement of Foreign Service personnel has vastly overcomplicated the assignment and promotion process. Foreign Service Officers intellectually and temperamentally divide themselves into four general groups: those with a gift for representation and reporting in the field; those able to contribute to the policy process at home; those skilled in negotiation; and those who are capable administrators. Since it normally takes time for these special talents to mature, a mix of assignments is desirable through the middle grades of a Foreign Service career. In the assignment process there should be a decided emphasis on field assignments and a strict rationing of staff jobs.

The principles of representivity and merit are not inherently antagonistic. They only become so when there is uncertainty about how they are being applied to the processes of recruitment, assignment, and promotion. Lateral entry into senior Foreign Service positions usually disserves both principles. It is in the recruitment of candidates for the Foreign Service who are both representative and qualified that the solution lies. An excellent way to enlarge the recruiting pool would be through the creation of a diplomatic ROTC by act of Congress.

The Foreign Service Manual states that all senior officers should speak fluently at least one "world" language and one "hard" language. The objective has never been seriously pursued. It should now be made a firm rule of personnel policy and a firm prerequisite for promotion into the Senior Foreign Service. If the American diplomatic service does not have demonstrable expertise in foreign languages and cultures there is no reason for it to exist.

Choosing and Using Good Ambassadors

To assure that the best talent is selected, the qualifications of candidates for ambassadorships, whether to foreign countries or to international organizations and conferences, should be reviewed by an independent panel whose members are knowledgeable about foreign affairs. Some members would come from outside the Foreign Service, others could be drawn from the ranks of retired diplomats. Both career and noncareer candidates would be screened by the panel, whose recommendations administrations would agree to support in advance. (This procedure would also allow competing candidacies to be evaluated when a deadlock developed between career and noncareer candidates.)

The habit of undermining and circumventing the authority of chiefs of mission, a deplorable practice that began as far back as the Franklin mission to Paris, should be ended. There is more benefit to be gained by an administration from building up its ambassadors than from tearing them down. The weight of responsibility they are permitted to carry relieves the foreign policy burdens of the president and the secretary of state. Transacting more diplomatic business through embassies and consulates permits the work to be done more quietly and usually more efficiently. If chiefs of mission abuse or misuse their authority they can be removed.

More Leadership, Less Management

If chiefs of mission were selected on the basis of demonstrated talent and competence, they could be allowed to run their mission with less interference from Washington in their administrative operations. The State Department as micromanager should be replaced by the State Department as leader of the foreign policy process. There should be more emphasis on the articulation of policy and the promotion of an active dialogue with the field and less on defensive and bureaucratically oriented paperwork.

Reducing marginal communications and travel would enable policy-makers to focus on reports and analyses that significantly affect foreign policy. Vertical lines of communication should be decongested and the secretary of state and his closest advisers made more accessible to senior officers in Washington for consultation. Chiefs of mission and "seventh-floor principals" would both benefit from being brought together for periodic exchanges of views. The Defense Department has shown how this can be done.

Changing the Professional Culture

There must also be a change in the culture of the Foreign Service itself, even if it requires amendment of the Foreign Service Act of 1980, and the mandated role of the American Foreign Service Association. Discipline of assignments must be restored. The best-qualified officers must be sent where the United States most needs them. This will cause inconvenience and discomfort in the assignment process. Some officers may decide that it does not suit their family circumstances or individual preferences. So be it. Sooner rather than later the leadership of the Foreign Service, those serving in its ranks, and those considering whether to enter them will have to decide whether they want a Foreign Service patterned more on the Marine Corps or the Postal Service. The model that will best serve the needs of American foreign policy is not in doubt.

Reforming the Personnel System

One of the most basic changes needed to prepare American diplomacy for its new frontiers is in the classification of diplomatic skills. The so-called cone system, dividing officers at the beginning of their careers into political, economic, administrative, consular, and information specialists, works badly today and is certainly not suited to future requirements.

The present system has unnecessarily rigidified the assignment

175

process without appreciably improving the ability of officers in each cone to deal with the kinds of problems that actually arise in these areas. The system recognizes that diplomats need to possess specialized skills but seems erroneously to assume that they also need to be specialists. A more flexible system would permit officers to develop specialized skills, in accordance with their aptitudes and preferences, but would not, as the present system does, make them (and the assignments process) prisoners within their cones. Since the profession of diplomacy calls for specialized technical skills to be used in a foreign culture, they will be used more often than not in a technically unspecialized way. The present system creates bureaucratic impediments to placing talent where American foreign policy needs it.

In one particularly egregious example of cone-headed personnel management, one of the Foreign Service's best Arabists encountered the personnel bureau's objections to his assuming an ambassadorial post in the Arab world because he was classified as an information specialist and his "career curve" indicated he should return to public affairs work. His ambassadorship eventually materialized, but the objections showed how liable the system is to being hamstrung by its own regulations.

THE NEED FOR MULTILATERALISTS

A more realistic division of labor, and one that has been used by other countries but not by the United States, is between specialists in bilateral and multilateral diplomacy. It is a division that corresponds to the emerging pattern of international affairs. These two forms of diplomacy involve different skills and, not infrequently, appeal to different temperaments. The officer who gains satisfaction from prolonged residence abroad, saturation in a foreign culture, and fluency in its language or languages will not always be at home in the more public and kaleidoscopic world of conference diplomacy. The multilateral specialist, on the other hand, is apt to become restless if confined to one country and the ups and downs of its bilateral relations with the United States.

There are other reasons to give multilateral diplomacy greater emphasis and to encourage young diplomats to specialize in it. For one thing, most diplomacy is already multilateral and the United States is a key player. For another, the demands of conference diplomacy—frequent travel and periods of tumultuous activity broken by longer and more serene intervals at home—may suit the family circumstances and life-styles of some Foreign Service officers better than do the longer absences from the United States that are inevitable in bilateral diplomacy. Working couples—in personnel jargon, "tandem couples"—can be easier to accommodate in large multilateral delegations than in small embassies. Lastly, in terms of their language skills, multilateralists can afford to concentrate on world languages—the languages of conference diplomacy—rather than the more exotic tongues spoken in regions where they might be posted to an embassy or consulate.

Under such a system of specialization, officers who chose to spend the bulk of their careers in conference diplomacy (in the past, rarely a fast track to the top of the Foreign Service) would be evaluated on criteria different from those applied to officers engaged in bilateral diplomacy. Their career goal would ordinarily be chief of delegation rather than chief of mission.

The new division of labor should be accompanied by the introduction of greater flexibility into the existing cone system, encouraging lateral movement within the service and permitting the development of a variety of skills that can be drawn on when officers assume senior positions of responsibility.

THE NEED FOR BILATERALISTS

For those who are more drawn and better adapted to the conditions of bilateral diplomacy, reforms are needed that will enhance the rewards of service abroad, especially for officers in difficult posts who speak hard languages and develop a depth of knowledge in specific regions and cultures. The diplomatic role models needed by young Foreign Service officers today are more likely to be provided by officers who have walked the back streets of Sarajevo, Mogadishu, and Kigali than by staff aides in Washington. They should be able, in Jefferson's words, to "ferret the people out of their hovels . . . look into their kettles, eat their bread," and make the American government understand what it tastes like.

This down-to-earth approach is actually quite well suited to the American temperament. Traditional diplomacy scorned it. Even so accomplished a British diplomat as Harold Nicolson was criticized by Edmund Wilson for being out of touch with reality because he looked at the world through embassy windows: "When you set out to read, say, [Nicolson's] account of the Peace Conference or his recent article on Boris of Bulgaria, you may be prepared to be taken behind the scenes; but what you find are merely pictures of persons and places which, neat and bright though they are, leave you with the conviction that, whatever was happening, Harold Nicolson did not know much about it."[10] Wilson concluded: "Throughout his travels [Nicolson] has only resided in one country: the British Foreign Office."

The Washington-dominated diplomacy of the United States runs the same risk. To minimize it, we need a diplomatic service equipped for both global and national diplomacy, capable of functioning effectively in either a multilateral or a bilateral context. The ability to "foresee and foretell" threats to the nation's security depends to an important extent on how promptly and accurately U.S. representatives abroad evaluate and report them. This is true whether the threat is the impending collapse of a nation-state or of an ecosystem.

Notes

PREFACE

1. This excerpt from a letter dated February 13, 1927, is quoted with the kind permission of Mrs. George W. B. Starkey, John Van A. MacMurray's daughter.

2. David E. Sanger, "This Is a Trade War! Get Your Popgun!" *New York Times*, February 12, 1995, sec. 4, p. 5.

3. Robert B. Reich, "Decline and Divergence," *Times Literary Supplement*, March 6, 1987, p. 232.

4. It is striking how few Foreign Service officers were included in U.S. delegations at summit meetings with Soviet leaders. FSO Charles E. Bohlen participated in the Tehran, Yalta, and Potsdam conferences in the closing phase of World War II, but his role was primarily that of Russian-language interpreter for President Roosevelt. Later, interpreting services at summit meetings, and for most other high-level purposes, were turned over to the State Department's Office of Language Services. Even this office was relegated to the sidelines by the Nixon administration. The president and his national security adviser, Henry A. Kissinger, chose at most summit encounters to rely on Soviet interpreters, in part to reassure the Soviets of U.S. good faith and in part to guard against possible leaks to the State Department.

5. George F. Kennan, *Memoirs, 1925–1950* (Boston and Toronto: Little, Brown and Company, 1967), 1:348.

CHAPTER ONE
THE NEW FRONTIERS OF AMERICAN DIPLOMACY

1. Serge Schmemann, "Solzhenitsyn Attacks Gorbachev and New 'Reforms,'" *New York Times*, May 29, 1994, p. 3.

2. Jane Tompkins, *West of Everything* (New York: Oxford University Press, 1992), p. 6.

3. Preamble to the Vienna Convention on Diplomatic Relations [italics in quotations are mine], signed in Vienna on April 18, 1961, entered into force on April 24, 1964, thirty days after the twenty-second instrument of ratification or accession had been deposited with the secretary-general of the United Nations. The United States signed the convention on June 29, 1961, and ratified it on November 13, 1972.

4. Vienna Convention, Article 41.

5. This figure was provided to me by a State Department officer whose

job included keeping tabs on such things, although he was rarely made aware of the content of the calls.

6. Alan Gotlieb, *I'll Be with You in a Minute, Mr. Ambassador. The Education of a Canadian Diplomat in Washington* (Toronto: University of Toronto Press, 1991). In this slender but significant volume, Ambassador Gotlieb refers at several points to his handling of the acid rain problem. It may be reflective of the changing perspectives of diplomacy that the new Canadian embassy in Washington, D.C., is located nearer to the houses of Congress than to the State Department.

7. Harold Nicolson, *The Evolution of the Diplomatic Method* (New York: Macmillan, 1954), p. 75.

8. In 1924 the Soviet Union reinstituted the diplomatic titles that had been formally recognized in 1815 at the Congress of Vienna and were standard among the powers with which the Soviets were beginning to establish relations. "Plenipotentiary representatives," being unrecognized outside the Soviet Union, were finding themselves seated below the salt in foreign capitals and generally dealing at a disadvantage with their capitalist counterparts.

CHAPTER TWO
THE DIPLOMACY OF REASON

1. I am indebted for this description to Peter D. Eicher, a career Foreign Service officer who has compiled an exceptionally interesting collection of historical American diplomatic despatches and from whose introduction to the series it is taken. Mr. Eicher's collection has proved a valuable reference in preparing the historical portions of this and other chapters of the present volume.

2. Theodore Lyman, *Diplomacy of the United States* (Boston: Wells and Lilly, State Street, 1826), p. 10.

3. Quoted in Jonathan Dull, *Franklin the Diplomat: The French Mission* (Philadelphia: American Philosophical Society, 1982), p. 4; from John Adams to Mercy Warren, August 8, 1807, Collections of the Massachusetts Historical Society, 5th ser. (1878) 4:446.

4. In discussing the problems of Franklin's mission I have drawn on several sources. Jonathan Dull's monograph, *Franklin the Diplomat*, is a fascinating account of the extraordinary difficulties under which Franklin labored; a fine, detailed analysis of the evolution of Franklin's views on foreign policy is contained in Gerald Stourzh's *Benjamin Franklin and American Foreign Policy* (Chicago: University of Chicago Press, 1954); and of course the public and private papers of Franklin himself while in France permit clear insights into both his problems and his consolations. In consulting Franklin's own writings I have relied primarily on the Library of America edition (New York: Literary Classics of the United States, 1987).

5. Dull, *Franklin the Diplomat*, p. 44.

6. Stourzh, *Benjamin Franklin*, p. 158.

7. Quoted by Dull, *Franklin the Diplomat*, p. 17.

8. Ibid., p. 27.

9. Stourzh, *Benjamin Franklin*, p. 151.

10. A particularly dangerous pitfall for American diplomats is to appear to adapt too comfortably to foreign, especially European, ceremonials. In 1784 the American press ridiculed Jay for having kissed the queen's hand in London. From what we know of Jay he may in fact have embraced court protocol with excessive enthusiasm. The American weakness for royalty still infects some diplomats and their spouses. I remember the sweeping curtsy made by the wife of an American chargé d'affaires to the Greek crown prince many years ago in an Athens movie theater where she was welcoming him to the premiere of an American film. He being at the time a teenager and she middle-aged, the gesture conferred little dignity on either one.

11. Quoted in Stourzh, *Benjamin Franklin*, p. 259.

12. Merrill D. Peterson, ed., *The Portable Thomas Jefferson* (New York: Penguin Books, 1985), p. 20.

13. Letter to James Madison, October 28, 1785, in ibid., p. 395.

14. Thomas Jefferson, "Observations on the Whale Fishery," *Jefferson: Public and Private Papers* (First Vintage Books/The Library of America Edition, September 1990), p. 66.

15. Bernard Bailyn, *Faces of Revolution* (New York: Alfred A. Knopf, 1990), p. 37.

16. Letter to Lafayette from Nice, April 11, 1787, in *The Portable Thomas Jefferson*, pp. 421–23.

17. Henry Adams, letter to Horace Gray, Jr., June 17, 1861, in Ernest Samuels, ed., *Henry Adams: Selected Letters* (Cambridge: Harvard University Press, 1992), pp. 38–39.

18. Henry Adams, *The Education of Henry Adams* (Boston: Houghton Mifflin, 1961), p. 115.

19. Ibid., p. 111.

20. Ernest Samuels, *Henry Adams* (Cambridge: Belknap Press of Harvard University Press, 1989), p. 44.

21. Since World War I consulates have also been responsible for issuing visas to foreigners who seek to enter the United States.

22. Andrew L. Steigman, *The Foreign Service of the United States* (Boulder: Westview Press, 1985), p. 124. At the beginning of 1994 the United States was maintaining 165 embassies and 96 consulates abroad.

23. Quoted in Tracy Hollingsworth Lay, *The Foreign Service of the United States* (New York: Prentice-Hall, 1925), p. 34.

24. Charles Evans Hughes, foreword to ibid., , pp. viii–ix.

CHAPTER THREE
THE DIPLOMACY OF DOCTRINE

1. Joseph Marion Jones, *The Fifteen Weeks, an Inside Account of the Genesis of the Marshall Plan* (New York: Harcourt Brace Jovanovich, 1965), p. 51.

2. Ibid., p. 155.

3. Dull, *Franklin the Diplomat*, p. 33.

4. In his fascinating 1991 biography of Wilson, August Heckscher makes the point that this was not a distinction without a difference: "The fact that the United States was free in principle to make a separate peace became Wilson's trump card in a last-ditch effort to secure from Allied leaders acceptance of his peace program." Heckscher, *Woodrow Wilson* (New York: Charles Scribner's Sons), p. 442.

5. Article 5 of the Brussels Treaty.

6. It is fair to add here that WEU, for all its sweeping language, has remained a passive force while NATO, despite its loopholes, has not. At the time of the Gulf War the WEU was used as a cover for military contributions by members of the anti-Iraq coalition, notably France, who were unwilling to concede to NATO an out-of-area role, but the organization has taken few initiatives and run few risks. Nevertheless, the different ways in which the NATO and WEU commitments are expressed reflect fundamental differences of approach to alliance diplomacy.

7. In the early writings of Franklin the theme of manifest destiny recurs frequently. It was his view, for example, that the leader who "acquires new Territory, if he finds it vacant or removes the Natives to give his own People Room" could properly be called the father of his nation (see Stourzh, *Benjamin Franklin*, p. 61). In his later years, after American independence was won, his philosophy became mellower and closer to the Enlightenment view that reason should play a larger role than force in foreign affairs.

8. See, for example, Bryan's speech "Imperialism," delivered August 8, 1900, in Indianapolis, accepting the Democratic nomination for president: "Behold a republic gradually but surely becoming the supreme moral factor in the world's progress and the accepted arbiter of the world's disputes." *Speeches of William Jennings Bryan* (New York: Funk & Wagnalls Company, 1913), 2: 49.

9. Henry A. Kissinger, *Hearings before the Committee on Foreign Relations, United States Senate, September 7, 1973* (Washington, DC: U.S. Government Printing Office), stock number 5270–02002, p. 7.

10. This point was made with particular force by a former secretary of defense, Robert S. McNamara, in his memoir and apologia, *In Retrospect: The Tragedy and Lessons of Vietnam* (New York: Times Books, Random House. 1995).

11. Thomas A, Bailey, *A Diplomatic History of the American People*, 10th ed., (Englewood Cliffs, NJ: Prentice Hall, 1980), p. 292.

12. Once again Peter D. Eicher's collection of historical American diplomatic despatches has been invaluable in supplying the full text of the Ostend Manifesto.

CHAPTER FOUR
THE DIPLOMACY OF PROCESS

1. The United States was responsible for about 25 percent in 1993.

2. Ambassador Paul Notredaeme to the author in New York, November 9, 1992.

3. Sir David Hannay to the author in New York, November 10, 1992.

4. Berndt von Staden, "The View from the Continent," in *As Others See Us: United States Diplomacy Viewed from Abroad*, ed. Margery Boichel Thompson (Washington, DC: Institute for the Study of Diplomacy, Edmund A. Walsh School of Foreign Service, Georgetown University, 1989), pp. 20–21.

5. Of these 4,300 officials, about 30 percent at any one time are serving in Washington. The remaining 70 percent are posted around the world in 246 American diplomatic and consular posts (figures from 1984). For purposes of comparison, the number of British diplomats, defined by the same criteria, is 2,420, of whom about 40 percent are usually serving at the Foreign Office in London and 60 percent at 214 British diplomatic and consular posts abroad (1992 figures). French diplomats currently number 1,164, 30 percent of whom are at the Quai d'Orsay in Paris and the remaining 70 percent at 284 (!) French diplomatic and consular posts abroad (1987 figures).

6. Much of the statistical data and other factual information in this chapter—updated when appropriate—is drawn from Andrew L. Steigman's *The Foreign Service of the United States* . This is certainly the best available manual on the American diplomatic service, and, since change comes slowly in the institutions conducting U.S. foreign policy, it remains an accurate guide to the organization, procedures, and conventions of the service.

7. Steigman notes that as terrorist organizations learned that diplomats were relatively "soft" targets, attacks on them increased significantly. His statistics show that by 1975, 30 percent of all international terrorist attacks were against diplomats; by 1980 it had risen to 54 percent (see Steigman, *The Foreign Service of the United States*, pp. 218–22). Stricter security precautions introduced in the 1980s by states, including the United States, whose diplomats were being targeted, and better international cooperation, have had their effect. The most recently available State Department figures indicate that in 1992 diplomats were targets in only 12.5 percent of terrorist

attacks. The total number of attacks of all kinds fell to the lowest level since 1975.

8. Conversation with the author in Paris, October 26, 1992.

9. Dean Acheson, *Present at the Creation* (New York: W. W. Norton, 1969), p. 88. Emphasis is mine.

10. Henry Adams, *The Education of Henry Adams*, pp. 274–75.

11. "Les 'Bouchons' du Ciel Européen," *Le Monde*, September 8, 1989, p. 1.

12. This brief description of negotiation of the Montreal Protocol, which barely touches on the number and complexity of the obstacles surmounted, is drawn from the fascinating and detailed account written by the chief U.S. negotiator, Ambassador Richard Elliot Benedick, *Ozone Diplomacy: New Directions in Safeguarding the Planet* (Cambridge: Harvard University Press, 1991).

13. Ibid., p. 76. Over one hundred states have now signed and ratified the treaty.

CHAPTER FIVE
DIPLOMACY AS REPRESENTATION

1. Diplomats are often specifically referred to as "representatives" or "envoys" (from the French word *envoyer*, to send), and the very word "diplomacy" derives from the Greek verb *diplono*, to fold, originating presumably in the folded letters of credence that representatives of one state carried when traveling in another.

2. Edmund A. Gullion, "The American Diplomatist in Developing Countries," in *The Secretary of State and the Ambassador: Jackson Subcommittee Papers on the Conduct of American Foreign Policy*, ed. Henry M. Jackson (New York: Frederick A. Praeger, 1964) p. 180.

3. Orville H. Bullitt, ed., *For the President: Personal and Secret* (Boston: Houghton Mifflin, 1972).

4. John O. Iatrides, ed., *Ambassador MacVeagh Reports: Greece, 1933–1947* (Princeton: Princeton University Press, 1980).

5. Harold Nicolson, *Diplomacy*, 2d ed. (Oxford: Oxford University Press, 1952), p. 126.

6. Personnel at U.S. embassies and consulates represent twenty-five different government agencies, ranging from the Department of Agriculture to the Treasury Department, and about two hundred entities within these agencies. State Department personnel make up only 25 percent of total personnel in embassies and consulates worldwide.

7. "Representation" in State Department jargon is what corporations refer to as "business entertaining"—social functions designed to serve official or company ends. In the U.S. Foreign Service reimbursement for such func-

tions is drawn from a single item in the embassy's budget, allocated for that purpose by the State Department. The amount varies according to the size and responsibilities of the embassy. Reimbursable functions are invariably those given for a specified official purpose—the annual Fourth of July reception, for example—where the number of foreign guests exceeds the number of American guests.

8. *Report of the Review Committee on Overseas Representation 1968–1969* (London: Her Majesty's Stationery Office, cmnd. 4107), p. 88.

9. For Kennan's own description of his dismissal, see George F. Kennan, *Memoirs, 1950–1963* (Boston: Little, Brown and Company, 1972), 2: 178.

10. Alexis de Tocqueville, *Democracy in America* (New York: Vintage Books, 1957), 1: 243–44.

11. Acheson, *Present at the Creation*, p. 250.

12. Genta Hawkins Holmes, director general of the Foreign Service, "Diversity in the Department of State and the Foreign Service," *State* (March 1994), p. 18. The remaining 9 percent of Foreign Service employees did not specify their race.

CHAPTER SIX
DIPLOMACY AS MANAGEMENT

1. This has been a demoralizing disability of many government agencies, especially since the time, somewhere between the Kennedy and Nixon administrations, when candidates for national office began routinely to present themselves as the adversaries of the career services of the federal government rather than their future leaders. In fact, the phrase itself comes from the comment of a former FBI agent about his own bureau.

2. *Toward a Modern Diplomacy* (Washington, DC: American Foreign Service Association, 1968).

3. *Diplomacy for the 70s* (Washington, DC: Department of State publication 8551, December 1970).

4. *The Foreign Service in 2001* (Washington, DC: Institute for the Study of Diplomacy, School of Foreign Service, Georgetown University, August 1992).

5. *Change at State* (Washington, DC: Department of State publication 10105, September 1993).

6. Plaques on the east and west sides of the State Department lobby carry the names of U.S. government personnel who have lost their lives "under heroic or other inspirational circumstances" while serving abroad. Eighty-eight names are listed, most of them employees of the State Department who have died since 1948. Since 1956, seven U.S. ambassadors have been assassinated at their posts.

7. Full text in Martin F. Herz, ed., *The Modern Ambassador: The Chal-*

lenge and the Search (Washington, DC: Institute for the Study of Diplomacy, School of Foreign Service, Georgetown University, 1983), p. 183.

8. See Lay, *The Foreign Service of the United States*, p. 72.

9. Acheson, *Present at the Creation*, p. 66.

10. James Bryce, *The American Commonwealth* (London: Macmillan, 1905), 1: 88.

11. "Back channel" means the CIA's communications capability linking CIA stations abroad with their headquarters in Langley, Virginia. It is separate from the State Department's communications net and in the past has frequently been used, especially by the staff of the National Security Council, to transmit messages to the ambassador that, for whatever reason, were not intended for general distribution. Henry Kissinger, as NSC director, was especially partial to this channel because it could be used to circumvent the secretary of state. As secretary, Kissinger continued to use it when he wished to convey messages to individual members of an ambassador's staff without the ambassador's knowledge. NSC staff members in other administrations have been equally partial to the channel. In the Reagan administration, Oliver North was a prolific author of back channel messages. Secretary Shultz in 1987 publicly reprimanded the U.S. ambassador to Lebanon for having acted on a back channel instruction from North without finding out whether it had been cleared by the State Department. Needless to say, it had not. Subsequently, the Reagan administration forswore such use of back channels, and later administrations have expressed the same determination. Nevertheless, as the process of clearing "front channel" messages becomes slower and more complicated, it is safe to predict that the back channel, in some form, will continue to exist.

12. Mary Curtius, "State Dept. Adrift over Baker Plans," *Boston Globe*, August 9, 1992, p. 1.

13. *1992 Application for the Foreign Service Officer Program* (Washington, DC: Department of State publication 9950, March 1992), p. 2.

14. See Steigman, *The Foreign Service of the United States*, pp. 54–55. Until recently, Foreign Service personnel from the State Department and AID were represented by AFSA; USIA personnel were represented by AFGE. In 1993 USIA employees joined State and AID by electing AFSA as their exclusive representative.

15. An excellent account of Henderson's career is given in H. W. Brands, *Inside the Cold War: Loy Henderson and the Rise of the American Empire* (New York: Oxford University Press, 1991).

16. William J. Crockett, *A Case Study of Change Efforts in a Government Agency*. In my files is an undated copy of this report, on which I have relied in describing Crockett's management program.

17. Ibid., p. 1.

18. Ibid., p. 3.

19. Dr. Chris Argyris, Beach Professor of Administrative Science, Yale University, 1965–1971.

20. These are two of the headings on my own "Decision Matrix Format," as the form was called in Athens, where I was serving as a young political officer when the exercise was conducted.

21. Crockett, *Case Study*, p. 10.

22. Ibid., p. 25.

23. In the 1980s the "management" positions abroad for which competition was most intense were deputy chief of mission in Dublin and consul general in Johannesburg. On the other hand, the department was having trouble filling "nonmanagement" positions like economic counselor in Moscow and political counselor in Manila. The trend continues. In 1994, for the same reason, one of the Foreign Service's most fluent Japanese-speaking officers chose a DCMship in Africa over the post of political counselor in Tokyo.

24. *Profiles in Diplomacy: The U.S. Foreign Service* (Washington, DC: Greater Washington Educational Telecommunications Association, 1990), p. 6. This is a teaching guide intended for use with the film "Profiles in Diplomacy."

25. *Report of the Commission on the Foreign Service Personnel System* (Washington, DC: Department of State publication 9713, June 1989), p. 27.

26. Sherman M. Funk, "The Foreign Service: An Endangered Species," *Foreign Service Journal* 71, 3 (March 1994): 19–20.

27. Foreign Service Act of 1980 (Public Law 96–465, as amended through December 1984), sec. 101, paras. 4 and 5.

28. John M. Goshko, "Foreign Service's Painful Passage to Looking More Like America," *Washington Post*, April 21, 1994, p. A29.

29. *Study of the Foreign Service Generalist Personnel System*, May 1, 1989 (Chairman, Ambassador L. Paul Bremer III), p. 20.

30. David Aaron, "The Role of Dissent in Formulating Foreign Policy in a Democracy," *Open Forum Journal*, no. 37 (January 1985): 26.

CHAPTER SEVEN
DIPLOMACY AS COMMUNICATION

1. Elihu Benjamin Washburn was American minister in Paris from 1869 to 1877. His reporting on the Franco-Prussian War, and that of his counterpart in Berlin, George Bancroft, is assessed by Sister Patricia Dougherty, O.P., in her interesting monograph, *American Diplomats and the Franco-Prussian War* (Washington, DC: Institute for the Study of Diplomacy, 1980).

2. State Department desks, offices, and bureaus that received embassy

despatches would automatically check the identity of the drafting officer first, the authorizing officer (on the lower right side of the first page) second, and usually only as an afterthought look to see whether the chief of mission, whose name appeared on the last page of the despatch, had actually signed off on it or initialed it.

3. Foreign Service Despatch 116, September 8, 1952, entitled "The Soviet Union and the Atlantic Pact." Most of the text of this despatch is printed as an appendix to volume 2 of Kennan's *Memoirs, 1950–1963* (Boston: Little, Brown and Company, 1972), pp. 328–51.

4. E-mail accounts for most of this traffic. Despatches have been eliminated. Newspapers, periodicals, and other bulky documents are the only official business still transmitted by diplomatic pouch.

5. *Change at State*, p. 67. The survey showed that 10.3 percent (1,680,596 messages) were Limited Official Use (the lowest form of classification); 13.1 percent (2,131,832 messages) were Confidential; 3.8 percent (619,002 messages) were Secret; and 0.02 percent (3,665 messages) were Top Secret.

6. Christian Schlaga, "German Officer Working Here Looks at the System—and Wow!"*State*, no. 380 (August 1994): 20.

7. David D. Newsom, *Diplomacy and the American Democracy* (Bloomington: Indiana University Press, 1988), p. 142.

8. *Change at State*, pp. 66, 162.

9. *Science and Technology in U.S. International Affairs*, report of the Carnegie Commission on Science, Technology, and Government, January 1992, p. 46.

10. *Change at State*, pp. 164–66, includes in its list of required reports that should be eliminated the "Bureau of the Mint Interrogatory," the "Semi-Annual Report on Retail Prices, Taxes and Duties on Petroleum Products," and the "Report on Lobbying Activities by Contractors." There are many more.

11. Reuters, "Britain Cuts Back on Foreign Office," *Boston Globe*, April 28, 1994, p. 13. The despatch quotes the permanent undersecretary of the British Foreign and Commonwealth Office as saying that Britain is looking at the feasibility of sharing embassies with Germany in Azerbaijan, Ecuador, and Iceland.

12. This reverses the usual priority in diplomatic reporting, which assumes the ambassador will faithfully carry out his instructions and calls for as complete an account as possible of what the ambassador's interlocutor had to say. During the secretaryship of John Foster Dulles there was one particularly loquacious foreign envoy in Washington whose initial lengthy report of a meeting with the secretary elicited from his foreign minister, according to the gossip of the day, a message commenting, "Your report

received and read with interest. Ministry would also appreciate an account of what Mr. Dulles said."

13. Harold Nicolson, *Peacemaking* (London: Constable & Company, 1945), p. 171.

14. Human intelligence reports emanating from "controlled American sources" led to use of the acronym "CAS" in State Department communications when referring to CIA stations abroad.

15. The episode is described in volume 1 of Kennan's *Memoirs, 1925–1950* (Boston: Little, Brown and Company, 1967), pp. 276–78.

16. In making computer runs of the officers who had been promoted across the threshold into the promised land of the Senior Foreign Service in three successive years, from 1983 through 1985, I found that only 41 of a total of 147 officers (or 28 percent) were certified as proficient in any hard language (at the ambiguously worded "professional" level). To spell out the message more clearly, this figure compared with 31 officers (or 21 percent) who had been promoted across the threshold with *no* certified proficiency in any foreign language whatsoever. These figures were flagrantly out of line with the objective that the Foreign Service itself had set for senior officers, as expressed in the State Department's Foreign Affairs Manual: "It is an objective of the Department [that each officer] . . . before reaching the senior level, be able to use two foreign languages at a minimum professional level of proficiency" (3 Foreign Affairs Manual 871.1–1a).

17. The Foreign Affairs Manual defines five levels of language proficiency and evaluates speaking (S) and reading (R) proficiency separately. In ascending order of fluency the definitions are as follows: S/R-1, Elementary Proficiency; S/R-2, Limited Working Proficiency; S/R-3, Minimum Professional Proficiency; S/R-4, Full Professional Proficiency; S/R-5, Native or Bilingual Proficiency (3 Foreign Affairs Manual 872.2-1 and 2).

18. "Report on Hard Language Proficiency in the Foreign Service," May 12, 1986. A slightly abbreviated version of this report was published in two issues of *State* magazine, nos. 296 and 298 (January 1987 and March 1987).

Chapter Eight
Diplomacy as Negotiation

1. François de Callières, "De la Manière de Négocier avec les Souverains," in *The Art of Diplomacy*, ed. H. M. Keens-Soper and Karl W. Schweizer (New York: Leicester University Press, 1983). Both the French and English texts of de Callières' work were originally published in 1716.

2. According to the State Department, 715 of these agreements are trea-

ties ratified by the U.S. Senate; 12,712 are executive agreements that did not require Senate ratification.

3. Adam Watson, *Diplomacy: The Dialogue between States* (New York: McGraw-Hill, 1983), pp. 84–85.

4. According to one U.S. participant in the crisis, the tactic of choosing the "yesable" letter became known on the American side as the "Trollope Ploy." The reference was to a young woman in a Trollope novel "who would construe even the tiniest gesture as a marriage proposal she could then eagerly accept." George W. Ball, *The Past Has Another Pattern* (New York: W. W. Norton, 1983), p. 307.

5. Vamik Volkan, director of the Center for the Study of Mind and Human Interaction in Charlottesville, Virginia, speaking at a conference held January 15–18, 1992, under the auspices of the Carter Center of Emory University in Atlanta, Georgia. The remarks appear in my notes on the conference.

6. Among the best known are Roger Fisher and William Ury, *Getting to Yes: Negotiating Agreement without Giving In* (Boston: Houghton Mifflin, 1981); Howard Raiffa, *The Art and Science of Negotiation* (Cambridge: Harvard University Press, 1982); and William I. Zartman and Maureen R. Berman, *The Practical Negotiator* (New Haven: Yale University Press, 1982).

7. The quote is from a brochure on INN published by the Carter Center.

8. John Dickie, *Inside the Foreign Office* (London: Chapmans Publishers, 1992), p. 66.

9. In May 1990 a new agreement was concluded extending the life of American bases in Greece for another eight years, although since that time the United States has closed all but one as part of a worldwide retrenchment in the American military presence overseas.

10. A more complete account of the problems involved in these and other military base negotiations conducted by the United States since world war can be found in John W. McDonald, Jr., and Diane B. Bendahmane, eds., *U.S. Bases Overseas: Negotiations with Spain, Greece, and the Philippines* (Boulder: Westview Press, 1990).

11. Ibid., p. 143.

12. Before becoming secretary of state in 1959 after the death of John Foster Dulles, Christian A. Herter had extensive experience in foreign affairs, including service as attaché in the American embassy in Berlin from 1916 to 1917. He was not, however, a commissioned Foreign Service officer, as Eagleburger had been.

13. McDonald and Bendahmane, *U.S. Bases Overseas*, p. 151.

14. Nicolson, *Diplomacy*, p. 63.

15. This remark was made with tongue in cheek by Tarasenko at a meet-

ing of retired American Foreign Service personnel at Brown University, which he and Sergei Khrushchev addressed on June 5, 1993. From my notes.

CHAPTER NINE
IMPROVING THE REACH OF AMERICAN FOREIGN POLICY

1. My reservations about the concept of "ripeness" in foreign policy were set forth in a previous work, *Entangled Allies: US Policy Toward Greece, Turkey, and Cyprus* (New York: Council on Foreign Relations, 1992), pp. 148–49. For present purposes it is sufficient to say that the "ripeness" school is as American as the school of Richelieu is European, and that the two schools reflect very different approaches to diplomacy.

2. These being, it will be recalled, not only "to form a more perfect union" but "establish justice, insure domestic tranquility, provide for the common defence, promote the general welfare, and secure the blessings of liberty to ourselves and our posterity."

3. Alexis de Toqueville, *Democracy in America* (New York: Vintage Books, 1957), 2:82.

4. George F. Kennan, *Memoirs: 1925–1950*, p. 326.

5. Eve Curie, *Journey among Warriors* (London: William Heineman, 1943), p. 19.

6. It is noteworthy that the U.S. officials who knew Yugoslavia best, Deputy Secretary of State Lawrence Eagleburger, a former American ambassador in Belgrade, and Warren Zimmerman, the ambassador when the crisis erupted, seem to have been in the forefront of those who advised against early recognition and who were criticized in the press for "opposing self-determination."

7. Niccolo Machiavelli, *The Prince* (Baltimore: Penguin Books, 1961), p. 39.

8. According to an official who was a member of the policy planning staff at the time.

9. This information comes from a senior White House official in the Bush administration who was involved in the NAFTA negotiations.

10. A legation is a diplomatic mission with a status one rung below that of an embassy. It is headed by a minister instead of an ambassador and normally has fewer personnel. Until 1893, when it adopted the title of "ambassador," the United States maintained only legations abroad. Today, almost all diplomatic missions, whatever the size of the receiving or sending state, are embassies.

11. See Charles William Maynes, "A Workable Clinton Doctrine," *Foreign Policy*, no. 93 (Winter 1993–94): 3–20.

CHAPTER TEN
IMPROVING THE GRASP OF AMERICAN DIPLOMACY

1. See Stanley Hoffmann, *Duties Beyond Borders* (Syracuse: Syracuse University Press, 1981), p. 106.

2. "Montreal Protocol on Substances that Deplete the Ozone Layer," September 1987, Article 8.

3. Strobe Talbott, "The Birth of the Global Nation," *Time*, July 20, 1992, p. 71.

4. Paul Lewis, "In Tune Now, U.N.'s Quintet Plays Themes Penned in '45," *New York Times*, January 3, 1993, p. E5.

5. *Rapport de la Commission de Réforme et de Modernisation*, Ministère des Affaires Etrangères, Paris, June 1987.

6. For a detailed description of the incident, see Samuel Pepys, *The Diary of Samuel Pepys* (Berkeley and Los Angeles: University of California Press, 1970), 2: 187–89.

7. Robert Dallek, *The American Style of Foreign Policy: Cultural Politics and Foreign Affairs* (New York: Oxford University Press, 1983), p. 18.

8. William Macomber, *The Angels' Game: A Handbook of Modern Diplomacy* (New York: Stein and Day, 1975), p. 80.

9. A similar observation was made of General Charles DeGaulle by Robert O. Paxton in his review of Jean Lacouture's biography of the general, *New York Review of Books*, April 23, 1992, p. 18.

10. Edmund Wilson, "Through the Embassy Window: Harold Nicolson," in *Classics and Commercials* (New York: Vintage Books, 1962), p. 122. And this was long before security precautions caused embassy windows to be coated with a viscous, shatter-resistant film called "Mylar."

Index

Aaron, David, 111
accountability, 88
Acheson, Dean, 67, 85, 86–87, 97, 154–55
acid rain, 12, 16–17, 180n. 6
ACORD (Crockett), 105 "Action for Organizational Development" (Crockett), 105
Acton, Lord, 18
Adams, Charles Francis, 31–33
Adams, Henry, 32, 67
Adams, John, 22, 23, 24, 25, 31
Adams, John Quincy, 31, 49–50
administrations: and political appointees, 158–59
AFGE (American Federation of Government Employees), 101, 186n. 14
Africa, 152
AFSA. See American Foreign Service Association
Agency for International Development (AID), 61, 186n. 14
Agnew, Spiro T., 139
agreements, diplomatic, 144–45
Agriculture Department, 61
AID (Agency for International Development), 61, 186n. 14
AIDS virus, 16–17
Alaska purchase, 20
alliances, nonentangling, 39, 43–45
ambassadors, 96; as chief negotiators, 139–41; and private interests, 78–80; qualifications of, 174; screening of, 80–82. See also diplomats; representatives
American Federation of Government Employees (AFGE), 101, 186n. 14
American Foreign Service Association (AFSA), 93, 101, 175, 186n. 14
American Revolution, 21–31
Arabic Language School, 128
Arab-Israeli problem, 7–8
Arafat, Yasser, 135
Armenia, 64

arms control, 16, 60, 137
Art of Diplomacy, The (Callières), 132
Asia Minor, 46
Azerbaijan, 64

"back channel" messages, 98, 186n. 11
Baker, James, 59, 159; and Bush, George, 97, 99
balance of power, 20, 45, 164–65
Balkans, xvi, 152
Bay of Pigs, 87, 122
Beijing Language Institute, 128
Berlind, Alan T., 141
Berrill Report, 94, 136
bilateral diplomacy, 177–78
Blackett, P. M. S., 145
Board of the Foreign Service, 101, 169
Bohlen, Charles, 31, 111, 179n. 4
Bolshevik revolution, 13
Bosnia, 163
Boston Globe, 99
Bourgoyne, 24
Boutros-Ghali, Boutros, 166
Bowie, Robert R., 154
Brazil, 65
Bremer report, 93, 110
Brezhnev "doctrine," 39
British Foreign Service, 62, 65–66, 118, 168–69, 188n. 11; and Berrill Report, 94, 136; leadership of, 101; personnel, 183n. 5. See also England; Great Britain
Brown, L. Dean, 73
Bruce, David, 74
Brussels Treaty Organization, 44
Bryan, William Jennings, 47
Bryce, Lord, 97
Buchanan, James, 52–53
Bullitt, William C., 74
Bundy, McGeorge, 48
Bunker, Ellsworth, 74

Bureau of International Organization Affairs (IO), 58–59
Bush, George, 6; and Baker, James, 97, 99; and domestic affairs, 89
Bush administration: election campaign of, 95; and former Yugoslavia, 152; and Gulf War, 6–8, 43, 53; and new world order, 56; and political appointees, 159; and Tiananmen Square, 89–90; and Turkey, 11

cables, diplomatic, 114
Callières, Francois de, 76, 132
Canada: and acid rain problem, 12, 180n. 6
Canning, George, 50
career officers, 82–83, 84
Caribbean, 45, 55
Carter, Jimmy: and Carter Center, 134; and foreign affairs, 89
Carter administration, 39, 111; and human rights, 10; and PLO, 59; and political appointees, 80–81; and Soviet Union, 122–23
Carter Center, 134–35
CAS, 189n. 14
Catherine the Great, 142
Caucasus, 18, 163
CCPS (Comprehensive Country Programming System), 104–6
Central Intelligence Agency. See CIA
Change of State (State Department), 94
chauvinism, 18
Chernobyl, 71
chief of mission, 74, 174–75
China, xvii; and Coolidge, xiii–xiv; language training in, 129; and Nixon, 53; and Tiananmen Square, 89–90; and Truman, 84–85; and Vietnam, 48, 161
Chinese Language School, 128
CIA, 95, 120–23, 156, 186n. 11; and CAS, 189n. 14
Civil Service, 108
Civil Service Commission, 33
Civil War, American, 14, 172; and Adams, Charles Francis, 31–32
classification: of documents, 114–15, 188n. 5
Clean Air Act (1977), 70
Cleveland administration, 35

Clinton administration, 163; and Bush administration, 95; and former Yugoslavia, 55; and political appointees, 159; and South Asia, 157
Cold War, xv, xvii–xviii
commerce: in eighteenth century, 33–34
Commerce Department, 61, 92
communication, 112–13; and electronics, 116–17; and language proficiency, 127–28. See also language training; reporting, diplomatic
communications revolution, xiv, xv
communism, 73
Comprehensive Country Programming System (CCPS), 104–6
compromise, 5–6
compulsion, 112
cone system, 175–76
conference diplomacy, 56–58, 146
conflict resolution, 133–34
Conflict Resolution Program, 134–35
Congress: and diplomats, 123–27; and human rights, 9–10
Congress of Vienna, 12, 170
consular corps, 35
consulates, 34–35, 181n. 21, 184n. 1
Continental Congress, 23, 28, 42, 51
continuity, 26
Cook, Captain James, 72–73, 165
Coolidge administration: and China, xiii–xiv
copyrights, xvii
Croatia, 14
Crockett, William J., 103–6
Cuba, 6, 87; and Bay of Pigs, 122; and Kennedy administration, 133; and Ostend Manifesto, 39, 51–53. See also Spanish Cuba
cultural affairs, 118
cultures, 173
Curie, Eve, 150–51
Cyprus, xvi

Deane, Silas, 22–23, 24, 25
Declaration of Independence, 26, 168
Defense Department, 92, 95, 172, 175
Demosthenes, 151
despatches, 113, 187–8n. 2

DGP (director general, Foreign Service), 101–2

Diego Garcia, 157

diplomacy, 184n. 1

diplomacy, bilateral, 177–78

diplomacy, conference, 56–58, 146

diplomacy, multilateral, 146, 176–77

diplomacy, nongovernmental, 134–35

Diplomacy for the 70s (State Department), 93

diplomatic negotiation, 136–37

diplomatic service, American, 35–36

diplomats, 123–27, 184n. 1; authority of, 58–59; and policymakers, 153–54; and political loyalty, 82–85; role of, xiii. See also ambassadors; representatives

director general, Foreign Service (DGP): authority of, 101–2

discipline, 108

doctrines, 38–41, 48–54

documents, diplomatic: classification of, 114–15, 188n. 5

domestic affairs: and foreign affairs, 86, 89

drug trade, 16–17

Dulles, John Foster, 50, 84–85, 97, 154–55, 188–9n. 12, 190n. 12

Duncan, Val, 79

Eagleburger, Lawrence, 140–41, 190n. 12, 191n. 6

eastern Europe, 15, 162, 163, 168

economic affairs, 118

Eisenhower, Dwight, 97

Eisenhower administration, 84, 85; and Nixon, 53

Eisenhower Doctrine, 39

E-mail, 188n. 4

embassy personnel, 184n. 1, 191n. 10; authority over, 96

England, 46; and Adams, Charles Francis, 31–32; and American Revolution, 23–25; colonial policy of, 27. See also British Foreign Service; Great Britain

Enlightenment, 20, 182n. 7

environmental pollution, 16–17. See also acid rain; ozone layer, depletion of

envoys, 184n. 1

ethnic cleansing, 39

EU. See European Union

Europe, 85–86, 149; and diplomatic uniforms, 20–21; and doctrines, 40; and private interests, 79; and Treaty of Westphalia, 9. See also European Union

European Air Transport Association, 69

European alliance system, 44

European diplomatic model, 41–44

European Union (EU), 57, 66, 68–69, 149. See also Europe

Export-Import Bank, 79

FBI, 185n. 1

FCS (Foreign Commercial Service), 61

Federal Bureau of Investigation (FBI), 185n. 1

Ferdinand, Franz, 36

Fillmore administration, 35

film: American western, 5

First World War. See World War I

Fletcher School of Law and Diplomacy, 74

Ford, John, 5

Ford administration, 97

foreign affairs: decentralization of, 88–91; and domestic affairs, 86

foreign affairs "aristocracy," 86

Foreign Affairs Manual, 189nn. 16, 17

Foreign Commercial Service (FCS), 61

foreign policy: control of, 85–87; coordination problems of, 59–61; decentralizing, 149–51

Foreign Service. See under specific countries

foreign service, national, 65

Foreign Service Act of 1946, 101

Foreign Service Act of 1980, 88, 93, 101, 114, 129, 175; flaws of, 106, 107–8; and representivity and merit, 109–10; and up-or-out policy, 110–11

Foreign Service examination, 110

Foreign Service in 2001, The, 93–94

Foreign Service Institute (FSI), 128–31

Foreign Service Manual, 173

Foreign Service Officers. See FSOs

former Yugoslavia, xv-xvi, 18, 152, 163; and Clinton administration, 55; ethnic cleansing in, 39

195

Fort Ticonderoga, 24

France, 142, 162, 170; and American Revolution, 23–24; and Franklin, Benjamin, 21–23; and Gulf War, 64, 182n. 6; and Indochina, 161; and Jefferson, Thomas, 27–30. *See also* French Foreign Service

Franco-Prussian War, 113

Franklin, Benjamin, 21–27, 30–31, 42, 51, 91, 165, 174; and Cook, Captain James, 72–73; and Manifest Destiny, 182n. 7

Franklin, William, 24

French Foreign Service, 62, 168; and American Foreign Service, 66–68; leadership of, 101; personnel, 183n. 5; and Viot report, 94–95. *See also* France

French Revolution, 27

"front-channel" messages, 186n. 11

FSI (Foreign Service Institute), 128–31

FSOs, 61–62, 64–65, 173; and AFSA, 186n. 14; appreciation of, 94–95, 185n. 6; and Foreign Service Act of 1980, 101; and Kennedy administration, 87; needs of, 95; and Nixon, Richard, 53; profile study of, 103–4, 106. *See also* personnel, foreign service

Funk, Sherman M., 108

Gadsden purchase, 20

Galbraith, John Kenneth, 76

GATT (General Agreement on Tariffs and Trade), 146

General Agreement on Tariffs and Trade (GATT), 146

General Services officer (GSO), 108

George III, 27

German Foreign Ministry, 115

German Foreign Service, 115

Germany, 63, 145

Glaspie, April, 53

global diplomacy: and national diplomacy, 164–65

Gore, Al, 94

Gotlieb, Ambassador, 180n. 6

government, American, xvi

Grant administration, 33, 67, 113

Great Britain, 79–80, 142. *See also* British Foreign Service; England

Greece, xvi, 39, 40, 46, 137; U.S. military bases in, 138, 139–41, 143, 190n. 9

Greek city-states, 12–13

Greek civil war, 48

Grenada, 157

Gresham's law, 114

Grew, Joseph C., xiii, xiv

Grey, Sir Edward, 36

Grierson, John, xiv

gross national product, 55, 183n. 1

Gulf War, 11, 56, 64; and Bush administration, 6–8, 43, 53; and Pickering, Thomas, 59; television coverage of, xiv; and WEU, 182n. 6

Gullion, Edmund A., 74

Harriman, Averell, 74

Hawaiian Islands, 72

Hawthorne, Nathaniel, 34

Heckscher, August, 182n. 4

Helsinki accords, 168

Helsinki Final Act, 165

Henderson, Loy W., 102–3

Herter, Christian A., 190n. 12

Home Civil Service, 136

Hughes, Charles Evans, 37, 38

Hull, Cordell, 67

human intelligence (HUMINT), 120, 189n. 14

human rights, 14–15; and Congress, 9–10; and diplomatic reporting, 118

HUMINT (human intelligence), 120, 189n. 14

Hungary, 85

Hurd, Sir Douglas, 66

Hussein, Saddam, 7, 8, 43

Indochina, 4, 126, 161

information: vs. knowledge, xv

information, secret, 121

INN (International Negotiation Network), 134

Institute for the Study of Diplomacy, 93–94

intelligence: and Gulf War, 64

intelligence reports, 120–23, 189n. 14

international agreements, 132, 189–90n. 2

international law, 21; and nation-states, 166–68

International Negotiation Network (INN), 134

interpreting services, 179n. 4

intervention, 165

IO (Bureau of International Organization Affairs), 58–59

Iran, 151, 162; and Reagan administration, 67

Iran, shah of, 90, 151, 163

Iran-Contra affair, 125, 154

Iraq, 7, 166. *See also* Gulf War

Israel, 135; and Truman administration, 102

Izard, Ralph, 26

Jackson, Andrew, 33

Japanese Language School, 128

Jay, John, 24, 181n. 10

Jefferson, Thomas, 26–30, 33, 162, 178; and alliances, 39, 43; and Declaration of Independence, 168; and Franklin, Benjamin, 21–22, 24, 25, 30–31

Johnson, Lyndon, 48; and Vietnam War, 60

Johnson administration, 87; and Greece, 139; and Vietnam War, 48–49

journalism, 123–27

Justice Department, 73

Kazakhstan, 64

Kennan, George, xviii, 31, 41, 45, 123, 150, 154; and Acheson, Dean, 85; and despatches, 113; and Kennedy administration, 111; vindication of, 53

Kennedy, John F., 74, 87; and embassy personnel, 96

Kennedy, Robert F., 103

Kennedy administration, 87; and Crockett, William J., 103; and Cuba, 122, 133; and Henderson, Loy W., 102; and Kennan, George, 111

KGB reports, 122

Khrushchev, Nikita, 133

Khrushchev, Sergei, 190–1n. 15

Kissinger, Henry, 6, 39, 40, 57, 154–55, 179n. 4; and "back channel" messages, 186n. 11; and Nixon Doctrine, 47

knowledge: vs. information, xv

knowledge, depth of, 26

Korean War, 31, 56

Kubisch, Jack B., 139

Kurds, 7, 166

Kuwait, 7

Lafayette, 30

language training, 4, 110–11, 127–31, 146, 173, 179n. 4; and proficiency, 189nn. 16, 17; and Soviet Foreign Service, 4, 129; and Vietnam War, 161. *See also* communication; reporting, diplomatic

Lansing, Robert, 35–36, 37

Laos, 126

Latin America, 39, 45, 55, 163

LCE (limited career extension), 108

Lee, Arthur, 23, 25, 26

legation, 161, 191n. 10

limited career extension (LCE), 108

Lincoln, Abraham, 32–33

localitis, 26

Lord, Winston, 155

Louisiana Purchase, 20

loyalty, 82–85

MacArthur, Douglas, 56

Machiavelli, 88, 153

MacMurray, John Van A., xiii, xiv

MacVeagh, Lincoln, 74

Madison, James, 27

management, 92–94

"Management by Objectives" (Crockett), 105

management positions, 105–6, 187n. 23

Manifest Destiny, 182n. 7

manufacturing, American, xvi; and multinationalism, 15–16

Man Who Shot Liberty Valence, The, 5

Marcos, President, 90

Marcy, William, 35

Marshall, George, 150, 154

Marshall Plan, 8

Matlock, Jack, 110

McCarthy, Joseph, 85

McKinley administration, 35

Mercouri, Melina, 73

merit, 109–10

messages, proliferation of, 114–15

Middle East, 39

Middle Eastern specialists, 7–8
military base agreements, 137, 138. *See also*
   Greece, U.S. military bases in
military power: vs. reason, 20
Milosevic "doctrine," 39
Monroe, James, 49–50
Monroe Doctrine, 31, 39, 49–50
Montreal Protocol, 69–70, 146, 165, 184n. 13
Moose, Richard M., 109
morality, 20
moral precision, 76, 82
Moscow State Institute for International Rela-
   tions, 4, 128
multilateral diplomacy, 146, 176–77

NAFTA, 16, 60, 159, 191n. 9
Nantucket whalers, 28–29
national diplomacy: and global diplomacy,
   164–65
National Foreign Affairs Training Center
   (NFATC), 65
National Guard, 172
nationalism, 14–15
National Security Council (NSC), 88, 186n.
   11; and new administrations, 159–60; and
   policy planning, 154, 155–56, 157–58
nation-state, 18; and international law, 166–
   68; and modern diplomacy, 11–14
NATO, xvi, 44, 58, 182n. 6
Navy Department, 143
negotiation, 132–33, 137–38, 145–47; and
   ambassadors, 139–41; effectiveness of,
   141–42; technical vs. diplomatic, 136–37
negotiators, U.S.: advantages of, 143–44; dis-
   advantages of, 142–43
neutrality, 45; in eighteenth century, 33–34
Newsom, David D., 117
new world order, 56
NFATC (National Foreign Affairs Training
   Center), 65
Nicolson, Harold, 13, 119, 142, 178; and
   moral precision, 76, 82
Nitze, Paul, 154
Nixon, Richard: and FSOs, 53
Nixon administration, 39; and Soviet Union,
   xvii-xviii, 90, 179n. 4; and Vietnam, 6

Nixon Doctrine, 39, 163; and Kissinger,
   Henry, 47
nonmanagement positions, 187n. 23
North, Oliver, 186n. 11
North American Free Trade Agreement. *See*
   NAFTA
North Atlantic Treaty Organization. *See*
   NATO
North Korea, 56
North Vietnam, 161
NSC. *See* National Security Council
NSC-68, 154
nuclear arms proliferation, 16

Observations on the Whale-Fishery (Jeffer-
   son), 28, 29
Office of the Special Trade Representative,
   159
Old World diplomacy, 63
Open Door policy, 39
Ostend Manifesto of 1854, 39, 51–53
Ottoman Empire, 46
ozone layer, depletion of, 16–17, 69–70. *See
   also* Montreal Protocol

Palestine Liberation Organization (PLO), 59,
   135
Panama Canal Treaty, 60
parochialism, 26
passports, 72–73
patents, xvii
peacekeeping operations, xvii
Penn family, 22
Pentagon, 143
personnel, foreign service, 88, 96, 175–76,
   183n. 5, 184n. 1, 191n. 10. *See also*
   FSOs
persuasion, 112
Philippines, 90
Pickering, Thomas, 59
Pierce, Franklin, 51–52
plenipotentiary representatives, 13, 180n. 8
PLO (Palestine Liberation Organization), 59,
   135
policymakers: and diplomats, 153–54
policy planning, 151–53; and NSC, 154, 155–

56; regional, 160–63; regional vs.
global, 156–58; and State Department,
154–55
political appointees, 80–82, 84; and new administrations, 158–59
political psychology, 134, 136, 137
political representation, 82–85
positions, foreign service, 105–6, 187n. 23
pouches, diplomatic, 114, 188n. 4
Powell, Enoch, 46
Presidential Reorganization Order (1965),
101
presidents: and secretaries of state, 96–99
press. *See* journalism
private interests, 78–80
process, diplomacy of, 55–56. *See also* conference diplomacy
Profiles in Diplomacy, 100
psychology, political, 134, 136, 137
public opinion, 125; and policy decisions, 89

Quai d'Orsay, 66. *See also* French Foreign
Service

Rabin, Yitzhak, 135
racism, 18
Reagan, Ronald, 159; and "evil empire," 9;
and Shultz, George, 97–98; and Trudeau,
Pierre, 12
Reagan administration: and Iran, 67; and
Oliver North, 186n. 11
reason, 20–21
recruitment, foreign service, 99–100
"Reinventing Government" (Gore), 94
religious affairs, 118
Renaissance Italy, 74
reporting, diplomatic, 113–16, 119–20, 188–
9n. 12; reforms in, 117–18. *See also* communication; language training
representation, 72–75, 82–85, 184–5n. 7
representatives, 184n. 1; essential qualities
of, 75–78. *See also* ambassadors;
diplomats
representivity, 109–10
Republic of Georgia, 135
Republic of the Ivory Coast, 65

Richelieu, Cardinal, 149, 191n. 1
Rogers Act of 1924, 33, 35, 37, 45
Roosevelt, Franklin, 67, 74–75, 179n. 4; and
Soviet Union, 102
Roosevelt, Theodore, 172
Root, Elihu, 35
Rough Riders, 172
Rouleau, Eric, 64
royalty: American weakness for, 181n. 10
Rubens, Peter Paul, 142
Rusk, Dean, 6
Russia, 4–5, 46, 163

SALT II, 60
satellite television, xiv
Scandinavian diplomatic model, 45
Schlesinger, Arthur, Jr., 87
secretaries of state, 169–71; and presidents,
96–99
security: embassy, 192n. 10; and foreign service, 63, 183–4n. 7
self-image, 45–47
self-interest, 21, 45–47
Senate Foreign Relations Committee, 81
Senior Foreign Service (SFS), 107–8, 129,
173; language training in, 189n. 16
Seward, William Henry, 33
SFS. *See* Senior Foreign Service
Shevardnadze, Eduard, 134, 135
Shiite Moslems, 7
Shultz, George, 15, 131, 186n. 11; and Reagan, Ronald, 97–98
SIGINT (signals intelligence), 120
signals intelligence (SIGINT), 120
Silberman, Laurence H., 82, 83, 85
Slovenia, 14
social functions, 184–5n. 7
Solzhenitsyn, Aleksandr, 5
Somalia, 4, 152, 162, 163
Soulé, Pierre, 52–53
South Asia, 157
South Korea, 56
South Vietnam, 161
sovereignty, 166
Soviet Foreign Service, 4, 129
Soviet republics, xv-xvi

Soviet Union, 6, 18, 46, 60, 64, 136, 162, 179n. 4; and Chernobyl, 71; and Cuba, 133; and diplomatic titles, 13, 180n. 8; and Greece and Turkey, 40; and KGB reports, 122; and negotiation, 144, 145–46; and Nixon administration, xvii-xviii, 90, 179n. 4; and Reagan, Ronald, 9; restructuring of, 14–15; and Roosevelt administration, 102; and Truman administration, 85; and Vietnam War, 48, 161

Spain, 170

Spanish-American War, 172

Spanish Cuba, 51–53

Spoils System, 32–33, 52, 61

State Department, 67, 92, 93, 94; and CIA, 120; decentralization of, 171–72; Foreign Affairs Manual, 189n. 16; and new administrations, 159–60; and NFATC, 65; Office of Language Services, 179n. 4; personnel, 184n. 1; and policy planning, 154–55, 156–58; reorganization of, 93; and social functions, 184–5n. 7

State Department Civil Service, 93

Strategic Arms Limitation Treaty (SALT II), 60

Suez Canal, 46

Summary View of the Rights of British America, A (Jefferson), 27

Sumner, William Graham, 47–48

superpower, 56

Swiss diplomatic model, 45

Switzerland, 42

Talbott, Strobe, 166

Talleyrand, 77, 78

Tarasenko, Sergei, 144, 190–1n. 15

technical negotiation, 136–37, 146–47

Tehran, 151

telephone diplomacy, 119

Tell el Amarna tablets, 132–33

tenure, 26

terrorism, international, 16–17

terrorist attacks: on American diplomats, 63, 183–4n. 7

Thailand, 126

Thatcher, Margaret, 65–66

Third World, xv; and diplomacy, 13–14

Thomas report, 93, 108

Tiananmen Square, 89–90; television coverage of, xiv

titles, diplomatic, 21; and Soviet Union, 13, 180n. 8

Tocqueville, Alexis de, 86, 87, 124, 150

Tolba, Mostopha, 70

Tonkin Gulf resolution, 59–60

Toward a Modern Diplomacy (AFSA), 93

Track One diplomacy, 135, 138

Track Two diplomacy, 134–35, 137, 138

trade: and Open Door policy, 39

trade negotiations, 143

transatlantic cable service, 113

transnationalism, economic, 15–16

transnationalism, social, 16–17

treaties, 144–45, 189–90n. 2

Treaty of Westphalia (1648), 9

Trollope Ploy, 190n. 4

Trudeau, Pierre, 12

Truman, Harry, 97

Truman administration, 50; and China, 84–84; and Israel, 102; and Nixon, Richard, 53

Truman Doctrine, 8, 39, 40, 41; and Vietnam, 48–50

Turkey, xvi, 39, 40; and Bush administration, 11; and Gulf War, 7

Tuscany, 26

U.N. General Assembly, 167

U.N. Security Council, 166, 167

Una Chapman Cox Foundation, 100

UNEP (United Nations Environmental Programme), 70

UNHCR (United Nations High Commissioner for Refugees), 15

uniforms, diplomatic, 21

United Nations, 18, 58–59; and Gulf War, 56

United Nations Charter: Article 41, 8

United Nations Environmental Programme (UNEP), 70

United Nations High Commissioner for Refugees (UNHCR), 15

United States Diplomatic Mission, 96

United States Trade Representative (USTR), 143

United States United Nations Mission in New York (USUN), 58–59

Up-or-out, 110–11

U.S. Foreign Service, 4; and French Foreign Service, 66–68; jurisdictional problems of, 95–99; leadership of, 101–2; management of, 92–94; personnel, 61–62, 88, 173, 175–76, 183n. 5; and policy planning, 151–53; and recruitment literature, 99–100; and social functions, 184–5n. 7; strengths and weaknesses of, 63–65; workforce (1993), 92

U.S. Information Agency (USIA), 61, 186n. 14

USIA (U.S. Information Agency), 61, 186n. 14

USUN (United States United Nations Mission in New York), 58–59

Veliotes report, 93

Vergennes, Count de, 23, 24, 26

Versailles Treaty, 145

Vienna Convention on Diplomatic Relations (1961), 8–10, 17, 165, 168, 179n. 3

Vietnam War, 31, 126, 160–61; and Johnson, Lyndon, 60; and Nixon administration, 6; and Truman Doctrine, 48–50

Viot, Jacques, 168

Viot report, 94–95

visas, 73, 181n. 21

Voice of America, 136

von Staden, Berndt, 60

war, ethnic, 18

War Department, 154

Warsaw Pact, 71

Washburn, Elihu Benjamin, 187n. 1

Washington, George, 28; and alliances, 43

Watson, Adam, 132–33

West Africa, 150

Western Europe, 163

Western European Union (WEU), 44, 182n. 6

WEU. See Western European Union

whale oil, 28–29

White House staff, 97

Wilson, Edmund, 178

Wilson, Woodrow, 182n. 4; and alliances, 43–44; and Fourteen Points, 39; and World War I, 9

witch hunts, 85

world leadership, U.S., xvii

World War I, 9, 31, 44, 145

World War II, 10–11, 31, 145

Wriston reforms, 93

xenophobia, 18

Young, Andrew, 59

Yugoslavia, 152, 162, 191n. 6; and nation-states, 18; restructuring of, 14–15

Zimmerman, Warren, 191n. 6

About the Author

MONTEAGLE STEARNS has served as a U.S. diplomat for over thirty years, including three years as ambassador to the Ivory Coast and four years as ambassador to Greece. He has served as Warburg Professor of International Relations at Simmons College and has held fellowships at the Woodrow Wilson International Center for Scholars, at the Council on Foreign Relations, and at Harvard University. He is the author of *Entangled Allies: U.S. Policy toward Greece, Turkey, and Cyprus.*